The First-Year Experience
Monograph Series No. 38

Transforming the First Year
of College for
Students
of Color

Laura I. Rendón
Mildred García
Dawn Person
Editors

NATIONAL RESOURCE CENTER FOR
THE FIRST-YEAR EXPERIENCE® & STUDENTS IN TRANSITION
UNIVERSITY OF SOUTH CAROLINA, 2004

Cite as:

 Rendón, L. I., García, M., & Person, D. (Eds.). (2004). *Transforming the first year of college for students of color* (Monograph No. 38). Columbia, SC: University of South Carolina, National Resource Center for The First-Year Experience and Students in Transition.

Sample chapter citation:

 Kinser, K., & Thomas, C. (2004). Pre-collegiate experiences, values, and goals of first-year students of color. In L. I. Rendón, M. García, & D. Person (Eds.), *Transforming the first year of college for students of color* (Monograph No. 38) (pp. 23-35). Columbia, SC: University of South Carolina, National Resource Center for The First-Year Experience and Students in Transition.

ISBN 1-889271-45-4
First Edition June 2004, Third Printing September 2004

The First-Year Experience® is a service mark of the University of South Carolina. A license may be granted upon written request to use the term "The First-Year Experience." This license is not transferable without written approval of the University of South Carolina.

Additional copies of this monograph may be obtained from the National Resource Center for The First-Year Experience and Students in Transition, University of South Carolina, 1728 College Street, Columbia, SC 29208. Telephone (803) 777-6029. Fax (803) 777-4699.

Special gratitude is expressed to Barbara F. Tobolowsky, Associate Director; Nina L. Glisson, Conference Coordinator; Tracy L. Skipper, Editorial Projects Coordinator; and Alicia Phillip, Editorial Assistant for the copy editing of this monograph; to Michelle Mouton, Editorial Assistant for proofing; and to Jenny Anderson, Composition Assistant, for layout and design.

Transforming the first year of college for students of color / Laura I. Rendón,
 Mildred García & Dawn Person, editors.
  p. cm. -- (The first-year experience monograph series ; no. 38)
 Includes bibliographical references.
 ISBN 1-889271-45-4
 1. College freshmen--United States. 2. Minority college students--United
States. 3. College student development programs--United States. I. Rendón,
Laura I. II. García, Mildred. III. Person, Dawn. IV. National Resource
Center for the First-Year Experience & Students in Transition (University of
South Carolina)
V. Series.
LB2343.32.T72 2004
378.19'8--dc22
         2004007750

Contents

Section Three
Working with Specific Populations

Section Four
Moving Toward the Future

Foreword

Gwendolyn Jordan Dungy

Now more than ever, it is important for educators to work toward enhancing the first year of college for students of color. The Supreme Court's decision to recognize race-conscious admissions highlights the need for a monograph offering a cornucopia of strategies to increase the success of these students. In addition to examples and strategies, this monograph helps educators understand that we must educate ourselves about how culture, history, class, and race influence the entire academic community. Then, it is the responsibility of all of us to *transform* the institution to provide what students of color need for successful learning and development.

While reading this monograph, I recalled my own collegiate experience of living bi-culturally and having pre-college experiences that made my perspective different than that of the traditional student. I did not feel validated by faculty, and the only way I could respond to the power differential between myself, as a student, and faculty was through a weak form of resistance—not paying attention to teachers who did not attend to me. Today, educators and students live in a much more complex and competitive world. For example, as devastating as segregation was during the earlier civil rights movement, the challenges were more easily identified because in the United States, the issues regarding students of color were literally and figuratively black and white. In contrast, today's challenges are more subtle, and must be discerned before they can be addressed.

As I read this monograph, I also had a deep empathy for all educators because I feel that the changing demographics of students are both positive and threatening, like an approaching tide for which faculty and administrators are inadequately prepared. In the United States, we are accustomed to categorizing people easily and then selecting particular stereotypes to use in our efforts to understand who our students are. Without a doubt, we are sorely underprepared for what the editors describe as a "complex, multifaceted student cohort that often defies categorization" (p. 4). Fortunately, the authors in this monograph have a precise sense of what is necessary to illustrate convincingly the diversity of backgrounds and experiences of students. They help us understand some of the common characteristics of groups based on history and experiences. However, it is also clear that students of color are linked, not necessarily by color, but by historical denials of access and inappropriate strategies for validating and educating them. This is particularly evident in the chapters where we hear students' voices.

I am particularly impressed with the manner in which the editors address the gaps in individual knowledge and institutional weaknesses. They understand that many educators with good intentions do not know enough about the complex tasks of transforming the learning environment to ask effective questions. In the following chapters, authors offer the questions, help with answers, and make suggestions on pragmatic initiatives to encourage action as well as cognitive understanding.

The necessity for total institutional transformation is poignantly clear when Wynetta Lee writes—"My initial optimism and passion for learning started to fade during the first week of college when I had my first encounter with an institutional staff person" (p. 93). This example demonstrates that while what goes on in the classroom between faculty and students is paramount, intentionally creating a welcoming and supportive campus environment can make the difference in retaining a student of color.

It is especially beneficial that this monograph is inclusive enough for a wide audience to find value. It is written for faculty and student affairs professionals who are already aware of the empirical findings that identify the traditional variables for success in college and want to expand their knowledge. It is also written for those educators who have less information about theories of student learning and development but do have a desire to learn how they can contribute to student success. All educators who care about the quality of their work and the impact of higher education on students will find this monograph enlightening. They will find useful strategies for using what they already know and viable suggestions for employing new knowledge in a manner that is sensitive to, appropriate for, and effective with students of color who span the continuum of personal characteristics, experiences, gifts, and needs.

Further, more than any other book on strategies to enhance the academic and personal success of first-year students, this monograph embraces the concept of collaboration. I am particularly interested in the possibilities for collaboration between academic and student affairs, not as an end itself, but as a way to acknowledge that learning is broader than intellectual cognition and involves the whole student. It is important that faculty and student affairs professionals create learning venues that draw on the multiple intelligences of students of color. Through collaborations, faculty and student affairs staff can better integrate experiences that all students bring with them into the curriculum, both inside and outside the classroom, in order to increase opportunities for successful learning and development.

While some books focus on the past and make suggestions for the present, this monograph uses predictive statistics about future student demographics as evidence that new knowledge and understanding about racial and ethnic identity will be critical for colleges and universities. Successful institutions will invite new student cohorts to be partners in creating relevant curricula, in designing effective pedagogy, and in promoting community for all students. Success for students of color will require that their cultural, spiritual, and emotional selves be included in their learning. In the final chapter of the book, Laura Rendón, writes that, "People of color become active owners of the institution and are actively involved in shaping the institutional culture as equal participants" (p. 171).

Faculty and administrators are discovering that today many students are juggling lives that include their education as just one of their multiple responsibilities. Often for students of color, managing it all is even more complex. In Chapter 3, where Laura Rendón and Romero Jalomo write about the "upside and downside of the transition to college," we recognize the strengths students of color bring to their learning. They tell us that, "negotiating separation and transition to college requires intelligence and resilience as well as formidable multicultural skills such as maneuvering the language, values, traditions, and conventions of home, work, and college" (p. 40). These students are truly non-traditional. Therefore, non-traditional and creative institutional transformations are necessary to serve them well.

While reading the chapters, I could sense how passionately the authors want to communicate what they have learned about students of color and what is necessary to prepare for them. It is because of this passion that I can emphatically say that regardless of who we are and what we think we know about students of color, there is still much to learn about the difficulties of transition into college life for students of color.

I applaud the authors for giving us a resource to help us continue to learn. In addition to this excellent resource and the learning we can glean from the students we encounter, we must value and engage in on-going research that adds to knowledge about students. From where I sit as a woman of color and the first in my family to attain a college education, I think that it is imperative that the scholarship on teaching and learning, especially in regard to students of color, be supported throughout higher education for the private benefit of students and the good of society.

It is my privilege to comment on this extraordinary and much needed work.

Gwendolyn Jordan Dungy
Executive Director
National Association of Student Personnel Administrators

Preface

Laura I. Rendón,
Mildred García,
and Dawn Person

This monograph is offered to first-year educators in American colleges and universities for two key purposes: (a) to assist educators in working with a growing number of students of color in higher education, many of whom are first-generation or low-income and (b) to provide a framework for the transformation of the first-year experience.

Dedication

We are proud to dedicate this monograph to all students of color who enter higher education full of dreams and hope for their futures. We write this monograph to help you in your new beginning and to assist those who will help you chart your journey. With conviction and passion, we tell all of you: "Believe in yourself! You can succeed!"

Audience

Transforming the First Year of College for Students of Color is designed for all faculty, counselors, administrators, paraprofessionals, and students who wish to understand how to improve the academic success and social adjustment of students of color during their first year of college. For these key audiences, this monograph provides essential information for understanding and addressing the complex, multifaceted educational and social issues that affect students of color. In addition, the monograph can be a useful tool to assist educational leaders as it provides concepts, models, and strategies for transforming the first-year experience.

Outline of Monograph

Section I provides a general introduction and overview of students of color in higher education. In Chapter 1, Laura I. Rendón, Mildred García, and Dawn Person review the richness and diversity within the overall population of students of color. The authors also discuss the importance of educating students of color and highlight critical educational issues for these students. In Chapter 2, Kevin Kinser and Corlisse D. Thomas analyze the values, career aspirations, and goals of students of color. Romero E. Jalomo and Laura I. Rendón (Chapter 3) discuss the multiple issues that students of color negotiate as they move from their own cultural contexts into their first-year experience in higher education, and offer strategies that can help students make the transition to college.

Section II emphasizes institutional readiness to work with students of color and to develop programs that promote their success. In Chapter 4, Nana Osei-Kofi, Sandra L. Richards, and Daryl G. Smith discuss the role of politics of knowledge in the struggle to create inclusive emancipatory teaching and learning environments. This chapter also includes a discussion of multiple ways in which educators can engage in the transformational process of creating inclusive classrooms that embody a commitment to a just social order. Jesús Treviño and Kris Ewing (Chapter 5) discuss models and strategies to foster positive intergroup relationships, as well as to reduce conflict and foster identity development within and between groups. In Chapter 6, James A. Anderson describes the factors that enhance or preclude the retention of students of color and provides models and strategies to promote persistence.

Section III is concerned with academic and student support strategies designed for specific populations of students of color. These chapters discuss the populations that have been historically underserved in American higher education. In Chapter 7, Wynetta Y. Lee addresses the first-year experience for African-American students. In Chapter 8, Kenneth Gonzalez, Louis Olivas, and Mistalene Calleroz outline first-year issues for Latino students. Xiaoyun Yang and Xiaomei Feng provide an overview of first-year issues for Asian-Pacific American students in Chapter 9. In Chapter 10, Charles R. Colbert, Joseph J. Saggio, and Dawn Tato discuss enhancing the first-year experience for American Indian/Alaska Native students. In Chapter 11, Raechele L. Pope, Timothy R. Ecklund, Teresa Miklitsch, and Radhika Suresh provide a discussion of first-year issues for biracial and multiracial students.

Section IV provides a summary of recommendations, as well as implications for practice and future research. In the concluding chapter, Laura I. Rendón offers a postscript for the monograph and a conceptual framework for the transformation of the first-year experience.

Acknowledgements

We wish to thank John Gardner for envisioning a volume addressing students of color and the first-year experience that was not only timely, but necessary, and for entrusting us with the challenge of completing this important work. We greatly appreciate the support of the staff at the National Resource Center for The First-Year Experience and Students in Transition, especially Barbara Tobolowsky, for her generous time, patience, and attention to detail without which this work might not have been accomplished and Tracy Skipper, for her meticulous attention to the editorial aspects of completing this monograph. Finally, we thank our friends, families, and colleagues who know in their hearts and minds that the effort to help students of color find success in every aspect of their college careers is not simply an academic exercise, it is a way of making a difference for students in our short lifetimes.

Laura I. Rendón
Long Beach, California

Mildred García
New York, New York

Dawn Person
Long Beach, California

Section 1

Identifying Students of Color
and Their Unique Needs

Chapter 1

A Call for Transformation

Laura I. Rendón,
Mildred García,
and Dawn Person

I am many different labels—of many colors, backgrounds, and heritages. I do not know all that I am, but I know that I do not fit into one box. I am multi-dimensional and I have much more to me than what any one label can describe.

I am a first-generation student of color. My first year of college was challenging, exciting, disappointing, and one of the most intense times of my life. My family was so proud of me and it was their support that helped me to complete the first year. It wasn't just me going to college; it was my extended family and community.

The above commentary from students of color illuminates two highly significant issues guiding the development of this book. The first is that educators in the nation's colleges and universities today cannot ignore the fact that college students are becoming more diverse and complex, not only in terms of race and ethnicity but also with respect to class, beliefs, lifestyles, educational preparation, sexuality, perspectives, language, and culture. The second issue concerns the importance of rethinking and transforming the first-year college experience in order to truly make a difference for students of color who come to college with hopes and dreams of attaining academic and economic success and becoming role models in their families and their communities.

The Growing Colorization and Demographic Complexity of America

The signs of a multiracial, multicultural future for American higher education are now glaringly apparent. The increasing diversity of the American population is bringing new challenges and opportunities to the nation's colleges and universities. In 1900, one out of every eight Americans was of a race other than White, but in 2000 one out of four Americans was non-White. Immigration and subsequent births to the new arrivals during the last few decades of the century are key reasons that the nation's minority population grew 11 times more rapidly than the White, non-Hispanic population between 1980 and 2000 (Hobbs & Stoops, 2002). Ochoa (2003) notes that immigration is playing a significant part in the changing American demographics, explaining that today one out of every five students in U.S. public schools is either an immigrant or the child of an immigrant, with a large number being Latino. Immigrant children represent the fastest-growing sector of the U.S. child population, and one of every five children in the U.S. lives in an immigrant household. This population represents a significant part of the potential future of student enrollment in American higher education.

America is growing ever more diverse. In the decade between 1990 and 2000, the White population diminished from 75% to 69.1%. In contrast, the Hispanic population surged from 9.3% to nearly 13%, and Hispanics have now surpassed Blacks as the nation's largest minority group (Schmitt, 2001). The national profile of race and ethnicity derived from the 2000 census reveals that Non-Hispanic Whites remain the majority, constituting 69% of the population. Hispanics comprise 12.5%; Blacks, 12.1%; Asians, 3.6%; American Indians, .7%; Native Hawaiians, .1%; and other races .2%.

The 2000 Census allowed for the identification of individuals who did not wish to classify themselves along traditional lines of race and ethnicity. For the first time, the Census gave people an opportunity to choose more than one race to classify themselves (choosing from six racial categories), and 2% of the nation's 281.4 million people complied. An overwhelming majority of these Americans, 93%, reported they were of two races, and 823 checked all six race categories. This segment of society is expected to grow in future decennial counts due to soaring intermarriage rates, especially for Asian Americans and Hispanics. Among children younger than 18, 4% were reported as multiracial. By 2050, about 21% of Americans are expected to claim mixed ancestry. These important trends are not only complicating the categorization of individuals, they are eroding the socially constructed notion of race as a basis of social distinctions and government policies. Already, every public and private entity that reports race and ethnicity data to the federal government has to rethink survey forms. Educational institutions will have to redesign enrollment forms and rethink how they report data (El Nasser & Overberg, 2001).

Within the next 10 years, a fast-growing generation of diverse students will arrive on American college campuses, revealing a complex, multifaceted student cohort that often defies categorization. Carnevale (1999) states that campuses are just beginning to enroll the leading edge of the biggest demographic wave of students since they were flooded by the baby-boom generation in the 1960s. Predicting that the entering undergraduate population will reach its peak in 2015 with more than 16 million students in colleges and universities, this new wave of students will be more racially and ethnically diverse than the baby boomers of the 1960s.

The Need to Transform the First-Year Experience

The first-year college experience is critical for students of color. Many, who despite having struggled with obstacles such as attending resource-poor schools, having low economic status, and lacking knowledge about higher education, are finding their way into two- and four-year colleges and universities. Given the obstacles these students have endured, it is fair to say that many students of color can be considered survivors. They have survived oppressive experiences such as poverty, racism, discrimination, prejudice, stereotyping, marginalization, and exploitation. They have endured schools that have offered them the least experienced teachers, the worst learning conditions, and the lowest expectations (Rendón & Hope, 1996; Tierney & Hagedorn, 2002). Some education models assume that students of color come to college only with deficits. However, educators should note that many students of color, who have managed to enroll in college as first-year students, bring some important assets such as mastering different languages, maneuvering multiple realities (i.e., the world of work, ghetto, barrio, reservation, gang culture, family, and schooling) and negotiating social, political, and economic hardships (Jalomo, 1995; Trueba, 2002). The last thing students of color need during their first year of college is a replication of their previous negative experiences. A well-designed first-year experience program can provide the tools and skills necessary for students to achieve their academic goals. A first-year program can propel students of color from matriculation to graduation by helping them understand and maneuver the culture of the campus, become informed participants, and ultimately change the culture. Yet, as Rendón elaborates in the last chapter in this volume, to transform the first-year experience requires that educators think beyond the notion of "offering services" to students of color. Transforming the first-year experience necessitates that first-year educators challenge their stereotypes and assumptions about these students. It entails faculty and staff's rethinking the way they design programs and services, as well as the way they interact with students of color. First-year faculty and staff must become transformative educators who actively engage in empowering students and challenging academic and student affairs structures that work against democratic participation and respect for cultural differences.

Transformation also calls for attention to what Tierney (1994) calls "cultural learning," the development of dialogue that supports understanding across differences. A first-year experience program can foster cultural learning through teaching and learning activities such as cross-cultural dialogues and readings. Offering diverse perspectives, which both complement and differ from each other, can be effective means of engaging students in difficult dialogues. Not only can students benefit from cultural learning, but faculty and staff are also afforded the opportunity to engage in obtaining knowledge about the populations they serve. Cultural learning may also help to uncover and change oppressive structures that bar student success such as feelings of marginalization and exclusion. It is also through cultural learning that first-year programs may build structures where no one group is privileged and where power is shared among those who become part of the community, thus creating a climate of respect and validation.

Transforming the first-year experience begins with an understanding of how students of color are defined and characterized and how these students are faring in the nation's K-12 system and in higher education. The information that follows in the next sections can be considered baseline, foundational knowledge that every first-year educator should have to acquire cultural competence (which requires viewing students as whole human beings who bring with them a wealth of strengths such as language and culture) when dealing with students of color.

Who Are Students of Color?

At the onset let us say that labeling groups of people is a difficult and politically charged endeavor. Labels referring to groups of people are constantly changing given political, economic, and social realities. Such is the nature of "socially constructed" terms defined by members of social groups. For instance, DeMarrais and LeCompte (1995) indicate that

the term African Americans is currently used to describe people who have been labeled as Black, Afro-American, and Negro during different historical periods. Often labels are ascribed by the dominant group in society, but, particularly in recent decades, ethnic groups have selected their preferred labels. (p. 29)

For example, "Latino" is a self-identified term growing in popularity to describe a group previously labeled "Hispanic" by the federal government. Complicating the matter is the notion that membership in a minority group does not limit minorities to a single identity based on race or ethnicity. Individuals also have identities based on class, generational status, gender, sexual orientation, abilities, and spirituality. These identities are constantly being reinterpreted on the basis of social interactions with others.

Racial/ethnic groups also differ within and across populations. An example of within group class and gender differences is noted when one compares the significantly different experiences of a working-class, African-American male to an upper-class, African-American woman. Moreover, all members of a particular group do not universally accept some labels. The term "Chicano" is offensive to some Mexican Americans who find the label derogatory but is accepted by others who embrace the political nature of the term. There are also individuals who have multiple racial or ethnic backgrounds such as biracial and multiracial students who resist being labeled as belonging to any one group. For instance, many African Americans can claim White, Hispanic, or Native-American ancestry. Asian-Pacific Americans are also a complex population composed of many different ethnic groups, some who have a century-long history as Americans and others who have recently arrived. Consequently, their composition and definition is not fixed, but fluid (Hune, 2000). Clearly, members of ethnic/racial groups do not fit easily into rigid categories.

"Students of color" is a socially constructed (as opposed to biologically determined) term often used interchangeably and in place of the word "minority," which historically was employed to define groups that were less numerically represented in American society. These minority groups—African Americans, Hispanics, Asians/Pacific Islanders, and American Indian/Alaska Natives—were classified as other than White and of European descent and were perceived to be different from the dominant European-American culture. It is worth noting that some scholars take issue with the term "students of color" because it implies that the White culture is the hidden norm and that being White is "colorless," when in fact all people have ethnic backgrounds. When Whites see themselves as the American norm without self-identifying an ethnic background, it is easy to label non-White groups as "ethnic" or "exotic" (DeMarrais & LeCompte, 1995).

Because within the past 20 years minorities have increased their proportional share of enrollment in colleges and universities, they are likely to become majority populations in many college campuses in the nation. Of course, there have always been institutions of higher education where minorities have been the majority, such as Historically Black Colleges and Universities (HBCUs), some Hispanic-Serving Institutions (though they were not labeled as such until the 1980s), and Tribal Colleges. However, being "majority minorities" does not necessarily imply that these groups will automatically benefit from privileges such as political power and social status. Historically, people of color have been viewed as "minority groups" in this country, no matter what their absolute numbers suggest. Numbers do not tell the whole story about people of color. Consequently, it is important to consider the psychological and social characteristics impacting these groups such as having "significantly less power, control, and influence over their own lives than do members of a dominant group" (Feldman, 2001, p. 81).

Another important factor to consider when defining students of color is the changing conception of the term "race," as some critical scholars are reshaping the intellectual discourse relating to issues of power relations and their connection to race and gender. To be sure, people of color in this nation have had multiple power struggles, including gaining full voting, language, and citizenship rights and equal opportunities for access to education and health care. San Juan (2002) explains that race "is a socially constructed term embedded in the structures of power and privilege in any social formation" and has "by scholarly consensus, no scientific referent" (p. 143). In other words, the concept of race develops not out of a biological basis, but out of group struggles over socially valued resources such as the struggle for power, prestige, education, and health (Weber, 2001). Barton and Coley (1997) point out that in 1996, Neil Rudenstine, then president of Harvard University, indicated in his President's Report, *Diversity and Learning*, that at one time "Irish American" was considered a race; and before 1970, U.S. census data were separated simply into "White" and "Non-White" (Hobbs & Stoops, 2002).

Because socially constructed terms are not biologically based and fixed, social constructions are flexible and subject to change. For example, although Caucasian, Mongoloid, and Negro were recognized in early anthropological writings as primary races, today these racial classifications based on physical attributes are no longer being accepted in the scientific community (DeMarrais & LeCompte, 1995; San Juan, 2002). Further, the terms race and ethnicity are imprecise, vague, and indistinct. For instance, Feldman (2001) notes that "race" is a biological term referring to classifications based on physical characteristics, while "ethnic group" is associated with cultural background, nationality, religion, and language. Nonetheless, race is commonly used as a broad descriptor covering everything from skin color to religion to culture. Ethnicity refers to common cultural ties, but many people have their cultural roots in several ethnic backgrounds. However, race does have social meaning considering that what people actually believe about race determines how individuals relate to others. Mistaken assumptions about different groups of people based on race often lead to discriminatory, ethnocentric, racist behaviors such as viewing students of color as inferior, incapable of doing college-level work, and lazy (DeMarrais & LeCompte, 1995).

Also important to consider is that we can no longer use a White/Black sociological paradigm to explain how difference manifests itself in society and in higher education. Historically, media and scholarly discussions of politics, the economy, and education have focused on White/Black differences, effectively dismissing other racial/ethnic cohorts. For example, Latinos and Asians are fast-growing in numbers and will have to be equally engaged in any discussion pertaining to the U.S. social structures such as education, health care, and the economy (Hune & Chan, 1997).

Considering the issues cited above, the term "students of color" may be employed to identify students who are (a) members of racial/ethnic groups that have been historically underrepresented and underserved in America's educational system and (b) socially defined as minorities who are most likely to become targets of oppression, prejudice, stereotyping, and discrimination regardless of numerical status and distribution. Students of color usually fall in one or more of the following groups, which are also discussed in greater detail in subsequent chapters in this monograph.

African Americans

African Americans, also often referred to as "Black," have historical links in many different countries of the world. There are African Americans with roots not only in Africa but also in the West Indies, the Caribbean, Canada, Central and South America, and the U.S. These regions constitute many languages, dialects, and cultural customs. McKinnon (2001) reports that 54% of the U.S. Black population resides in the South, 18% lives in the northeast, and 10% lives in the West.

Like other marginalized groups, African Americans have had a history of oppression. Many Africans were enslaved and taken to the Americas where they were stripped of their native languages, history, and customs. What evolved was a blending of African traditions with the new world. New customs and languages developed out of necessity so that Africans from different regions of the continent could communicate in the Americas. As time passed, African people migrated to other areas of the Americas, while some returned to Africa— either by force or out of necessity. In 1857, the Supreme Court ruled in the *Dred Scott v. John F. A. Sanford* decision that a slave was not a citizen of the U.S. and had no right to sue in federal court. The Fourteenth Amendment gave newly freed slaves the right to vote, but limited the vote to males. While the Fifteenth Amendment guaranteed all male citizens the right to vote regardless of race or color, men of color continued to face obstacles to voting such as literacy tests, dual registration, and poll taxes. The Nineteenth Amendment extended voting privileges to both sexes, but, as in the past, men and women of color continued to face obstacles to voting (Weber, 2001). Even more recently, African Americans have also had to deal with discriminatory experiences such as racial profiling, hate crimes, stereotyping, and racism. Despite the *Brown v. Board of Education* (1954) case that declared segregated schools unconstitutional, African Americans and other minority children disproportionately attend separate and unequal schools that yield significantly different outcomes in terms of preparation for college (Rendón & Hope, 1996; Tierney & Hagedorn, 2002).

American Indian/Alaska Natives

American Indians and Alaska Natives (AI/ANs) are a very diverse group. There are now 557 federally recognized tribes in the United States, and 220 of these are in Alaska (Russell, 1997). American Indian tribes with at least 100,000 members are Cherokee, Navajo, Latin American Indian, Choctaw, Sioux, and Chippewa (Ogunwole, 2002). The state of Arizona is home to 21 different American Indian tribes. Alaska is home to three distinct Native groups: (a) Eskimos (Inupiak and Yupik); (b) American Indian tribes (Athabaskan, Tlingit, Tsimshian, and Haida); and (c) Aleuts. There are some 20 Alaska Native languages and more than 200 Native villages, with roughly 60% living in Alaska's rural areas. Most American Indians and Alaska Natives live in the western part of the nation (Ogunwole).

Demmert (1996) indicates that AI/AN people, unlike other racial/ethnic groups, have a special fiduciary relationship with the U.S. because the federal government maintains a trust responsibility as guardian of Native lands and resources. Consequently, the federal government must follow strict codes of conduct in their dealings with AI/AN people. Native residents to the U.S., AI/AN people were denied access to their lands and freedom to practice their spiritual beliefs and language in an attempt to socialize them into a new America based on Puritan beliefs and ethics (1996). These oppressive experiences caused a lifestyle incongruent with their culture and traditions. Atrocities experienced by these communities continue to affect their resources, land ownership, health, education, and cultural wholeness. It was not until 1924 that Native Americans were granted citizenship in the U.S., though some states continued to disenfranchise them. In 1948, for the first time, Native Americans in Arizona and New Mexico were allowed to vote in state and national elections. In 1957, Utah was the last state to allow Native Americans living on reservations to vote (Weber, 2001).

The colonization of AI/AN people is a well-documented, yet often ignored tragedy. DeJong (1993) indicates that Europeans embarked on America to change the cultural orientation of native peoples. He writes:

Concepts such as individualism, competition, and time—all of which were foreign to most Indian communities—were thrust upon the Indian students along with the Europeans' manners and styles of clothing and hair dress. Educational methods, such as the use of the written word, daily classroom routine, and indoor study soon became a burden to many Indian students, who were used to oral tradition and experiential learning. Moreover, Europeans attempted to change the Indians' spiritual orientation; almost all educational endeavors focused on religious instruction. (p. 22)

Also devastating to Indians was the use of boarding schools beginning early in the 18th century for the purposes of "civilizing" them. Tragically, many Indian children perished with this changed environment, diet, and manner of living (DeJong, 1993).

Asian/Pacific Americans

The Asian/Pacific American (APA) population is large, fast growing, and culturally heterogeneous. Asian refers to people from the Far East, Southeast Asia, or the Indian sub-continent (e.g., Cambodia, China, India, Japan, Korea, Malaysia, Pakistan, the Philippine Islands, Thailand, and Vietnam). Pacific Islander refers to people from Hawaii, Guam, Samoa, or other Pacific islands. More than 20% of Asians and Pacific Islanders live in Hawaii, California, Washington, New York, and New Jersey (U.S. Census Bureau, 2000a). Hune (2000) notes that "over the past three decades, APAs changed from a largely U.S.-born population to a predominantly foreign-born population of new immigrants and refugees who speak a language other than English" (p. 161). The adoption of the Immigration and Naturalization Act of 1965, which gave citizens of all nations equal opportunity to immigrate to the U.S., has been a major contributing factor to the growth of Asian and Pacific Island populations.

Within Asian and Pacific Islander groups, there is a significant difference in when, how, and why they found their residence in the U.S. Kim (1997) notes that Asian immigrants have been coming to America since the middle of the 19th century. The Chinese were the earliest to arrive around 1840, followed by the Japanese who arrived between 1890 and 1920. Koreans followed in smaller numbers around 1903. The last of the early Asian immigrants were Asian Indians and Filipinos. The early immigrants made major contributions to the economic growth and development of the West Coast and Hawaii, taking jobs in railroads, canneries, mines, and sugar and pineapple plantations. Hmong and Vietnamese are recent immigrants who fled their countries to find refuge in America. APAs have faced discrimination and prejudice because their culture, language, and values are quite different from the White majority.

APAs have sought access and equity in education, resulting in the 1974 *Lau v. Nichols* decision, which provided for bilingual programs, teachers, and teacher assistants that have benefited all immigrant and non-English speaking groups of students. APAs have challenged higher education admissions policies charging that some institutions were setting quotas on APA enrollment (Hune, 2000). Often characterized as a "model minority," APAs have sought to erase this kind of stereotyping, arguing that the stereotype does not consider large numbers of uneducated, illiterate Asians and many who have not achieved high levels of economic success such as Vietnamese, Cambodians, Laotians, and Hmongs (Kim, 1997).

Latinos/as

The U.S. government initiated the term "Hispanic," while "Latino/a" is a self-designated term. Though it is difficult to ascertain a clear preference for either term, it appears that "Latino/a" is gaining in popularity. Latino/a is employed to define individuals who are usually Spanish-speaking of Latin American descent who live in the U.S. People referred to as Hispanic or Latino/a can be of any race or ethnicity. Mexican Americans are the largest group in the Latino/a population. In 2000, Mexican Americans accounted for 58.5% of the Latino/a population. Puerto Ricans were 9.6% of this population and Cubans were 3.5%. The remaining 28.4% were of other Hispanic origin (i.e., Spanish, South American, Central American, and Dominican), and these "other" Hispanics have experienced significant growth since 1990. Half of the Latino/a population resides in two states: California and Texas. States with one million or more Latinos include: California, Texas, New York, Florida, Illinois, Arizona, and New Jersey (Guzman, 2001).

Within the Latino/a population, immigrants from Mexico and Central and South America continue to arrive in the United States each year. After 1900, significant numbers of Puerto Ricans came to the U.S., but the bulk of the migration occurred in the 1950s and 1960s. Puerto Ricans became American citizens by birthright in 1917. Cuban immigration rose sharply in the 1950s as a result of political turmoil in Cuba. Wealthy, well-educated Cubans fled their country to escape political dictatorship. The next wave of immigrants included the relatives of the first group and poor people looking for work. These Cuban immigrants were followed by *Marielitos*, about 125,000, mostly poor and ill-educated people that the government wanted to get out of Cuba.

The Mexican-origin population sometimes referred to as Chicanos, *mexicanos*, or Mexican Americans, has deep roots in this country that extend even before the establishment of Jamestown (Rendón & Hope, 1996). The U.S. southwest, consisting of Texas, New Mexico, Arizona, California, and parts of Nevada, Utah, and Colorado were part of Mexico until U.S. troops overtook Mexican forces in the U.S.-Mexican War. These lands were signed away to the U.S. on February 2, 1848 in the Treaty of Guadalupe-Hidalgo in exchange for $15 million. Language and cultural rights of new citizens were not protected, and over the next 50 years language laws restricted Mexican-American participation in voting, legal processes, and education (Weber, 2001).

In terms of economic status, few Latinos come from affluent families where both parents have attended college and graduate school. A large number come from working class, low-income families where neither parent has finished high school. One in five Latinos is poor, and Latino/a children represent 30.4% of all children in poverty (Ochoa, 2003). The Latino/a population has challenged policies such as inequitable school financing through the courts (i.e., *San Antonio ISD* v. *Rodriguez* in 1973 and *Edgewood v. Kirby* in 1987), cases that illuminated the financial limitations of poor school districts, which serve a preponderance of Mexican-American students in Texas. Another case in Texas, *LULAC v. Richards* (1992) highlighted inequities in funding to institutions of higher education located along the Texas-Mexican border, which is two-thirds Mexican American and the poorest area in Texas. Even though the Texas Supreme Court ruled that disparities in funding were not the result of intentional discrimination against Mexican Americans, the state of Texas moved toward correcting inequities in funding formulas (Rendón & Hope, 1996).

In summary, it can be discerned from the discussion above that first-year educators are dealing with issues related to a very complex, rapidly growing, fluid, and dynamic group of students of color. These issues include diversity within and across racial/ethnic groups and legacies of oppression connected to not only social and economic policies, but also to educational issues related to language, access to college, equitable schooling, and college admissions requirements.

College Participation and Degree Attainment

Making a difference for students of color during their first year in college requires having a grasp of the characteristics of students and what they bring to the college environment. It is also important to understand where these students tend to enroll, how they are faring in college, and why it is important to educate students of color.

Participation

Examining percentage distribution of enrollment of 18- to 24-year-olds in colleges and universities between 1980 and 2000 (Table 1), shows that Whites experienced a loss in their share of enrollment during that 20-year period, while a larger proportion of students of color attended college in 2000 than in 1980. Regardless, White students remain the majority population in the nation's two- and four-year institutions (Llagas & Snyder, 2003).

Table 1.
Percentage Distribution of Enrollment in Colleges and Universities, by Race/ethnicity: 1980 and 2000

Race/Ethnicity	1980			2000		
	Total	Two-year	Four-year	Total	Two-year	Four-year
White, non-Hispanic	81	79	83	68	64	71
Black, non-Hispanic	9	10	8	11	12	11
Hispanic	4	6	3	10	14	7
Asian/Pacific Islander	2	3	2	6	7	6
American Indian/ Alaska Native	1	1	0	1	1	1
Nonresidential alien	3	1	3	3	1	5

Note. Includes two-year and four-year degree-granting institutions that were participating in Title IV federal financial aid programs. Details may not add to 100 due to rounding.
Source: U.S. Department of Education, National Center for Education Statistics, Digest of Education Statistics, 2002, based on Higher Education General Information Survey (HEGIS). "Fall Enrollment in Colleges and Universities" survey, 1980-81, and Integrated Postsecondary Education Data System (IPEDS), "Fall Enrollment" survey, 2000-01.

Table 2 illustrates that students of color are not equally distributed in the nation's two- and four-year college systems. In Fall 2000, nearly 58% of all Hispanics enrolled in public and private two- and four-year colleges and universities were found in two-year institutions (42% in four-year). In the same year, out of all students in their cohort enrolled in college, roughly 49% of American Indian, 41% of Asian, 43% of Black, and 36 % of White students were enrolled in two-year institutions. Conversely, out of all students in their cohort enrolled in college, about 64% of Whites, 59% of Asians, 58% of Blacks, and 51% of American Indians were participating in four-year institutions (*Chronicle of Higher Education*, 2003).

Table 2.
College Enrollment by Racial and Ethnic Group, Fall 2000

Race/Ethnic Group	Public/Private Four-year		Public/Private Two-Year		Total
	Number	Percent	Number	Percent	
All Students (grad & undergrad)	9,363,900	61.2	5,948,400	38.8	15,312,300
American Indian	76,500	50.6	74,600	49.4	151,100
Asian	576,300	58.9	401,900	41.1	978,200
Black	995,400	57.5	734,900	42.5	1,730,300
Hispanic	617,900	42.3	843,900	57.7	1,461,800
White	6,658,100	63.6	3,804,000	36.4	10,462,100
Foreign	439,700	83.2	89,000	16.8	528,700

Source: Chronicle of Higher Education Almanac Issue, 2003-4 (2003, August 29), p. 15.

Degree Attainment

In terms of degree attainment, Table 3 (Llagas & Snyder, 2003) shows that White students still earn the majority of undergraduate and graduate degrees. Examining college degree attainment for students of color, Hispanic and Black students are better represented in the percentage distribution of associate and bachelor's degrees, but less represented in graduate degree attainment, especially doctoral and first professional degrees. Asian/Pacific Islanders are better represented in the percentage distribution of first professional degree. American Indian/Alaska Native students represent a very small share of undergraduate and graduate degrees earned. It is alarming to note that non-resident alien students earned a higher proportion of doctoral degrees (25.1%) than all minority students combined (13.6%). Retaining minority students so that they are better represented in the share of undergraduate and graduate degrees earned remains an important priority, and the first-year experience can certainly play a key role in providing the foundation for persistence behavior.

Importance of Educating Students of Color

A key reason that educators need to be concerned about educating students of color is that national and world societal structures require a well-educated and trained workforce with a high degree of social consciousness. Students must be prepared to work anywhere in the world on a multitude of social issues in a way that values and respects cultural differences and diverse ways of solving problems. Further, as work requirements change to address new technologies, use of information systems, and skills to work in an international world market, individuals will need advanced levels of education. Today's high school diploma is only the first step on the journey to earning a passport to the future. The link between education, employment, and earnings is clear, and is reflected in data published by Postsecondary Education Opportunity (2001). Unemployment rates in 2001 were higher for individuals who had less than a high school diploma (7.3%) or only a high

Table 3.

Number and Percentage Distribution of Degrees Conferred by Colleges and Universities, by Race/ Ethnicity and Degree Level: 1999-2000

	Number of Degrees Conferred						
Degree Level	Total	White Non-Hispanic	Hispanic	Black Non-Hispanic	Asian/ Pacific Islander	American Indian/ Alaska Native	Non-Resident Alien
Associate Degree	564,933	408,508	60,181	51,541	27,764	6,494	10,445
Bachelor's Degree	1,237,875	928,013	107,891	74,963	77,793	8,711	40,504
Master's Degree	457,056	317,999	35,625	19,093	22,899	2,232	59,208
Doctor's Degree	44,780	27,492	2,220	1,291	2,380	159	11,238
First Professional	80,057	59,601	5,552	3,865	8,576	546	1,899

	Percentage Distribution of Degrees Conferred						
Associate Degree	100	72.3	10.7	9.1	4.9	1.1	1.8
Bachelor's Degree	100	75.0	8.7	6.1	6.3	0.7	3.3
Master's Degree	100	69.6	7.8	4.2	5.0	0.5	13.0
Doctor's Degree	100	61.4	5.0	2.9	5.3	0.4	25.1
First Professional	100	74.4	6.9	4.8	10.7	0.7	2.4

Note. Includes two- and four-year degree-granting institutions that were participating in Title IV federal financial aid programs. Detail may not add to totals due to rounding.
Source: U.S. Department of Education, National Center for Education Statistics, Digest of Education Statistics, 2001, based on Integrated Postsecondary Education Data System (IPEDS), "Completion Survey," 1999-2000.

school diploma (4.2%) than those who earned associate degrees (2.9%), bachelor's degrees (2.5%), doctorates (1.1%), and professional degrees (1.2%). Similarly, median earnings in 2001 were higher for those who earned professional degrees ($82,421), doctorates ($75,182), master's degrees ($56,589), bachelor's degrees ($46,969), and associate degrees ($36,399) than those who stopped at graduation from high school ($29,187) or had less than a high school diploma ($22,350).

The future of the American economy is tied to the education of students of color. As these individuals join the ranks of well-paid citizens, their taxable wealth could translate into billions of dollars of revenue for federal, state, and local communities, benefiting all citizens. Not only can the nation as a whole benefit, but higher education can also provide students of color a path to the middle and upper class. Further, well-educated students of color can bring the perspectives of their communities into the workforce (Carnevale & Stone, 1995). A college education can provide societal role models, individuals who become pillars of society who have the time to engage in civic responsibilities. These individuals are also likely to become informed citizens who are able to engage in political activism and perhaps even become political leaders.

Economic arguments supporting the education of students of color often neglect the moral and ethical rationale for educating groups of people who have histories of oppression. It was President Franklin D. Roosevelt who said: "We seek to build an America where not one is left out." Given the history of people of color who know first-hand what it is like to be left out of American social and economic structures, and given the pernicious persistence of stereotyping and marginalization of racial/ethnic groups, doing what is morally right for students of color is reason enough to embark on transforming the first-year experience. As first-year educators, we cannot forget that our task is two-fold. First, we must be involved in providing students of color the intellectual and social tools they need to function as contributing members of society. It is these highly prepared individuals who, along with their White counterparts, will be able to shape a world that values diversity, democracy, community, and hope for humanity. Second, we must remain cognizant that as we work to make a difference for students of color during the first year of college, we are also playing a significant part in erasing legacies of neglect and in shaping a better future for higher education and our society.

Critical Educational Issues for Students of Color

Faculty and administrators need to be aware of the issues that impact students of color in higher education. Beyond understanding diversity within and across the racial/ethnic groups, educational achievement patterns, and reasons to educate racial/ethnic groups, there are critical educational issues that need to be understood and addressed if students of color are to have a successful and meaningful first-year college experience.

Negotiating the Transition to College

Students of color, particularly those from working-class backgrounds and who are the first in their families to attend college, are likely to find the transition to college a disruptive and somewhat traumatic experience. Some of these students are coming to college with excellent academic skills, while others have not fully developed reading, writing, speaking, and computational skills. However, even some students with average and above-average high school GPA's may experience feelings of inadequacy, isolation, and cultural shock, as well as discrimination, stereotyping, lack of confidence, particularly on predominantly White college campuses (Terenzini et al., 1993). Clearly, students with low levels of academic preparation will need curricular initiatives that promote reading, writing, math, and high-level thinking skills. Student and academic activities and services are also needed to reduce isolation and foster involvement. These include summer bridge programs, learning communities, and first-generation student programs, as well as counseling and mentoring from culturally competent educators (Rendón, Jalomo, & Nora, 2000).

Educators need to know that the transition to college can be a time of great disequilibrium for students of color. These students are entering a new college world that is often drastically different from their home realities. They are assuming a new college identity that makes them appear different to their friends and families who have often not participated in higher education. Many of these students experience cultural assaults from some students who view them as less competent individuals who do not really belong in college. The transition to college is a time when students of color need to acquire confidence in their ability to be successful college students, negotiate the new world of college, maneuver themselves through multiple worlds (i.e., the world of college, work, family, community) negotiate changes in identity development, and develop a positive self-esteem that can counteract any discrimination or stereotyping they may experience (Jalomo, 1995; Rendón, 1994; Terenzini et al., 1993).

Retaining Students of Color

> *No one in my family ever went to college. I remember that first day vividly as I walked into my first college classroom. The professor gave out a syllabus with a long list of expectations, assignments, and due dates. I was completely overwhelmed and felt totally alone. When I returned back home, I felt I had no one in my neighborhood or family to turn to for help. Would they understand my anxiety? So I went into my room looked at the syllabus and began to cry.*

The above statement from a student is an example of why colleges and universities must do a better job of addressing the needs of first-generation, low-income students, many of whom are students of color. First-year attrition rates indicate that in public two-year institutions 54.2% of the student body leaves after the first year, a dire consequence for Hispanics and American Indians who are clustered in two-year colleges. The attrition rate at public four-year institutions after the first year is 30%, and at private two- and four-year institutions the rate is 29.6% and 25.4%, respectively (Carnevale, 1999).

Data from the National Education Longitudinal Study (NELS) of 1988, Fourth Follow-up 2000 (NCES, 2003) illustrate racial/ethnic differences in meeting educational milestones such as graduating from high school, entering college, and earning a college degree. The NELS survey tracks students who were in the eighth grade in 1988 and who were 8 years beyond their expected (1992) high school graduation in 2000. Racial/ethnic differences were found in the first milestone, the receipt of an on-time, regular high school diploma, with Asian (91%) students followed by White students (82%) being more likely than Black (72%) and Hispanic (67%) students to receive a regular on-time diploma. At the second milestone (i.e., enrolling in a postsecondary institution within the year following high school graduation), Asian (83%) students who received an on-time high school diploma were more likely than White (71%), Black (61%), and Hispanic (66%) students to immediately enroll in a postsecondary institution. At the third milestone, earning a college degree within the scheduled time frame (e.g., two years for an associate degree) Black (10%) and Hispanic (9%) students who had graduated from high school on time and immediately enrolled in a postsecondary institution were found to have lower credential attainment rates than Asian (31%) and White (26%) students. However, these differences were reduced when "nontraditional" completion indicators were introduced (i.e., taking a longer time to earn a high school diploma or GED and taking a longer time to enroll in college and to complete a postsecondary credential). Of the students in the nontraditional category, 55% of Asians, 57% of Whites, 77% of Blacks, and 74% of Hispanics earned a postsecondary credential, suggesting that flexibility in meeting educational milestones can reduce differences in attainment (NCES, 2003).

Many students of color will need academic and student support strategies to allow them to persist in the first year of college and beyond. Retention strategies are critical if students are going to stay in college until they attain two- or four-year college degrees. The mean time to complete a bachelor's degree is about five years. However, on average, students who complete the college-prep curriculum, earn high test scores, and graduate from high school with high GPAs take roughly 4.45 years to earn a BA. Students who do not leave the institution and are continuously enrolled complete the BA in about 4.33 years (Adelman, 1999). College retention and academic success are shaped by experiences students have before and after enrolling in college.

Pre-College Experiences Relating to Success in College

We believe it is important to consider the pre-college experiences that shape the potential for doing college academic work early in a student's life. The extent that students of color gain access to and succeed in college is shaped by the following:

- *Tracking policies that result in failing to complete the high school college-prep sequence.* Blacks and Latinos are disproportionately enrolled in a less demanding high school curriculum, because they are likely to attend schools in low-income areas that may not offer a rigorous, comprehensive curriculum. The college-prep sequence is critical to college access and academic success (Adelman, 1999; Oakes & Lipton, 1996). Tracking and ability grouping in high schools place students in course-taking patterns that do not lead to college entry or college success. "Slow" students almost never catch up, while advanced students are likely to engage in high-order thinking skills (Oakes, 1985).
- *Setting low expectations.* Students who do not see themselves as capable college students lower their aspirations. In a study of urban 6th, 8th, 10th, and 12th graders, Rendón and Nora (1997) found that although all students had high aspirations (i.e., wanting to graduate from high school, attend college, and graduate from college) these aspirations diminished somewhat between the 6th and the 12th grade. By the time students were seniors in high school, they were less likely to believe that they had the financial resources and family encouragement to attend college (social capital). Further, they were less inclined to believe that they had the grades and intelligence to attend college (academic capital). Moreover, some K-12 faculty and counselors do not see students of color as a professional class. Some students are also misdiagnosed as slow learners or as having learning disabilities (Rendón, 2002; Rendón & Hope, 1996).
- *Attending resource-poor schools.* There are serious educational disparities between affluent and poor school districts. Low-income schools operate with a less demanding curriculum; lack textbooks, computer technology, and certified teachers; and produce fewer students qualified to enter selective and relatively selective colleges and universities (Oakes, 2003).
- *Growing up in poverty.* Poor students' life histories may include deficiencies in nutrition and health, as well as invalidating experiences such as being told they are remedial and on a dead-end track. Many attend poorly funded schools with scarce resources and grow up in communities removed from academics. The culture of poverty is a breeding ground for failure to take advantage of educational opportunities; to set high expectations; and to view college as an affordable, realistic possibility (Nora, 2003; Oakes, 2003; Rendón, 1997).

College Attendance Factors Affecting Retention and Academic Success

To prevent students from leaving college, first-year educators need to be aware of the factors that are related to dropout behavior, including the following:

- *Stopping out of college.* Students who are not continuously enrolled and interrupt their studies for more than one year are less likely to complete college (Adelman, 1999).
- *Attending college part-time.* Students who attend college on a part-time basis are less likely to get involved in institutional life and to develop an affiliation with the academic and social life of the college. This includes students who have jobs outside the campus, although working on campus has a positive effect on retention. Work opportunities on campus and financial aid allow students to spend more time on campus and their academic work (Nora, 2003).
- *Being married with family obligations such as taking care of a sibling, grandparent, or an entire family.* Unless these students negotiate family responsibilities and the work of college, they are likely to spend little time on academics (Nora & Wedham, 1991).
- *Being a first-generation student.* Students with a family history of little to no college attendance are likely to experience feelings of confusion and trauma as they enter the new world of college (Rendón, 1992; 1994).
- *Lacking validation, encouragement, and support from family and friends.* Students who are teased about attending college or told they will never succeed in college are likely to lack confidence about being in college (Jalomo, 1995; Rendón, 2002).
- *Experiencing cultural shock or cultural assaults in college.* Students of color who are perceived as "different" from mainstream, White students may experience discrimination and racism. Nora and Cabrera (1996) found that Hispanic students were more likely than Whites to sense discrimination and prejudice in the classroom and on campus. These experiences negatively affected their academic interactions with faculty, social experiences on campus, academic and intellectual development, and commitment to the institution, all of which are considered important to student retention.
- *Setting high educational aspirations.* Goal setting and dedication to studies can positively affect intentions to return to college for the second year (Cabrera, Nora, & Castaneda, 1993).
- *Receiving financial aid.* The actual awarding of financial aid, as well as attitudes associated with having received financial assistance, have been known to influence the decision of Latino students to remain in college (Cabrera et al., 1993). The importance of financial aid as a means of fostering retention has also been noted in studies by Stampen and Cabrera (1988) and Cabrera, Stampen, and Hansen (1990).
- *Interacting formally and informally with faculty.* Academic and social integration can be fostered by formal and informal contact between students and faculty (Nora & Cabrera, 1996; Tinto, 1993).
- *Being validated, supported, and encouraged by significant others.* Many students of color are not likely to get involved in college on their own. They need what Rendón (1994) calls "validation," which can occur in and out of the

classroom when faculty and staff take the initiative to reach out to students in an attempt to confirm them as capable knowers who can be a valuable asset to the college community. Out-of-class validation from family members has also been found to positively affect the determination of students of color to do well in college. This form of validation can come in the form of parental, spouse, mentor, or counselor encouragement and support (Nora & Cabrera, 1996; Rendón, 1994; 2002).

The need to improve first-year college retention rates is very important given that a successful first year is likely to provide the motivating impetus for students to persist until college graduation (Nora, 2003). As noted earlier, students of color need to persist in college to earn a higher share of undergraduate and graduate degrees.

Fostering Intergroup Relations

Racist incidents where students of color are the victims of hateful acts such as caricatures, jokes, discrimination, and stereotyping occur every year, especially at predominantly White institutions. A first-year program should be concerned with fostering positive, respectful relations between and among different student groups on campus representing diverse identities based on race and ethnicity, class, sexuality, spirituality, and disabilities. Many students of color, as well as White students, enter college with little understanding of the cultural values, traditions, language, and worldview of students who are different from themselves. This lack of awareness can lead to uncertainty, confusion, hostility, and mistrust among minority and majority students. Programs that address intergroup conflict and promote tolerance of, respect for, and dignity of all students are typically a part of Intergroup Relations Centers and Multicultural Student Centers. Such programs can assist first-year educators deal with these sensitive issues.

Addressing Teaching and Learning

The increased presence of students of color on two- and four-year college campuses creates a significant opportunity for first-year faculty and staff to rethink epistemological issues and pedagogical approaches based on perspectives that address issues of social justice, democracy, and equity. Critical educators such as Paulo Freire (1970/2000), Antonia Darder (1989), and Peter McLaren (1998), among others argue for teaching and learning contexts that create liberated as opposed to oppressed learners. Moreover, critical educators question the traditional view of faculty as sole experts who dispense knowledge in classrooms where students are passive learners. Critical educators advocate for active learning and a liberatory pedagogy that calls for teaching and learning to be democratic, participatory, and relational and allows both faculty and students to be holders and beneficiaries of knowledge.

Along similar lines, feminist scholars (Belenky, Clinchy, Goldberger, & Tarule, 1986) propose the concept of "connected teaching," a relational model of teaching and learning that gives students voice and confirmation, builds relationships among faculty and students, and welcomes diversity and the creation of non-hierarchical learning communities. In addition, holistic teaching and learning advocated by educators such as Palmer (1998), hooks (1994), and Rendón (2000) provide paradigms that address the educational development of the whole student, including intellectual, social, emotional, and spiritual growth. Indeed, learning communities that incorporate holistic learning have been shown to demonstrate significant potential to foster academic success and personal development for students of color (Burgis, 2000). With regard to what gets taught in college classrooms, Smith and García (1996) maintain that core curriculum should be multicultural—inclusive of the contributions of groups that represent diverse ethnic/racial, gender, and sexual perspectives. Essentially, educating students of color will require attention to transformation of the college curriculum and a shift in the way instruction is actualized.

A first-year program that embraces diversity should also attend to the representation of culturally competent faculty and staff who take the time to learn about these students and what matters in promoting academic success for students of color. The presence of faculty and staff of color can have positive effects on both minority and majority students. For instance, minority faculty may encourage non-minorities to reconsider stereotypes about culturally different groups and allow for positive interaction between Whites and non-Whites. Moreover, a significant representation of minority faculty can reduce feelings of isolation on the part of minority students who see these faculty members as role models and validating agents. The mere presence of minority faculty can attract larger numbers of minority students, as well as faculty and administrators to a particular campus, creating a critical mass of racial/ethnic group representation. Along the same lines, the presence of minority administrators may benefit the level of satisfaction and well-being of minority faculty and students as they validate the campus as an accepting environment that is concerned with the educational attainment of ethnic/racial minorities (Harris & Nettles, 1996).

The first year of college is one of the most exciting and challenging times in the life of a student of color. As the nation prepares to deal with greater numbers of students of color, a first-year program can stand at the forefront of innovation and transformative change. First-year educators can make a significant difference in the academic and social lives of students of color, and it is our privilege to join them in helping to accomplish this most important purpose of higher education.

Authors' Note

All student quotes in this chapter are taken from conversations with Dawn Person.

References

Adelman, C. (1999). *Answers in the toolbox*. Jessup, MD: Education Publications Center.

Barton, P. E., & Coley, R. J. (1997). Foreword. In H. Kim (Ed.), *Diversity among Asian American high school students*. Princeton, NJ: Educational Testing Service.

Belenky, M. F., Clinchy, B. M., Goldberger, N. R., & Tarule, J. M. (1986). *Women's ways of knowing: The development of self, voice, and mind*. New York: Basic Books.

Burgis, L. (2000). *How learning communities foster intellectual, social and spiritual growth in students*. Unpublished doctoral dissertation, Arizona State University, Tempe, AZ.

Cabrera, A. F., Nora, A., & Castaneda, M. B. (1993). College persistence: Structural equation modeling test of an integrated model of student retention. *Journal of Higher Education*, 64(2), 123-137.

Cabrera, A. F., Stampen, J. O., & Hansen, W. L. (1990). Exploring the effects of ability to pay on persistence in college. *Review of Higher Education*, 13(3), 303-336.

Carnevale, A. P. (1999). *Education = success: Empowering Hispanic youth and adults*. Princeton, NJ: Educational Testing Service.

Carnevale, A. P., & Stone, S. C. (1995). *The American mosaic: An in-depth report on the future of diversity at work.* New York: McGraw Hill.

   Chronicle of Higher Education Almanac Issue 2003-4. (2003, August 29). *L*(1), 15.

   Darder, A. (1989). *Critical pedagogy, cultural democracy and biculturalism. The foundation for a critical theory of bicultural education.* Unpublished doctoral dissertation, Claremont Graduate University, Claremont, CA.

   DeJong, D. H. (1993). *Promises of the past. A history of Indian education.* Golden, CO: North American Press.

   De Marrais, K. B., & LeCompte, M. (1995). *The way schools work: A sociological analysis of education.* New York: Addison Wesley Longman.

   Demmert, W. G., Jr. (1996). Indian nations at risk: An educational strategy for action. In L. I. Rendón, & R. O. Hope (Eds.), *Educating a new majority* (pp. 231-262). San Francisco: Jossey-Bass.

   El Nasser, H., & Overberg, P. (2001). *USA TODAY index charts rise in nation's diversity.* Retrieved September 25, 2002, from http://www.usatoday.com/news/census/2001-03-14-diversityindex.htm

   Feldman, R. S. (2001). *Social psychology.* Upper Saddle River, NJ: Prentice Hall.

   Freire, P. (2000). *Pedagogy of the oppressed.* (3rd ed.). New York: Continuum. (Original work published 1970)

   Guzman, B. (2001, May). *The Hispanic population, Census 2000 brief.* Washington, DC: U.S. Department of Commerce. Economics and Statistics Administration. U.S. Census Bureau.

   Harris, S. M., & Nettles, M. T. (1996). Ensuring campus climates that embrace diversity. In L. I. Rendón, & R. O. Hope (Eds.), *Educating a new majority* (pp. 330-371). San Francisco: Jossey-Bass.

   Hobbs, F., & Stoops, N. (2002). Demographic trends in the 20th century. U.S. Census Bureau. *Census 2000 Special Reports*, Series CENSR-4. U.S. Government Printing Office, Washington, D.C.

   hooks, b. (1994). *Teaching to transgress.* New York: Routledge.

   Hune, S. (2000). Doing gender with a feminist gaze: Toward a historical reconstruction of Asian America. In M. Zhou & J. V. Gatewood (Eds.), *Contemporary Asian America: A multidisciplinary reader.* New York: New York University Press.

   Hune, S., & Chan, K. (1997). Special focus: Asian Pacific American demographic and educational trends. In D. Carter, & R. Wilson (Eds.), *Minorities in education (1996–1997), Vol. 15* (pp. 39-67, 103-107). Washington, DC: American Council on Education.

   Jalomo, R. E. (1995). *Latino students in transition: An analysis of the first-year experience in the community college.* Unpublished doctoral dissertation, Arizona State University, Tempe, AZ.

   Kim, H. (1997). *Diversity among Asian America high school students.* Princeton, NJ: Educational Testing Service.

   Llagas, C., & Snyder, T. D. (2003, April). *Status and trends in the education of Hispanics.* Washington, DC: U.S. Department of Education. National Institute of Education Sciences. National Center for Education Statistics.

   McKinnon, J. (2001). *The Black Population, Census 2000 brief.* Washington, DC: U.S. Department of Commerce. Economics and Statistics Administration. U.S. Census Bureau.

   McLaren, P. (1998). *Life in schools: An introduction to critical pedagogy in the foundations of education* (3rd ed.). New York: Longman.

   National Center for Education Statistics (2003, June). Racial/ethnic differences in the path to a postsecondary credential. *Issue Brief, NCES 2003-005.* Washington, DC: U.S. Department of Education, Institute of Education Sciences.

Nora, A. (2003). Access to higher education for Hispanics: Real or illusory? In J. Castellanos, & L. Jones (Eds.), *The majority in the minority* (pp. 47-68). Sterling, VA: Stylus Press.

Nora, A., & Cabrera, A. F. (1996). The role and perceptions of prejudice and discrimination on the adjustment of minority students to college. *Journal of Higher Education, 67*(2), 119-148.

Nora, A., & Wedham, E. (1991, April). *Off-campus experiences: The pull factors affecting freshman-year attrition on a commuter campus.* Paper presented at the annual meeting of the American Educational Research Association, Chicago, IL.

Oakes, J., & Lipton, M. (1996). Developing alternatives to tracking and grading. In L. I. Rendón, & R. O. Hope (Eds.), *Educating a new majority: Transforming America's educational system for diversity* (pp. 168-200). San Francisco: Jossey-Bass.

Oakes, J. (1985). *Keeping track: How schools structure inequality.* New Haven, CT: Yale University Press.

Oakes, J. (2003). *Education inadequacy, inequality, and failed state policy: What Williams v. State of California reveals about accountability.* Veffie Milstead Jones Distinguished Lecture, California State University-Long Beach.

Ochoa, A. (2003, July 20). *Succeeding in America.* Retrieved August 17, 2003, from http://www.signonsandiego.com/news

Ogunwole, S. U. (2002). *The American Indian and Alaska Native population. 2000 Census brief.* Washington, DC: U.S. Department of Commerce. Economics and Statistics Administration. U.S. Census Bureau.

Palmer, P. (1998). *The courage to teach.* San Francisco: Jossey-Bass.

Postsecondary Education Opportunity. (2001). *Education and training pay.* Oskaloosa, IA: Author.

Rendón, L. I. (1992). From the barrio to the academy: Revelations of a Mexican American "scholarship girl." In L. S. Zwerling, & H. B. London (Eds.), *First generation students: Confronting the cultural issues* (New Directions for Community Colleges, No. 80). (pp 55-64). San Francisco: Jossey-Bass.

Rendón, L. I. (1994). Validating culturally diverse students: Toward a new model of learning and student development. *Innovative Higher Education, 19*(1), 33-50.

Rendón, L. I. (1997). *Access in a democracy: Narrowing the opportunity gap.* Commissioned Report for the Policy Panel on access of the National Postsecondary Education Cooperative, Washington, DC.

Rendón, L. I. (2000). Academics of the heart. *About Campus, 5*(3), 3-5.

Rendón, L. I. (2002). Community college Puente: A validating model of education. *Journal of Educational Policy, 16*(4), 642-667.

Rendón, L. I., & Hope, R. O. (1996). An educational system in crisis. In L. I. Rendón, & R.O. Hope (Eds.), *Educating a new majority: Transforming America's educational system for diversity* (pp. 1-32). San Francisco: Jossey-Bass.

Rendón, L. I., Jalomo, R. E., & Nora, A. (2000). Theoretical considerations in the study of minority student retention in higher education. In J. M. Braxton (Ed.), *Reworking the student departure puzzle* (pp. 127-156). Nashville, TN: Vanderbilt University Press.

Rendón, L. I., & Nora, A. (1997). *Student academic progress: Key data trends.* Report prepared for the National Center for Urban Partnerships, The Ford Foundation, New York.

Russell, G. (1997). *American Indian facts of life: A profile of tribes and reservations.* Phoenix AZ: Russell Publication.

San Juan, E., Jr. (2002). *Racism and cultural studies.* Durham, NC: Duke University Press.

Schmitt, E. (2001). *Census figures show Hispanics pulling even with blacks.* Retrieved from http://www.nytimes.com/2001/03/08/national/08CENS.html

Smith, D., & García, M. (1996). Reflecting inclusiveness in the college curriculum. In L. I. Rendón, & R. O. Hope (Eds.), *Educating a new majority* (pp. 265-288). San Francisco: Jossey-Bass.

Spring, J. (1996). *The American school: 1642-1996* (4th ed.). New York: McGraw-Hill.

Stampen, J. O., & Cabrera, A. F. (1988). Is the student aid system achieving its objectives: Evidence on targeting and attrition. *Economics of Education Review, 7*, 29-46.

Terenzini, P. T, Allison, K., Gregg, P., Jalomo, R., Millar, S., & Rendón, L. I. (1993). *The transition to college: Easing the passage.* Pennsylvania State University: National Center on Postsecondary Teaching, Learning, and Assessment.

Tierney, W. G. (1994). *Building communities of difference: Higher education in the twenty-first century.* Westport, CT: Bergin & Garvey.

Tierney, W. F., & Hagedorn, L. (Eds.). (2002). *Increasing access to college: Extending possibilities for all students.* New York: SUNY Press.

Tinto, V. (1993*). Leaving college: Rethinking the causes and cures of student attrition* (2nd ed.). Chicago: University of Chicago Press.

Trueba, H. T. (2002). Multiple ethic, racial and cultural identities in action: From marginality to a new cultural capital in modern society. *Journal of Latinos in Education, 1*(1), 7-28.

U.S. Census Bureau. (2000a). *The Asian and Asian Pacific Islander population in the United States.* Retrieved April 24, 2001, from http://www.census.gov/prod/2000pubs/p20-529.pdf

U.S. Census Bureau. (2000b). *Hispanic origin.* Retrieved April 24, 2001, from http://quickfacts.census.gov/qfd/meta/long_68188.htm

Weber, L. (2001). *Understanding race, class gender and sexuality.* New York: McGraw-Hill.

Chapter 2

Pre-Collegiate Experiences, Values, and Goals of First-Year Students of Color

Kevin Kinser
and Corlisse Thomas

I come from a traditional family on the reservation. I went to high school on the reservation. My parents only went to boarding school, my father didn't graduate. But they told me to go to college. They didn't understand exactly what it was but they thought it was good, that it would help me. They knew it was far away and they didn't mind that as long as I came back for ceremonies. They told me to study hard. (Native-American student in Tierney, 1992)

In high school in South Florida, I never thought about being Latino—I just was. In New England, a really Waspy society, I really felt that I did not belong, that my manner of interacting with people, partying and values were more similar to other Latinos and other minorities on campus. (Latino student in Saylor & Aries, 1999)

I remember once when I was sitting at the table where black students sit in one of the dining halls here, and they were saying, "You know when I first came here it was a culture shock, totally" or saying all these things that I couldn't relate to because I'm used to seeing five black people and 100 white people, and...I'm so accustomed to it that it doesn't create any insecurity in me. I don't feel like I need to run to the closest black person and hold onto them. I found out how to be independent and feel like I can be self-sufficient because if there's only five black people and you don't like any of them, and you're in school with 600 kids, you'd better learn how to depend on something! (Black student in Smith & Moore, 2000)

Each year, 600,000 first-year students of color, diverse in background and experience, enroll in institutions of higher education for the first time (National Center for Education Statistics, 2001, table 209). Many are the only ones in their families to ever go to college. Others are following in the footsteps of parents and grandparents. Some come from the best college prep schools in the country, while others have attended high schools with few resources to aid them as college-bound seniors. These new students include valedictorians with expectations of continued academic success, as well as those who approach college concerned about their ability to meet the educational challenges ahead. Demographically, students of color include Asian student populations whose origins can be traced to more than 30 countries in Asia and the Pacific; Native-American students from more than 500 federally recognized tribes; Hispanic students whose origins are based in 20 western Spanish-speaking countries, in addition to those who do not speak Spanish but ethnically identify as Latino; and Black students whose history is primarily traced to the many countries of Africa and the Caribbean (Brown & Rivas, 1995). All of these individuals, no matter how different they may be from one another, share at least one thing in common—they are college students.

Remarkably little is known about how students of color make the decision to attend college (Perna, 2000). Similarly, data regarding the values, aspirations, and goals of this population are not readily available to those interested in knowing more about the entering characteristics of first-year students of color (Freeman, 1997). On the other hand, the perspectives, experiences, failures, and successes of students of color enrolled in college have been extensively documented. We know much about how college affects students of color, but our knowledge about who these students are when they arrive on our campuses and in our classrooms is far from complete.

This chapter will highlight some of the characteristics of students of color as they enter college. We draw on research on college choice conducted by the United States Department of Education and on available data regarding the academic and social experiences of high school students of color. A variety of perspectives will be offered on the more subjective dimension of who first-year students of color are, including their academic and career goals, cultural values, and identity. It is difficult to paint a comprehensive picture of this population given the state of the research. Generalizations are always false. Yet in this chapter, we offer a range of the experiences and values of entering students of color, recognizing that our descriptions are necessarily incomplete.

Pre-College Decision Making, Preparation, and Experiences

The end of high school represents a period of transition for students of color. They, like all high school seniors, can either continue their education or move directly into the world of work. Most prefer to continue their education. Approximately three quarters of all 12th-graders, regardless of race and ethnicity, state that they intend to enroll in a postsecondary institution immediately after high school graduation (National Center for Education Statistics, 1995). However, concrete steps must be taken in order for these intentions to become a reality. To realize this goal, most students take an admissions test (e.g., the ACT or SAT) and submit an application for admission to at least one postsecondary institution. It is at this point that, despite similar intentions, racial and ethnic differences show their impact. Hispanic and Black seniors are less likely than Whites and Asians to take entrance examinations, and Hispanic high school seniors are less likely than their White classmates to apply to college (National Center for Education Statistics, 1995). For instance, more than 70% of Hispanics plan to continue their education immediately after high school, but only 51% have applied to a college and only 44% have taken an entrance exam. Overall, 6 out of 10 high school seniors have completed both of these tasks (National Center for Education Statistics, 1995).

Consequently, the impact of these data on enrollment patterns is striking. Half of all graduating Hispanics enroll in two-year institutions. They are less likely than Whites, Blacks, and Asians to attend a private, four-year college and are also less likely than Whites (but not Blacks or Asians) to attend a public four-year college (National Center for Education Statistics, 1996). Regardless of student preferences, opportunities to attend baccalaureate degree-granting institutions, particularly more selective private colleges and universities, are severely restricted for those students of color who do not take the minimal steps necessary for admission. Kao and Tienda (1998) argue that the divide between aspirations and achievement for Black and Hispanic students represents a paradox that is not easily resolved. Their data suggest that a combination of social segregation and simple misinformation may hold the key: Blacks and Hispanics are more likely to compare their performance and judge their aspirations against other Blacks and Hispanics, resulting in a self-perpetuating paucity of information and role models in these communities. Therefore, these students may have the ambition to go to college but remain unaware of the basic steps they must take to realize their ambitions.

When information is available about attending college, students of color, especially those in the top academic quartile, react similarly to White students (National Center for Education Statistics, 1996). All students, regardless of race or ethnicity, consider institutional reputation to be an important factor in the selection of a college or university. Hispanic and Black students, like their White counterparts, view academic program availability and financial aid as significant considerations. However, Blacks tend to view the expense of attending college and financial aid availability as being more important than do Whites, while Hispanics consider distance from home to have a greater weight in their decision-making process. Nevertheless, these differences (except for Blacks' stronger consideration of financial aid availability) disappear for the most academically qualified students (National Center For Education Statistics, 1996). In fact, the overall impression is that students in any racial group are more alike than different.

Nevertheless, some differences do exist. White students are more likely to consider the social atmosphere of the institution, while African Americans and Hispanics tend to weigh distance from home more heavily. Hispanics show a preference for campuses with a diverse student population (Carreras, 1998), but this finding does not hold for African-American students (Goldsmith-Caruso, 1999).

Carreras (1998) and Goldsmith-Caruso (1999) found that factors such as a diverse faculty and the availability of identity-based student organizations seem not to make a difference in Hispanic and African-American students' college decisions. These findings do not contradict assertions about the importance of a diverse faculty and student population and identity-based organizations elsewhere in this monograph. While these factors may not be a major consideration in a student's initial college choice, they provide strong support for students of color once they are enrolled. Making students aware of the benefits of diversity and social support can be a powerful recruitment tool as students of color decide among a variety of college campuses.

Students of color and White students alike report that they are able to attend their first or second choice institution (National Center for Education Statistics, 1996). This indicates that after all the decision making is over, high school students generally can attend the college of their choice, regardless of race or ethnicity. Enrollment trends offer some support for this: Students of color are accessing higher education at levels equivalent to or greater than their distribution in the overall population (National Center for Education Statistics, 2001, Table 208). Students of color currently represent 27% of all first-time, first-year students and 33% of all other first-year students (National Center for Education Statistics, 2001, Table 209).

Two caveats should be considered. First, many students of color drop out of the educational "pipeline" and never attend college. Therefore, one must take into account all those students who never plan to attend college or who have limited college options when noting the percentage of students of color who are enrolled in their preferred institution. Second, access does not equal completion. Looking at graduation rates for those starting at four-year institutions, White and Asian-American students are more likely to complete a degree than are Black and Hispanic students (National Center for Education Statistics, 2001, Table 311). While initial enrollment in a two-year institution reduces the likelihood of degree attainment for all racial and ethnic categories, the effect is disproportionate for Black students: Over half of all African Americans (54%) who begin at community colleges stop their education before earning a degree or certificate (National Center for Education Statistics, 2001, Table 311).

Reasons for the discrepancy in enrollment versus graduation rates are a source of debate, demanding political, social, and educational diagnoses. For example, compared to all other racial or ethnic groups with the exception of Asian Americans, Whites score higher on the ACT and on the verbal and math sections of the SAT (*Chronicle of Higher Education*, 2000; National Center for Education Statistics, 2001, Table 133). While these standardized tests are used for admissions purposes by approximately 68% of all colleges and universities (National Center for Education Statistics, 2001,Table 309), they are not generally considered predictive of academic success beyond the first year and ought not in themselves explain the graduation rate discrepancy. However, since there is a strong relationship between high standardized test scores and enrollment in a top college or university (Owings, Madigan, & Daniel, 1998), students with lower test scores may be more likely to enroll in less selective institutions. Less selective institutions have lower graduation rates, thereby reducing the likelihood that the matriculated student will in fact graduate. Thus, preparation and academic skills, as evidenced by test scores, combine with institutional factors to explain the gap between enrollment and graduation rates for some students of color.

A high school student's proficiency in various academic areas is of considerable importance to college success. The National Assessment of Educational Progress (NAEP) is a congressionally mandated program that measures the academic proficiency of elementary and secondary students in certain subjects or skills. In the NAEP test of reading proficiency, 40% of all 17-year-old high school students scored at the highest level. The averages for Black and Hispanic students were substantially lower, with only 17% and 24%, respectively, scoring that high (National Center for Education Statistics, 2001, Table 113). A similar situation exists with respect to math and science proficiencies. In math, 61% of all 17-year-olds could perform "moderately complex procedures and reasoning," while in science, 47% could "analyze scientific procedures and data." Only 27% of Black students and 38% of Hispanic students met that standard in math, and just 12% of the Black students and 27% of the Hispanic students were able to perform at that level in science (National Center for Education Statistics, 2001, Tables 123 and 129). In the NAEP writing assessment, the average score for 11th-graders was 283 points out of a possible 500. Again, Black and Hispanic students gave poorer performances, scoring an average of 267 points and 269 points respectively on this exam (National Center for Education Statistics, 2001, Table 117). In history, 12th-grade Whites and Asians were, respectively, three and four times more likely to score at a proficient level or higher than were Blacks and Hispanics (National Center for Education Statistics, 2001, Table 119). In geography, the final NAEP assessment for which racial and ethnic data are readily available, the situation is equally dramatic: In the 12th grade, 33% of Whites and 32% of Asians were assessed to be proficient while just 10% of Hispanics and only 5% of African Americans reached that level (National Center for Education Statistics, 2001, Table 121).

High school grade point average (GPA) is another indication of a students' preparation for a postsecondary education that may impact access, performance, and opportunity to succeed in college. According to research conducted by The College Board (2002), White students who take the SAT have GPAs that are consistently higher than test-taking Black, Hispanic, and Native-American students. The average GPA in 2002 for a White student was 3.37. Black students, on the other hand, had an average GPA of 2.95, Native-Americans earned a 3.15, and Hispanics had GPAs ranging from 3.07 to 3.21. (The College Board divides Hispanics into several categories based on national origin.) Asian Americans, the only group in The College Board study with a higher GPA than Whites, had a high school average of 3.43. The College Board's 10-year trend analysis shows that the gap between high school GPAs of White students and Blacks, Hispanics, and Native-Americans is actually increasing. In 1992, White students had a GPA 0.17 points higher than all students of color with the exception of Asian Americans; the difference grew to 0.24 points by 2002. This indicates that Blacks, Hispanics, and Native-American students are falling further behind their White peers in high school academic achievement, potentially affecting their ability not only to compete for spaces in selective colleges and universities but also to compete academically once admitted.

Such dramatically different scores on the NAEP assessments and high school GPA may be linked to the characteristics of the school or school district in which the student completed his or her pre-collegiate education. As Kozol (1991) points out in his book *Savage Inequalities*, students attending low-income schools have fewer educational opportunities than students attending wealthier schools. Current statistics suggest that students of color continue to be disproportionately represented in low socioeconomic-status schools (as measured by the level of federally funded services offered to low-income students). Two-thirds of all Blacks and three-fourths of all Hispanics attend schools with more than 50% minority enrollment (National Center for Education Statistics, 2001, Table 96). In public secondary schools where students of color are in the majority, nearly two out of every five students (39%) receive federally funded free or reduced-price lunches. And, compared to those schools with lower proportions of students of color, four times as many secondary students receive Title I services in public high schools where students of color are in the majority (National Center for Education Statistics, 2001, Tables 372 and 373). The level of student participation in school lunch programs and other federally funded programs can be seen as an index of the relative size of the tax base for a school district. Higher participation in these programs suggests a lower tax base and, consequently, a smaller funding source for academic programs. The poverty of these schools means that students of color are not as likely to have access to opportunities available in wealthier schools, such as advanced academic or college preparatory courses (Kozol, 1991).

Safety issues that affect the learning environment comprise an additional set of factors that also seem to have an adverse effect on students of color. For example, compared to their White counterparts, twice as many 12th-grade minority students reported that they did not feel safe at school (National Center for Education Statistics, 2001, Table 144). Unspecified "disruptions" by other students interfered with the learning of between 38% and 41% of 12th-grade Blacks, Hispanics, Asian Americans, and Native Americans, compared to 31% of White 12th-graders (National Center for Education Statistics, 2001, Table 144). Finally, crime is more prevalent in schools with high minority enrollment (National Center for Education Statistics, 2001, Table 151).

Offsetting these factors are extracurricular activities, where few differences in participation rates exist among racial and ethnic groups. All 12th-graders report that they perform volunteer and community service; take music, art, or dance classes; participate in academic clubs and athletics; and read for pleasure at similar levels, regardless of racial or ethnic background. One discrepancy is in the amount of television watched: Black 12th-graders are twice as likely to watch more than five hours of television on a week day than are students from other racial and ethnic backgrounds (National Center for Education Statistics, 2001, Tables 146 and 147). Since watching television takes time away from studying or participating in school-sponsored activities (such as extracurricular activities or volunteer work), this represents a potential disadvantage to students in a selective admissions process.

Finally, given that computer skills have become essential for academic success in college, it is important to consider trends in this area. In 1997, two-thirds (61%) of White, non-Hispanic high school students used computers at home, compared to just 21% of African Americans and 22% of Hispanics (National Center for Education Statistics, 2001, Table 424). In the realm of technology, however, 1997 data is ancient history and should be viewed with caution. Indeed, later studies have indicated that the "Digital Divide" among racial and ethnic groups may, in fact, be closing (U.S. Department of Commerce, 2000).

Values, Aspirations, and Goals

In addition to the wide array of pre-college educational experiences among students of color, a diverse set of values, goals, and aspirations also exist within this population. These values, goals, and aspirations are heavily influenced by myriad familial, societal, and environmental factors. Socioeconomic status, for example, not only affects access to education but also impacts the educational goals and career aspirations of students of color once they enroll in college. Kim and Sedlacek (1996) cited getting a better job and making more money as being among the top expectations of first-year African-American students. Among Native-American students attending tribal colleges, job training was the top priority when asked about their goals for college attendance (Laanan, 2000). Liu and Sedlacek (1999) found that Asian first-year students ranked preparation for graduate school and getting a good job among the most important reasons for attending a large, eastern, state university. Other studies reported that for many students, the lack of socioeconomic resources prior to college served as the underlying motivation for their desire to succeed (Terenzini et al., 1994; White & Shelley, 1996).

The desire to do well financially after college was explored by Leppel (2001) in her study of majors selected by college students. She found that humanities and social science disciplines were the most commonly selected majors overall within her diverse sample of students. However, Leppel's particular focus on the business major yielded interesting findings. A closer look at major selection by race indicated that Hispanic students were more likely than Asian, Black, or White students to select business as a major, and that among the three students of color groups analyzed, Asians were least likely to select a business major. A higher proportion of Whites, Asians, and Blacks could be found in humanities and social sciences, science and engineering, and in "other" majors including education and health fields. Factors affecting the choice of a business major included socioeconomic status, level of parental education, and type of parental occupation. In short, students from families with high socioeconomic status, college-educated parents, and parents with professional occupations—characteristics more commonly found among White and Asian students in this study—were less likely to select a business major. The perception that a business major was linked to financial success made its selection more likely among many students who named a desire to do well financially as a goal. Leppel speculates that the number of Black and Hispanic business majors is likely to decrease if these groups begin to experience increased educational and financial success.

A major study of first-time, full-time, first-year students conducted by the Cooperative Institutional Research Program (CIRP) offers further insight into the educational and career goals of students of color enrolled in community colleges. More than two thirds of White students and two thirds of students of color participating in the study indicated their intention to complete an associate's degree. A desire to transfer to a four-year institution and complete a bachelor's degree was also expressed by a similar proportion of the White students and the students of color in the sample. Both groups of students expressed the desire to get a better job and to make more money as primary goals. The major difference between White students and students of color in the study emerged with respect to their motivation to attend college. When asked to select the most important factors affecting their decision to go to college from a pre-determined list, students of color more frequently selected parental influence, the desire to improve study skills, the desire to learn more things, the desire to get a general education, and to become more cultured (Laanan, 2000). While some differences do exist, Laanan's findings seem to point out that within this particular population, more similarities than differences are apparent in their goals and aspirations.

Though many students of color do not make it to college, those who do attend have widely varying attitudes toward and expectations of college based on their pre-college experiences. Brown and Rivas (1995) note that many students of color arrive on college campuses as high academic achievers who are dedicated and hardworking. They further note that despite previous academic success for some students, factors such as lower quality of high school preparation, first-generation status, or a highly supportive pre-college environment (i.e., family, community) may combine to create unrealistic expectations of the college experience. Students from these backgrounds may be academically underprepared, lack information about how to manage the college experience that is typically shared within families that have members that are college graduates, or expect college to provide a more supportive environment than it does in some cases. Entrance into unexpectedly competitive college environments that offer little support can challenge the academic and social integration of these college students. Additionally, Rowser's (1997) study of Black student perceptions at a Midwestern university suggests that some students might expect to make unrealistically high grades and to graduate in four years even though they are academically underprepared.

While unrealistic expectations about college are not unique to students of color, both Rowser (1997) and Brown and Rivas (1995) point to the negative effect of these expectations on these students' attitude toward their own ability to succeed, their integration into the college experience, and ultimately, on their retention. The effect is particularly salient among students who have had little exposure to college prior to attending, a common experience among students of color. In fact, the students themselves cited the importance of their attitude toward work in determining their success (Terenzini et al., 1994; White & Shelley, 1996). Managing expectations and addressing social and academic issues are essential to the design of retention efforts focused on first-year students of color.

At a very elemental level, these students aspire simply to achieve a sense of belonging within the college communities in which they are enrolled. They want to be accepted, just like any other student (Terenzini et al., 1994; White & Shelley, 1996). Unfortunately, numerous accounts detail the ways in which some college campuses are not receptive to these students and the diversity of cultures and viewpoints they bring to college. Some schools do support model programs that address the needs of first-year students of color and issues relating to campus climate. These programs range in nature from academic to personal and psychosocial. They include such initiatives as, revising curricula to include diverse viewpoints, designing programs to improve specific skill sets, hiring a culturally diverse faculty and staff, raising the level of sensitivity of college and university staff through workshops and training programs, and revising the programmatic and service elements of campus life (e.g., orientation, student activities, counseling and advising services) to better serve a diverse college community (Carreathers, Beekmann, Coatie, & Nelson, 1996; Clements, 2000; Suzuki, 1994).

Another factor affecting the values, goals, and aspirations of students of color is the family. A student's family can play an important role in decisions about all aspects of the college experience from college choice to major selection. Some students cite family influence as a deciding factor in the college admission process. Others name family support as essential to their survival in school, while still others note family responsibility as a driving force in their need to succeed in college. Some students have listed family input as pivotal to their academic choices (e.g., major selection) (Kenny & Stryker, 1996; Laanan, 2000; Saggio, 2001). Simultaneously, some students also acknowledge the drawback of the weight of family responsibility (Brown & Rivas, 1995; Terenzini et al., 1994) to their goals and aspirations. While they attempt to become members of a new college community, they remain accountable to family and community values and obligations that may be in direct conflict with those encountered in the college environment.

These findings point to the significant impact of culture upon the values, goals, and aspirations of students of color. According to Wilson (1978), culture defines values, beliefs, and objectives, and reinforces these through reward and punishment. He notes that culture offers a lens to interpret the world and world events and that it determines and explains behavior. More specifically, Hoare (1995) and Myers (1993) explore the power of culture on worldview and personal values among populations of color. Each points to the link between family and community, and the interdependence of group members as defining characteristics of the identity of people of color in American society. In accord with these identity frameworks, students of color repeatedly point to family, church, and peers as primary influences on their goals, aspirations, and attitudes (Kidwell, 1994; Olszewski-Kubilius & Scott, 1992; Saggio, 2001; Terenzini et al., 1994). While some research indicates that students of color aspire to high achievement or to careers that they perceive to yield high incomes (Leppel, 2001; Olszewski-Kubilius & Scott, 1992), the cultural value of connection to community is also evidenced in the frequent aspiration among students of color to enter professions geared toward helping individuals or serving the community (Laanan, 2000; Olszewski-Kubilius & Scott, 1992; Walsh & Vacha-Haase, 1996).

The far-reaching effects of culture on the values and goals of students of color suggest the importance of understanding these students' beliefs about their ability to manage the cultural environment in college. A study of first-year students at a university in the western United States examined the concept of "bicultural efficacy," or the student's attitude about whether he or she was able to manage the stress of living in two different cultural environments simultaneously (Coleman, 1992). Surprisingly, the research did not support the expectation that students of color with a high level of bicultural efficacy were more comfortable with the adjustment to the college environment. In fact, among these students it was found that although a high level of bicultural efficacy was correlated with a supportive social network, they did not perform or adjust as well as those who were determined to have a low level of bicultural efficacy. The highest level of successful adjustment among first-year students of color was found among those who were more closely affiliated with White culture (and had a lower level of bicultural efficacy). In this study, affiliation with White culture was determined by examining the level of acculturation of participants or the degree to which they maintained or discarded their own cultural characteristics or adopted the cultural characteristics of White culture when interacting with it. Coleman used an acculturation scale that measured such factors as language familiarity and usage, personal and familial ethnic identity (self-described), social relationships, and cultural interests to rate the level of affiliation. In this study, a high level of acculturation among participants (i. e., greater identification with White culture) was correlated with a high level of socioeconomic status, giving rise to the possibility that economic success influences a students' cultural expression and as a result affects their adjustment experience during college. Though the study was small, it aptly illustrates the impact that culture may have on the college experiences of first-year students of color and raises many questions regarding the demands that the college environment places on these students as they endeavor to succeed.

Freeman (1997) also noted the effect of culture on college student success in her study of African-American participation in higher education. She asked African- American high school students to describe the barriers to higher education that they perceived. The students described economic and psychological barriers, and emphasized the importance of cultural awareness in meeting their needs. The value of higher education, Freeman found, was interpreted through a cultural context. The African Americans in her study agreed that the benefits of higher education were worth the costs, but their "passion for learning" was muted by encounters with cultural ignorance and thus transformed into "acting White." Freeman suggests listening to the voices of students of color in the creation of policy and paying attention to the cultural values that are important in their lives. Listening to these voices may take many forms including researching the backgrounds of the students that we serve; assessing their abilities, needs, and attitudes before creating programs and policies; and enlisting their input on committees in the creation of policies and programs for their use.

Saylor and Aries (1999) also attempted to explain the relationship of ethnic identity to first-year college adjustment. Here again, the research shows that culture acts as a basis for student identity throughout the transition to college. They found that a strong sense of ethnic identity was maintained and strengthened by intentional involvement on the part of the students in a variety of ethnically oriented practices and activities. Liu and Sedlacek (1999) concur based on their findings from a study of leadership activities among Asian/Pacific American students in the college environment. They go further to suggest that definitions of traditional leadership and leadership styles may need to be expanded to recognize other styles that emerge with the cultural characteristics of Asian-American student leaders. Interestingly, in the Saylor and Aries study, strong ethnic identity appeared to support racial identity development that was balanced and inclusive both of the students' own and the dominant culture causing, among other things, a greater degree of involvement in non-ethnically oriented activities. This finding suggests that having the security and acceptance of their own cultural norms provides some students of color with a firm basis upon which to get involved in activities that are culturally dissimilar.

It is important not to assume that students of color are a culturally monolithic group with like backgrounds, motivation, values, and goals. Unlike many studies examining the values and attitudes of students of color, Saylor and Aries (1999) also looked at students of color who have grown up in predominantly White environments. Although students of color from these backgrounds at times elect to distance themselves from communities of color and their associated activities, Saylor and Aries found these students overwhelmingly chose to join ethnic organizations and, in many cases, to learn about their own ethnic identities for the first time. Smith and Moore's (2000) study of intra-racial diversity and relations among Black college students addressed the important issue of within-group differences among students of color. The study investigated similarities in values, attitudes, experiences, and feelings of closeness among Black undergraduates, in the context of the social, economic, and cultural differences within the sample. They found that biracial students, Black students from predominantly White backgrounds, and those from low socioeconomic backgrounds experienced reduced closeness to other Blacks on campus and differences in values and attitudes based on their background characteristics. For example, biracial students' identification with both of their racial heritages often led to differences in attitudes toward social experiences (e.g., interracial dating), while Black students from predominantly White backgrounds expressed values, aspirations, expectations, and experiences more closely aligned with their White peers.

Studies involving intraracial differences naturally lead to a further examination of acculturation, an important factor related to culture's influence on students' values, attitudes, goals, and levels of adjustment. As mentioned earlier, acculturation may be defined as the manner in which one relates to one's own ethnicity and that of others. Phinney, Chavira, and Williamson (1992) outline four levels of acculturation, namely, assimilation, integration, separation, and marginality. The four levels reflect a continuum of relating to ethnicity that ranges from complete identification with the dominant culture (assimilation) to complete lack of involvement with the dominant culture (marginality). Their study of nearly 650 high school and college students concluded that the preferred level of cultural identification was the middle ground of the continuum, integration, defined as identification with both the dominant culture and one's own ethnicity.

Integration may be becoming less of a goal to strive for and more of the status quo for today's college population. This possibility is well illustrated by the influence of popular culture in student's lives. New technology, media, and music have crossed cultural lines in their impact on students. A 1999 survey on the impact of hip hop culture and music on students at four northeastern universities (Thomas & Daniels, 1999) revealed a very diverse listening audience including male and female students of every race, socioeconomic class, and year in school. The demographics of the sample were interesting because hip hop is a musical art form with Caribbean and Latino influences firmly rooted in the young, urban, Black cultural experience. The students surveyed considered themselves participants in hip hop culture and so went beyond participation in the commonly accepted cultural manifestations of hip hop (e.g., music, breakdancing, graffiti art, deejaying, speech, and dress) to adopt many of the ideas and beliefs that spawned the culture. They regularly participated in conversations that examined and supported the issues of oppressed and underrepresented groups. They stated that hip hop influenced their values and beliefs by reflecting their lives, valuing youth struggle and experiences, and raising their consciousness (Thomas & Daniels, 1999). The findings of this survey point to new factors that may contribute to our understanding of today's students. For example, the survey suggests it is no longer appropriate to view diverse student experiences in isolation because in some ways our advancing society has blurred the cultural lines separating student populations.

Conclusion

In view of the rapidly changing demographic landscape of American society, it is important to recognize that there is no single college or university experience that represents students of color. The challenge of enhancing the first-year experience for this immensely diverse population is made even greater by pre-college and external factors that impact first-year students and are well beyond the control of college administrators and faculty. For many years, these students have been regarded as homogeneous, special populations, often considered "at-risk," and requiring particular academic and personal support. Current research and experience dictate that although support for these students may still be required, the nature of it is bound to be relative to the students' pre-college background and the values, aspirations, and goals that they hold as college students. Our students' voices implore us to be attentive to their differences, and our professional responsibility requires that we recognize and incorporate their diversity as we seek to enhance their first-year experience.

References

Brown, T., & Rivas, M. (1995). Pluralistic advising: Facilitating the development and achievement of first year students of color. In M. L. Upcraft & G. L. Kramer (Eds.), *First-year academic advising: Patterns in the present, pathways to the future* (Monograph Series No. 18). Columbia, SC: University of South Carolina, National Resource Center for the Freshman Year Experience and Students in Transition.

Carreathers, K. R., Beekmann, L, Coatie, R. M., & Nelson, W. L. (1996). Three exemplary retention programs. In I. H. Johnson & A. J. Ottens (Eds.), *Leveling the playing field: Promoting academic success for students of color* (pp. 35-52). San Francisco: Jossey-Bass.

Carreras, I. E. (1998). *Institutional characteristics of importance at the college search stage among Latino high school students.* Unpublished Dissertation. Boston College.

Chronicle of Higher Education. (2000). *Almanac: 2000-2001.* Washington, DC: Author.

Clements, E. (2000). Creating a campus climate in which diversity is truly valued. In S. R. Aragon (Ed.), *Beyond access: Methods and models for increasing retention and learning among minority students* (pp. 63-72). San Francisco: Jossey-Bass.

Coleman, H. L. K. (1992). *Bicultural efficacy and college adjustment.* (ERIC Document Reproduction Service No. ED 345 608)

The College Board. (2002). *College bound seniors: A profile of SAT program test takers.* New York: College Entrance Examination Board.

Freeman, K. (1997). Increasing African Americans' participation in higher education: African American high school students' perspectives. *Journal of Higher Education, 68,* 523-550.

Goldsmith-Caruso, N. E. (1999). *Reexamining college choice: Ethnicity and college search.* Unpublished Dissertation. Boston College.

Hoare, C. H. (1995). Psychosocial identity development and cultural others. *Journal of Counseling and Development, 70,* 45-53.

Kao, G. & Tienda, M. (1998). Educational aspirations of minority youth. *American Journal of Education, 106*(3), 349-336.

Kenny, M. E., & Stryker, S. (1996). Social network characteristics and college adjustment among racially and ethnically diverse first-year students. *Journal of College Student Development, 37,* 649-658.

Kidwell, C. S. (1994). Higher education issues in Native-American communities. In M. J. Justiz, R. Wilson, & L. G. Bjork (Eds.), *Minorities in higher education* (pp. 240-258). Phoenix: Oryx Press.

Kim, S. H., & Sedlacek, W. E. (1996). *Gender differences among incoming African-American freshmen on academic and social expectations.* (ERIC Document Reproduction Service No. ED 387 768)

Kozol, J. (1991). *Savage inequalities: Children in America's schools.* New York: Crown Publishers.

Laanan, F. S. (2000). Community college students' career and educational goals. In S. R. Aragon (Ed.), *Beyond access: Methods and models for increasing retention and learning among minority student* (pp. 19-33). San Francisco: Jossey-Bass.

Leppel, K. (2001). Race, Hispanic ethnicity, and the future of the college business major in the United States. *Journal of Education for Business, 76,* 209-216.

Liu, W. M., & Sedlacek, W. E. (1999). Differences in leadership and co-curricular perception among entering male and female Asian-Pacific-American college students. *Journal of the First-Year Experience and Students in Transition, 11,* 93-114.

Myers, L. J. (1993). *Understanding an Afrocentric world view: Introduction to an optimal psychology* (2nd ed.). Dubuque, IA: Kendal/Hunt.

National Center for Education Statistics. (1995). *A profile of the American high school senior in 1992.* Statistical Analysis Report. (National Center For Education Statistics 95-384). Washington DC: U.S. Department of Education.

National Center for Education Statistics. (1996). *National education longitudinal study: 1988-1994: Descriptive summary report with an essay on access and choice in postsecondary education.* Statistical Analysis Report. (National Center For Education Statistics 96-175). Washington DC: U.S. Department of Education.

National Center for Education Statistics. (2001). *Digest of education statistics 2000.* Thomas D. Snyder, Project Director. Charlene M. Hoffman, Production Manager. (National Center For Education Statistics 2001-034). Washington, DC: U.S. Department of Education.

Olszewski-Kubilius, P. M., & Scott, J. M. (1992). An investigation of the college and career counseling needs of economically disadvantaged, minority gifted students. *Roeper Review, 14,* 141-149.

Owings, J., Madigan, T., & Daniel, B. (1998, November). *Who goes to America's highly ranked "national" universities?* Statistics in Brief. (National Center For Education Statistics 98-095). Washington, DC: U.S. Department of Education, Office of Educational Research and Improvement.

Perna, L. W. (2000). Racial and ethnic differences in college enrollment decisions. In A. F. Cabrera & S. M. La Nasa (Eds.), *Understanding the college choice of disadvantaged students.* (New Directions for Institutional Research No. 107) (pp. 65-83). San Francisco: Jossey-Bass.

Phinney, J. S., Chavira, V., & Williamson, L. (1992). Acculturation attitudes and self-esteem among high school and college students. *Youth & Society, 23,* 299-323.

Rowser, J. F. (1997). Do African-American students' perceptions of their needs have implications for retention? *Journal of Black Studies, 27,* 718-726.

Saggio, J. J. (2001). *The influence of institutional culture on institutional choice and post-freshman persistence of American Indian/Alaska Native students at a bible college.* (ERIC Document Reproduction Service No. ED 451 978)

Saylor, E. S., & Aries, E. (1999). Ethnic identity and change in social context. *Journal of Social Psychology, 139,* 549-567.

Smith, S. A., & Moore, M. R. (2000). Intraracial diversity and relations among African-Americans: Closeness among Black students at a predominantly white university. *American Journal of Sociology, 106,* 1-39.

Suzuki, B. H. (1994). Higher education issues in the Asian-American community. In M. J. Justiz, R. Wilson, & L. G. Bjork (Eds.), *Minorities in higher education* (pp. 258-285). Phoenix: Oryx Press.

Terenzini, P. T., Rendón, L. I., Upcraft, M. L., Millar, S. B., Allison, K. W., Gregg, P. L., & Jalomo, R. (1994). The transition to college: Diverse students, diverse stories. *Research in Higher Education, 35,* 57-73.

Tierney, W. G. (1992). *Official encouragement, institutional discouragement: Minorities in academe—The Native-American experience.* Norwood, NJ: Ablex Publishing.

Thomas, C. D., & Daniels, A. M. (1999). *Hip hop culture and its effects on college student values.* Unpublished manuscript.

U.S. Department of Commerce. (2000, October). *Falling through the net: Toward digital inclusion.* Retrieved on June 21, 2003, from http://www.digitaldivide.gov/reports.htm.

Walsh, B. D., & Vacha-Haase, T. (1996). The values scale: Differences across grade levels for ethnic minority students. *Educational & Psychological Measurement, 56,* 263-276.

White, C. J., & Shelley, C. (1996). Telling stories: Students and administrators talk about retention. In I. H. Johnson & A. J. Ottens (Eds.), *Leveling the playing field: Promoting academic success of students of color.* San Francisco: Jossey-Bass.

Wilson, L. N. (1978). *African-American psychology: Compelling issues and views.* Washington, DC: University Press of America.

Chapter 3

Moving to a New Culture: The Upside and Downside of the Transition to College

Romero E. Jalomo, Jr.
and Laura I. Rendón

I always look forward to coming to college. I feel good because I am putting something back.

I'm the first to go to college. A few years ago, I wasn't planning to go to college. Now I'm coming here. It's something!

I feel like my future is here. I feel like—sometimes I get emotional. This is where I'm coming to get my education and it makes me feel good...I like this place.

Sometimes family members get threatened or friends get threatened. They start thinking that now that you're in college, you think you're better than them.

[Before college] I'd say, "I'm never going to forget my friends." But little by little, I've realized that a lot of my friends are breaking away.

The voices of these students of color exemplify that the transition to college can be both a period of great jubilation and a time of trauma and angst. On the one hand, students can become excited about realizing their dreams of attending college; living on-campus; making new friends; developing greater personal independence; learning new concepts; serving as role models to younger siblings, relatives, and friends; and forming ideas about improving their communities. On the other hand, because many students of color come from worlds removed from academics—ethnic and racial enclaves, housing projects, barrios, or reservations where few have completed college—they have a tremendously difficult time transitioning to college life. Many are first-generation college students, the first in their family to attend college. Their families provide varying amounts of emotional support, but limited advice on how to make a successful transition. In many cases, these families are initially apprehensive about the benefits of college and may feel threatened by the sheer fact that a family member has decided to be "different" by breaking away from the family unit (Jalomo, 1995; London, 1989; Rendón, 1992; Terenzini et al., 1994).

Making a successful transition to college is shaped by early-life experiences and prior schooling. Many students of color exhibit risk factors associated with poor performance in college—a lower socioeconomic-status (SES) quartile, a single-parent background, academic underpreparedness, and a pattern of dropout behavior in the family. Prior schooling experiences can also be risk factors, for instance, changing schools two or more times, earning average grades of 'C' or lower, and having to repeat one or more grade levels (Choy, Horn, Nunez, & Chen, 2000). Other factors that may affect poor performance in college are failure to complete the college-prep sequence in high school; little time spent on academics; poor performance on standardized tests; invalidation by family, teachers, or peers; being the first in the family to attend college; as well as lack of financial resources and encouragement needed to do well in college (Adelman, 1999; Nora, 2003; Rendón, 1994).

Adding to the complexity of their transition, students of color who are also the first in their family to attend college have added considerations. Most will seek advice regarding college participation from someone outside their immediate family. Many will return to an academic setting after a prolonged period of time since leaving high school. Some will first enter the job market or choose military service. Others will first choose to marry and start a family. Still others will choose to "hang out" with friends before making a decision to enroll in college. The transition to college for first-generation college students, especially for those who delayed entry to college, can be unsettling given the academic and social demands of college (Jalomo, 1995).

Consequently, the importance of fostering a successful transition to college for students of color, particularly those from high-risk backgrounds, cannot be overstated. First-year students of color represent an expanding diversity of academic skills, social interests, and life experiences. For these students, having a meaningful and rewarding first-year experience is crucial to academic success and social adjustment in a new academic world that is vastly different from the students' home realities (Noel, Levitz, & Saluri, 1985; Upcraft & Gardner, 1989). Yet, a successful transition from high school or work to college is still a challenge for many of these students (Jalomo, 1995; Rendón, 1994; Terenzini et al., 1994).

Negotiating the Transition to College

Educators concerned with facilitating the transition to college for students of color must understand three critical processes involved in moving from one's former reality or home life to a new context that focuses on the college participation experience: (a) separation, (b) validation, and (c) involvement.

The Separation Process

Separation is a phase that students experience when they move away from the everyday realities with which they are most familiar to join the new world of college life. This transitional phase is a very critical period for many first-generation, low-income, or "at risk" students of color, often not well understood by policymakers and educators who come from middle- and upper-class backgrounds. Consider the following statements made by students of color:

> *Since we come from… lower-class families everybody is always telling us, "Well, just get yourself a job. You're not going anywhere. You guys make great blue-collar workers." That's a bunch of nonsense.*

Just because you're gifted doesn't mean that anyone's going to pay attention to you…Because we're not their kids…You're not expected to accomplish anything.

The problem is that a lot of people have to recognize that we're coming from a community where education isn't a priority.

Despite the fact that many of these students believe they are often considered "non-college material," they take the risk of attending college, often to develop career skills, pursue a new lifestyle that is different from their former one, and contribute to the well-being of their local communities.

The Transitional Experience for Traditional Students

The transition to college can be quite different for traditional and nontraditional students. For traditional students (i.e., recent high school graduates with above average grades, those who enter college less than two years after high school, students from middle- and upper-socioeconomic backgrounds, or those that come from a family with college experience), college attendance is a normal rite of passage. Traditional students often are simply expected to attend college. College enrollment for these students is often an expectation formed by contact with parents, friends, relatives, and significant others who have at least attended, if not completed college (Terenzini et al., 1994). While there are growing numbers of students of color who can be considered "traditional students" based on their family's socioeconomic status, the majority of students in this category are likely to be White. The following student comments exemplify the college-going decision for traditional students:

Going to college…was never even, like, a question! Both my parents went to college and I guess they figured that all their kids would go to college. I mean…it was never even too much a question. Both my sister and I did pretty well in school and so college was just like the definite thing to follow high school.

Going to college was never a question. You know, that's never something I thought about, whether I'm gonna go to college or not, that was kind of, a given.

The Transitional Experience for Nontraditional Students

Nontraditional students (i.e., low-income, first-generation students, with below average grades or those who have been out of school for some time) often find the transition to college to be a major disjuncture in their lives. Many White and non-White students from low-income backgrounds fall into the nontraditional student category. The following student commentary provides examples of the transitional experience for nontraditional students:

I was discouraged toward the end of high school. I realized I could have done better. I was too caught up in other things. I thought those things would get me what I wanted—happiness. . . [When applying to college] I was thinking, "My college counselor will do it; my mom will help; or there is always my brother, he knows." But my brother has his family; my mother has her obligations; and the college counselor has to take care of the whole senior class. There was nobody there telling me what to do or how to do it.

In a way [coming to college has] affected my friends because I come from the barrio. I see a lot of my friends just drinking, smoking, standing against the walls, and kicking back. I tell them, "Hey, man, I bet you're not going to do that for the rest of your life. I know you want to do something else. You don't want to be one of those guys." I don't waste my life away drinking, smoking, doing whatever. I don't get into trouble with the law or anything like that. That's more or less what they see in me. I talk to them about going to college.

I expected to fail. Two weeks and I was out. I didn't think I could study. I didn't think I could learn.

Clearly, not everything about making the decision to attend college is positive in nature. For many of these students, college-going is often not a part of their family's tradition or expectations. Nontraditional students tend to break, not continue, their family traditions when they enroll in college. As they do so, they are at once redefining their family history and beginning the process of assuming a new identity that makes them different from their family. It is also the time when students navigate and step in and out of multiple worlds—worlds that involve most of the following: ethnic and racial enclaves; housing projects and shelters; barrios; reservations; as well as the work, family, spiritual, and gang worlds (Jalomo, 1995). Many fear that they will no longer be fully accepted in some of these worlds (Weis, 1985).

Furthermore, nontraditional students must balance living in these multiple worlds while concurrently learning the values, traditions, conventions, and practices of their new college environment that are often vastly different from those of their familiar home life. For example, students learn a new terminology; work with a curriculum that often excludes the voices of people of color; learn in classrooms where they may be the only person of color; and may even experience cultural assaults such as stereotyping, racism, and various forms of discrimination. All of this can be daunting and frightening. Therefore, negotiating separation and transition to college requires intelligence and resilience as well as formidable multicultural skills such as maneuvering the language, values, traditions, and conventions of home, work, and college.

The Benefits and Challenges of Separation

Separation is an internal and external process that involves cultural dislocation and relocation (Levy-Warren, 1988). Internally, a student is reforming his or her identity and assuming a new, redefined sense of self as a college student. Externally, students are also making some key changes. Separation involves geographical relocation, which is tied to moving away from family and friends and the loss of familiar objects and people. Separating from family and friends who did not choose to attend college can generate benefits and drawbacks. Among the benefits are that many students find the transition to college to be exciting and exhilarating. They enjoy their newfound autonomy. They form new social networks and take pride in the fact that they are taking the necessary steps toward a new, brighter future. Further, breaking away from certain family norms and behaviors can foster a heightened self-concept, improved self-esteem, and reinforced identity (Jalomo, 1995; London, 1989).

However, a drawback to attending college involves families' and friends' perceiving students as different. In addition, students find themselves redefining old high school friendships and testing cultural ties and family codes of unity (Rendón, 1992; Rodriguez, 1982). Separation can lead to feelings of isolation, alienation, self-doubt, and psychological distress. Of course, these factors can have a detrimental impact on self-concept, persistence, and attainment of educational goals. Consequently, separation needs to occur gradually, allowing students to move slowly toward healthy individuation, while still maintaining ties to their family and culture. Total separation from a students' culture is unnecessary and potentially harmful. What is needed is a modified separation-individuation model that allows students to engage in self-definition and increasing degrees of separateness, autonomy, and relatedness (Bloom-Feshbach & Bloom-Feshbach, 1987).

What is desirable is not complete disengagement from previous relationships, but a modified relationship. Bloom (1987) indicates that the family system is a critical separation variable because it has the potential to both generate problems and solutions. When a student leaves home, the family has to reorganize to maintain some kind of balance in the relationship. Family members will learn to communicate and get their needs met in new ways. In families that do not tolerate separation well, pathological solutions such as parents' developing illnesses to forestall separation or create a dependency that results in failing at work or at school may emerge. Families with a well-established history of college-going behavior will have the flexibility and consistency of communication to promote separation without serious problems.

However, among families where college attendance is not the norm, a tendency to create challenging, difficult, and painful separation situations can be potentially harmful to a student's college success. To ease the transition, colleges and universities can facilitate personal development; provide culturally-sensitive counseling and mentoring; encourage contact with faculty, students, and staff of color; and expose students to multi-cultural centers, classes, art, and music that celebrate a wide variety of diverse cultures. These strategies can evoke a sense of comfort and inclusion (Rendón, 1996).

Separation involves trauma and loss. Students begin to notice changes in the way they relate to family and friends, especially those who have not pursued a higher education. They begin to experience feelings of loss, guilt, and anxiety that are associated with separation. They struggle to fulfill the demands of college work while trying to meet family, work, and cultural expectations. For example, in American-Indian cultures, students are expected to return to the reservation when a relative passes away or when a family member is ill. In Hispanic families, the eldest son or daughter is expected to take over family responsibilities when a parent is absent from the home (Jaloma, 1995). It is evident that students of color need assistance undergoing one of the most complex passages in their lives: the transition to college. Two processes can help students do this: validation and involvement.

The Validation Experience

Many students of color bring invalidating life experiences to the college transition process. Here are examples of this kind of invalidation:

I was identified as a gifted child by the time I was in my fourth grade. But in my freshman year in high school, my counselor told me to be a brick mason because somewhere in my records they thought my dad was one.

[In high school] you have the college corner. Do you know how hard it was to get into the college corner? You had to make a high grade point average. If you didn't have a particular grade point average, it wasn't worth it for you to join them because you're not going to be able to go to Cal State or UCLA.

These types of students are likely to drop out early in their college careers if they continue to have invalidating experiences. Sadly, there is a great deal of invalidation taking place in colleges and universities. Students have reported being called by social security numbers, told they're not going to go very far in life, told they are going to fail the class the first time they turn in their assignment, treated as incompetent, never called on to participate in class discussions, and had their culture and past experiences discounted as insignificant (Rendón, 1994). Many faculty and staff expect students to take the initiative to seek help. However, students cannot ask questions when they do not know what to ask. When students are the first in their family to attend college, they are unaware of what college has to offer and are afraid to ask questions that they feel may make them appear stupid or lazy.

In a transition to college study (Terenzini et al., 1994), first-year students of color completing their first semester of college were asked what made the most difference for them during their first semester. Interestingly, students did not point out that getting involved in college was what made the most significant difference for them. Instead, they usually cited instances when someone, in or out of college, reached out to them to affirm that they were capable of doing college work and being a valuable member of the college learning community. This is not to say that involvement is not important. However, students who have been invalidated in the past are not likely to get involved on their own (Rendón, 1994).

The hope for many students of color is what Rendón (1994) calls validation, an enabling, confirming, and supportive process initiated by in- and out-of-class agents that fosters academic and personal development. While involvement theory (Astin, 1985) leans toward students taking the initiative to get involved, validation does not assume students can form connections on their own. In the validation model, institutional agents are expected to take the first step toward helping students believe in themselves and their inherent capacity to learn.

Examples of in-class validation include structuring learning so that students are able to see themselves as capable of learning early in the semester. Conversely, negative practices, such as weeding students out through fierce competition and fostering fear by telling students to look to the right and left because their peers may not persist to graduation, prove particularly damaging to first-generation students of color. There are many other examples of ways educators can provide in-class validation. For instance, faculty can share knowledge with students and become partners in learning so that teaching and learning become relationship-centered processes. Additionally, having faculty meet with students both in- and out-of-class can result in affirming experiences that encourage students to do their best. Students also express appreciation when faculty give them their pager, home phone number, or e-mail address. Further, faculty can employ active modes of teaching that allow for student collaboration and ensure that the core curriculum is inclusive of the contributions of diverse groups, so that students can see themselves in what is being learned, which fosters validating experiences.

The following student comments offer examples of in-class validation:

My communications instructor became like an idol to me…when I came to school, my life had fallen apart and I didn't have structure or direction. She gave me the direction with which I wish to mold myself.

Recently I got a 'C' on a test in zoology where I was an 'A' student. I was [feeling like] "Give up!" You know, I cried a little bit. I was ticked off. But then I had someone constantly behind me saying, "You're going to do this. Sit down and study, and you can do it! Don't worry about it."

I had a reading teacher last semester, and she helped me a lot…When I got here…she told me to start studying…I have problems reading…I can read it, but then I'll forget. So she helped me study in ways that I would not forget.

My English teacher last semester, she explained things and talked to you…She went over your essays and told you what was wrong and how to fix it…While you were writing your essay, she would come and look at your thesis and tell you what's wrong and what you needed to change in it and how to improve on it.

Validation can be very powerful. Students who are validated begin to believe they can be successful; become excited about learning; feel a part of the learning community; become motivated; and feel cared about as a person, not just as a student. In-class validating agents can include faculty, coaches, counselors, advisors, tutors, and teaching assistants. These individuals typically validate a student's academic competence by providing positive oral feedback; acknowledging competence on quizzes, exams, class projects, term papers, and other class assignments; and providing casual compliments on a student's academic knowledge, skills, and effort (Jalomo, 1995; Rendón, 1994; Terenzini et al., 1994). Out-of-class validation agents can be spouses, partners, co-workers, family members, and college staff (i.e., faculty, coaches, counselors, mentors, tutors, teaching assistants, and resident advisors) who meet with students out of class to affirm their capabilities and efforts and support their academic and social adjustment to college. Out-of-class agents help foster adjustment and provide reassurance during a student's transition to college.

Some faculty and staff believe that validating actions coddle or "spoon-feed" students. They believe that caring support and encouragement actually make students weaker. However, validation is not about condescending to students or making them weaker or totally dependent on others. Special programs such as The Hispanic Mother/Daughter Program at Arizona State University; the Summer Scholars Transfer Institute at Santa Ana College in California; the national Mathematics, Engineering, and Science Achievement (MESA) program; the national Advancement Via Individual Determination (AVID) program; and California's Puente Project are examples of validation in action. Participants in these programs begin to believe in themselves as successful college students. Research has demonstrated the powerful transformative impact of validation (Rendón 1994, 2002).

When administered with respect and dignity for the student, validation has the effect of strengthening self-esteem and capacity to learn. Once students are validated, it becomes much easier for them to get involved on their own. Students express both personal and academic confidence as they speak of their validating experiences. For example, one student indicated she was "in awe" of herself and how she had blossomed as a college learner. Puente Project students related that they gained confidence in their academic ability, indicating that they improved writing skills, learned to take notes, and became confident in their pursuit of future educational goals (Rendón, 1994; 2002).

The Involvement Process

Involvement is about making connections on campus and getting involved in the academic and social life of the college (Astin, 1985). However, it should never be assumed that all students can get easily involved or that merely offering opportunities for involvement will foster connections with the college. A campus "field of dreams" perspective (i.e., "If you build it, they will come") does not work for many students of color. It is not that colleges have not made the effort to provide services to students. The key problem is that many educators fail to understand that many nontraditional students want to get involved, but don't know how to do so. These students often must work off campus to help their families survive. Others do not understand how college life is structured. As one student stated: "I didn't know what to expect from college because I've never been taught what to expect from college." As a result, students can feel lost, because they do not know to whom to turn for help. They may also worry that they may be perceived as incompetent.

In addition, students often experience a cultural clash when they enter college. In their study of the academic and social experiences of Black and Hispanic students, Malaney and Shively (1995) reported that these students often experienced discrimination and harassment and became disillusioned about their first year of college. In addition, Nora and Cabrera (1996) surveyed commuter students at a predominantly White institution and found that minority students were more likely than White students to perceive discrimination on campus, feel more prejudice from faculty and staff, and report negative classroom experiences, which may lead to separation from the academic and social life of the college. The following statements made by students of color reflect some of these experiences.

> *Some [students of color], who do go to college,…they think it's going to be easy. When it's not easy, they get overwhelmed. They experience culture shock because their high school was all Chicano and they go to college and see that they're actually in the minority.*

> *A lot of older people…stereotype us. They're like, "Don't talk to him, he's a punk."*

Furthermore, students of color often perceive themselves as less worthy than other students and can be the victims of stereotyping. They assume all college faculty and staff understand their issues and what they are going through, but often this is a false assumption. Therefore, they make mistakes that are typical of a college dropout. They take a heavy course load, do not interact with faculty, fail to use campus services and resources, work long hours off campus, and become disconnected from college life. This detachment behavior is the " kiss of death" for students of color, and educators must take proactive steps to assist students to get involved. The following commentary from students of color exemplify this point:

> *None of my teachers…ever seemed to care. One time I had to drop a class because I asked for help and racquetball was more important for that person than to help me, although it was his office hours.*

> *I think the least helpful…are the counselors…. They don't really care about you. You're the one who's supposed to go there and visit them…Well, maybe they care, but they don't have the time for you. They're too busy.*

> *[Students] are overwhelmed. They can't handle it or they take too heavy a course load. There's nobody to guide them through…. They end up tangling themselves up.*

These situations impact student involvement, which is reduced when students experience uncaring, invalidating faculty and staff. Involvement can also be restricted through the fast pace of college life, limited institutional offerings during evening hours (e.g., libraries closing before 10 p.m. and other offices closing at 5 p.m.), and financial realities that require many students to work at least part-time.

Elements that make involvement easier include bridge programs where students are exposed to different cultures and helped to establish friendships and networks. Other elements facilitating involvement include instructors, counselors, coaches, tutors, student services staff, peers, and lab assistants who provide a sense of caring and support and allow students to work on projects with them. Students also appreciate their instructors covering material at a slow, comfortable pace. They enjoy being exposed to authors, leaders, and sports figures who represent their own cultural backgrounds and have attained success in life. Special programs focusing on their unique cultural backgrounds such as the Puente Project in California also create involvement opportunities such as close and continuous in- and out-of-class interactions among students, faculty, counselors, and mentors through group work and one-on-one meetings. Financial aid can also foster involvement, as students will be able to work less and spend more time on campus and on academic work. The enthusiasm generated by these involvement opportunities is exemplified in the following comments:

The teachers are really nice here. I mean they really help you.

If we have any problems, we can always go to [the teacher's office] and talk to her about any problem. [She helps] in the classroom, in her office, outside the classroom.

The coach is really helpful. He beats my butt every time. He keeps telling me that I have to turn in certain assignments and have them in when the teacher asks...I have good grades and stuff.

If it wasn't for my counselor, I think I would have been coming to school just to come.

Fostering involvement among nontraditional students and students of color requires assistance from what de Anda (1984) calls cultural translators, cultural mediators, and role models. Cultural translators are individuals from the student's native world who assist in bridging the native culture with the mainstream majority culture. However, it is important to note that higher education still has relatively few Latino, African-American, Asian/Pacific Islander, American Indian/Alaska Native faculty, counselors, and advisers. This is a serious deficiency as these cultural translators can pass on valuable heuristic and normative behavior information to students (Jalomo, 1995).

Cultural mediators are members of the mainstream culture who can assist individuals in deciphering and understanding the behaviors and manners of the majority culture. Role models "are individuals in the minority person's environment whose behavior serves as a pattern to emulate in order to develop a behavioral repertoire consistent with the norms of the majority or minority culture" (de Anda, 1984, p. 104). While White faculty can assume these roles and to their credit often do, it is essential that faculty and staff of color be present for students to know that someone on campus understands their issues and can be of assistance. Older, more sophisticated students can also be cultural translators, mediators, and role models. The University of Texas-El Paso has a program in which minority upper-class students mentor their first-year counterparts. The peer mentors help students select courses, develop study habits, and solve personal problems (Comarow, 2001).

Programmatic Initiatives that Facilitate the Transition to College

Programmatic initiatives that facilitate the transition to college must focus on four areas: (a) preparing students for college early in their schooling, (b) assisting students with the delicate process of separation, (c) creating validating in- and out-of-class environments, and (d) fostering involvement opportunities. Educators seeking to keep more students of color in college must also reframe their thinking about why students of color have difficulty staying in college. For example, some educators may place the blame for lack of integration, adjustment problems, and poor academic performance solely on students without understanding the complexities involved with separation and acknowledging that involvement is as much the responsibility of the institution as the student. Moreover, placing blame solely on students of color without examining institutional barriers to success (e.g., Euro-centered curriculum, lack of faculty and staff of color, racist incidents, invalidating in- and out-of-class environments) is an inappropriate and insensitive way to respond to transition issues. Students of color should not be the only ones making adjustments. As noted in this volume's last chapter, truly responsive institutions will seek to transform teaching, learning, counseling, and mentoring practices in order to ensure that students will have a successful first-year experience and beyond.

The following are examples of initiatives colleges and universities can undertake to facilitate the transition to college for students of color.

Early Outreach Programs

Students with many failures in their lives, who view college as too long term, whose daily lives are about survival, and who feel college is not for them need intensive assistance to shape their aspirations and to fulfill their hopes and dreams (Nora, 2003). For these students, college success begins long before they are ready to make the transition to college. As noted earlier in this chapter, the transition to college is in large part shaped by academic and social experiences students have early in their lives and in prior schooling. Therefore, early outreach programs targeting students no later than the seventh grade are important to instill in students and their parents the idea that college participation is an attainable goal. Nationwide, there are a multitude of programs that now do this, including Project GRAD, which began in Houston, Texas; New Mexico State University's *Generaciones* program which educates fifth grade Latinas and their mothers about the future expectations of college-going behaviors for the student and her family; and the federally funded GEAR-UP initiative, with numerous projects located throughout the nation. The elements of these programs typically include: early college awareness, summer bridge/readiness programs, parental involvement, basic skills instruction and tutoring, test preparation workshops, visits to colleges and universities, advance placement testing preparation, and financial aid workshops.

Bridge Programs

Programs that provide a bridge to college are becoming more prevalent in an effort to promote success among entering college students. Examples of such programs include California's The Puente (Bridge) Program, Arizona's and Texas' Hispanic Mother/Daughter Program, and the federally funded Upward Bound Program designed for high-risk, low-income, and minority students (Santa Rita & Bacote, 1997).

The Puente Project resides in 21 high schools and 38 California community colleges. This program serves about 6,500 students annually, and some 45,000 benefit from the extended impact of Puente's programs. The Puente mission is to increase the number of educationally underserved students who succeed in high school and in community colleges, enroll in four-year colleges and universities, earn degrees, and return to the community as mentors and leaders. Puente staff believe that students need three basic things to succeed in college: (a) writing skills, (b) information about going to college, and (c) information about career opportunities. Accordingly, three people guide each Puente student: (a) an English faculty member, (b) a counselor, and (c) a mentor. Counselors develop an education plan for each student detailing every course a student needs to take to complete a degree. English instructors use the Bay Area Writing Project model to teach composition. The composition model is not deficit-based; rather, students are allowed to write and re-write until a satisfactory paper is submitted. They also read and react to authors representing their own cultural backgrounds. Mentors from the community work with Puente students, take them to their work sites, and help them set high goals—higher than what they think they can attain (Rendón, 2002). Santa Ana College in California based its first-year classes/first-year experience on the teaching and counseling model of the Puente Project.

Results are impressive. About 48% of Puente community college students who complete the program transfer to four-year colleges and universities within three years (compared to less than 7% of non-Puente students). Puente students make up 19% of all Latino transfer students entering the University of California from community colleges participating in the Puente Project. Students participating in High School Puente attended four-year colleges at almost twice the rate of non-Puente students—43% compared to 24%. An additional 41% of Puente students attend California community colleges, for a total college-going rate of 84% (Gandara, Mejorado, Gutierrez, & Molina, 1998).

Similarly, summer bridge and readiness programs such as Upward Bound build academic and social support networks for the transition to college process. In some of these programs, counselors talk with students about issues of racial isolation, cultural differences, and academic preparedness. High-risk students participating in semester long-bridge courses recorded significantly larger gains in academic self-confidence than students in the general population (Hardy & Karathanos, 1992).

Arizona State University's Hispanic Mother/Daughter Program identifies eighth-grade girls and their mothers and consults with them until college graduation. During that time, students and their mothers are provided information about college preparation and success, receive assistance with the financial aid process, and participate in workshops on study skills and cultural issues, as well as adjustment to college life.

Orientation Programs

Orientation programs are perhaps the most popular intervention policy to facilitate student persistence (Brawer, 1996). Perigo and Upcraft (1989) described orientation efforts as those activities, programs, and courses designed to help first-year students make a successful transition to college with the goal of enhancing their overall academic experiences. These programs are delivered in many different formats, beginning prior to a student's enrollment on campus and lasting from one day to an entire semester. Despite some variation in purpose, content, and scheduling, most colleges offer some form of student orientation that contains information regarding academic programs and provides advice about using campus resources and student services. Orientation programs also begin the process of initiating students to the prevailing campus climate (Robinson, Burns, & Gaw, 1996) and allow first-year students to collaborate with faculty, administrative staff, and their peers.

One other component of orientation is the extended orientation or first-year seminar, which involves student enrollment in a multi-week or semester-long course. Empirical studies conducted at multiple colleges across the country document the effectiveness of first-year seminars in fostering retention (Santa Rita & Bacote, 1997). The first-year orientation seminar frequently includes topics that are associated with academic persistence, such as time management, memory techniques, handling test anxiety, writing research papers, and stress reduction.

First-Generation Student Programs

The University of La Verne in California launched a First Generation Student Success Program for its nontraditional, diverse student population. The program includes summer workshops that assist and support parents and students as they endure the separation phase. Program features include educational and career goal development, values clarification, cultural enrichment, and coping mechanisms to help address new academic pressures. Academic and personal counseling services are also a focal point of the program (Comarow, 2001).

Learning Communities

Learning communities help students engage the academic and social aspects of college life. For example, the benefits of learning communities include increased student-faculty interaction and opportunities for collaborative learning, group study, and socializing. Many campuses, including Sonoma State University in California, place students in small (about 20 students) learning communities with linked or paired classes. Learning communities at LaGuardia Community College in New York feature thematically linked courses. Two or three college-level courses are linked with a developmental course. Students in learning communities take all their courses together and develop close friendships, which help foster a healthy transition to college. Furthermore, the instructors who teach in the learning communities carefully monitor the progress of their students by consulting each other on a regular basis. LaGuardia Community College's New Student House is a learning community designed especially for first-year students who require basic skills development. This learning community allows groups of entering students to enroll in thematically linked basic skills courses where they are the only members of the classes. In addition, students are required to enroll in an integrated seminar that includes academic advising, problem solving, study skills, and test-taking strategies (Tinto, Goodsell, & Russo, 1994).

Research findings derived from studies conducted at Seattle Central Community College, the University of Washington, and LaGuardia Community College suggest that participation in a first-year learning community enables students to develop a network of supportive peers and fosters more positive views and greater rates of involvement in learning activities than non-participation (Tinto, Goodsell, & Russo, 1994). The positive academic and interpersonal outcomes of these and other learning communities initiatives have increased their popularity across the country.

Coordinated Freshman Programs

The City University of New York funds programs such as the Coordinated Freshman Program (CFP) in its community colleges. Although each campus has its own CFP, the overall goal is to increase the persistence and strengthen the academic skills of first-year students. Since many community college first-year students require some form of remedial coursework, the CFP offers underprepared students the opportunity to develop academic skills that are essential for academic success. At LaGuardia Community College, for example, the CFP addresses the needs of students who encounter difficulties moving through the remedial sequence.

To help students gain a head start in college, all entering students requiring remediation in one or more basic skills are able to enroll in the summer immersion program. Students register for remedial courses to make up for any academic deficiencies. Since the summer immersion program is not capable of serving all students, the program is filled on a first-come, first-serve basis. This is a drawback at LaGuardia, as in the other community colleges studied, because the programs cannot serve the many first-year students requiring basic skill development.

At the University of Houston's Downtown campus, a new initiative, Learners' Community Program, was launched to boost the retention and graduation rates of diverse, first-time students. The Initiative has four components:

1. *Coordination of existing academic programs* that includes course linkages, which allow students to take a first-year seminar that is a developmental course in reading, writing, or math, and a core curriculum course taught by faculty trained to work with developmental students.
2. *Academic advising and counseling systems* that enable advisors and counselors to work with students to identify federal and state financial assistance opportunities including grants and scholarships. There is also a Probation Recovery Program targeting students who earn a low grade point average at the end of the first semester.
3. *Academic support services and student success programs*, which include a collaborative relationship between academic and student affairs. This program sends peer mentors and first-year student orientation leaders to local high schools to talk with students who will enter the University in the following year.
4. *Institutional support for student success and retention* provides outcomes assessment of activities and objectives and informs all stakeholders of the profile of factors impacting student retention and persistence (Thielemann, 2001).

Educators should note that all of these programs provide multiple validating in- and out-of-class experiences such as, faculty, counselors, and mentors who encourage and support students, the use of a culturally relevant curriculum, opportunities for student and faculty collaboration, and recognition of achievement. In addition, these programs provide involvement opportunities such as field trips, visits to libraries, tutoring, and ceremonial events that foster networking, friendships, and in- and out-of-class contact among faculty, counselors, mentors, and students.

Conclusion

The transition to college is an often misunderstood and romanticized phenomenon that is thought to have only positive consequences. Students who experience difficulties traversing the path to college may be thought to be poor college material. Yet, transitional events in life tend to trigger a loss response that entails surrendering an attachment of some kind, leaving behind what is familiar. According to psychologists

Bloom-Feshbach and Bloom-Feshbach (1987): "The dynamics of separation responses include anxiety at being apart from the love object; anger, rage, and sadness at the loss; conflict over negative feelings toward the yearned-for figure; defensive attachment and depression" (p. 2). An individual's psychological heritage, such as quality of early upbringing and history of separation and loss experiences, shape the separation reaction and response. This chapter notes that there are major differences between the early experiences of traditional and non-traditional students of color. Traditional students who have privileged cultural upbringing will tend to shape their separation response quite differently than students from less privileged backgrounds. Therefore, the transition to college cannot be considered to be the same for all students. Colleges and universities can do much to help students develop autonomy and academic identity by creating in- and out-of-class validating environments and fostering opportunities that engage students with faculty and peers. Truly responsive educators must understand and come to terms with the positive and negative aspects of separation for different kinds of students. Indeed, this approach can facilitate the transition to college, while making it much more rewarding for all students.

Authors' Note

All student quotations used in this chapter are taken from *The Transition to College Project of the National Center for Postsecondary Teaching, Learning and Assessment* funded by the U.S. Office of Education, Office of Educational Research and Improvement, under Grant No. R117G100037. The opinions expressed herein do not necessarily reflect the position or policies of OERI, and no official endorsement should be inferred.

References

Adelman, C. (1999). *Answers in the tool box: Academic intensity, attendance patterns, and bachelor's degree attainment*. Washington, DC: Office of Educational Research and Improvement, U.S. Department of Education.

Astin, A. (1985). *Achieving educational excellence: A critical assessment of priorities and practices in higher education*. San Francisco: Jossey-Bass.

Bloom, M. V. (1987). Leaving home: A family transition. In J. B. Bloom-Feshbach, S. B. Bloom-Feshbach, & Associates, *The psychology of separation and loss*. San Francisco: Jossey-Bass.

Bloom-Feshbach, J. B., Bloom-Feshbach, S. B., & Associates. (1987). *The psychology of separation and loss*. San Francisco: Jossey-Bass.

Brawer, F. B. (1996). *Retention-attrition in the nineties*. Los Angeles: ERIC Clearinghouse for Community Colleges. (ERIC Document Reproduction Service No. ED 393 510)

Choy, S. P., Horn, L. J., Nunez, A. M., & Chen, X. (2000). Transition to college: What helps at-risk students and students whose parents did not attend college. In A. F. Cabrera & S. M. La Nasa (Eds.), *Understanding the college choice of disadvantaged students*. (New Directions for Institutional Research No. 107) (pp.45-63). San Francisco: Jossey-Bass.

Comarow, A. (2001, May 3). Vanishing freshmen. *U. S. News and World Reports*. Retrieved from http://www.usnews.com/usnews/edu/college/articles/coreten.htm

De Anda, D. (1984, March-April). Bicultural socialization: Factors affecting theminority experience. *Social Work, 29*(2), 101-107.

Gandara, P., Mejorado, M., Gutierrez, D., & Molina, M. (1998). *Final report of the evaluation of High School Puente, 1994-1998.* Unpublished manuscript, University of California, Davis.

Hardy, C. D., & Karathanos, D. (1992). A bridge course for the high-risk freshmen: Evaluating outcomes. *NASPA Journal, 29,* 213-220.

Jalomo, R. E. (1995). *Latino students in transition: An analysis of the first-year experience in the community college.* Unpublished doctoral dissertation. Arizona State University, Tempe, AZ.

Levy-Warren, M. H. (1988). Moving to a new culture: Cultural identity, loss, and mourning. In J. B. Bloom-Feshbach, S. B. Bloom-Feshbach, & Associates. *The psychology of separation and loss.* San Francisco: Jossey-Bass.

London, H. (1989). Breaking away: A study of first-generation college students and their families. *American Journal of Education, 97,* 144-170.

Malaney, G. D., & Shively, M. (1995). Academic and social expectations and experiences of first-year students of color. *NASPA Journal, 33,* 3-17.

Noel, L., Levitz, R., & Saluri, D. (1985). *Increasing student retention: Effective programs and practices for reducing the dropout rate.* San Francisco: Jossey-Bass.

Nora, A. (2003). Access to higher education for Hispanic students: Real or illusory? In L. Jones & J. Castellanos (Eds.), *The majority in the majority: Retaining Latina/o faculty, administrators and students in the 21st century.* Sterling, VA: Stylus Press.

Nora, A., & Cabrera, A. F. (1996). The role of perceptions of prejudice and discrimination on the adjustment of minority students to college. *Journal of Higher Education, 67,* 119-148.

Perigo, D. J., & Upcraft, M. L. (1989). Orientation Programs. In M. L. Upcraft, & J. N. Gardner, *The freshman year experience* (pp. 82-94). San Francisco: Jossey-Bass.

Rendón, L. I. (1992). From the barrio to the academy: Revelations of a Mexican-American "scholarship girl." In L. S. Zwerling, & H. London (Eds.), *First generation students: Confronting the cultural issues.* (New Directions For Community Colleges No. 80) (pp.55-64). San Francisco: Jossey-Bass.

Rendón, L. I. (1994). Validating culturally diverse students: Toward a new model of learning and student development. *Innovative Higher Education, 19,* 33-51.

Rendón L. I. (1996, November-December). Life on the Border. *About Campus,* 27-30.

Rendón, L. I. (2002). Community College Puente: A validating model of education. *Journal of Educational Policy and Practice, 16*(4), 642-667.

Robinson, D. A., Burns, C. F., & Gaw, K. F. (1996). Orientation programs: A foundation for student learning and success. (New Directions for Student Services No. 75) (pp. 55- 68). San Francisco: Jossey-Bass.

Rodriguez, R. (1982). *Hunger of memory.* Boston: David R. Godine Publishers.

Santa Rita, E., & Bacote, J. B. (1997). The benefit of college discovery pre-freshmen summer programs for minority and low-income students. *Journal of College Student Development, 31,* 161-173.

Terenzini, P. T., Rendón, L. I., Upcraft, M. L., Millar, S. B., Allison, K.W., Gregg, P. L., & Jalomo, R. (1994). The transition to college: Diverse students, diverse stories. *Research in Higher Education, 35,* 57-73.

Thielemann, J. (2001). 1.9 Million to UHD for Learners' Community Program. *Hispanic Outlook in Higher Education, 11*(14), 36-38.

Tinto, V., Goodsell, A., & Russo, P. (1994). *Building learning communities for new college students.* Philadelphia: The Pennsylvania State University, National Center on Postsecondary Teaching, Learning, and Assessment.

Upcraft, M. L., & Gardner, J. N. (1989). *The freshman year experience.* San Francisco: Jossey-Bass.

Weis, L. (1985). *Between two worlds: Black students in an urban community college.* Boston: Routledge and Kegan Paul.

Zwerling, L. S., & London, H. (Eds.). (1992). *First generation students: Confronting the cultural issues* (New Directions For Community Colleges No. 80). San Francisco: Jossey-Bass.

Section 2

Supporting Students of Color in the Classroom and Beyond

Chapter 4

Inclusion, Reflection, and the Politics of Knowledge: On Working Toward the Realization of Inclusive Classroom Environments

Nana Osei-Kofi,
Sandra L. Richards,
and Daryl G. Smith[1]

As a teacher and a social activist I cannot take an "objective" look at oppression and define it outside academic discourse. For me, multicultural teaching is about transforming the self, the classroom and ultimately the society; the places where oppression is real, lived and resisted.— Gail Dines, 1994

Struggles for inclusion have been a part of American higher education since its inception in the 17th century. At that time, higher education exclusively served the interests of a select group of elite men. The struggle then, just as today, has been to broaden access to higher education. Throughout history, rationales for greater inclusiveness have centered on various combinations of moral, demographic, civic, intellectual, and political imperatives (Border & Chism, 1992).

Today, rationales for inclusion primarily focus on the underrepresentation of people of color and are dominated by economic and demographic arguments (e.g., Hurtado, Milem, & Clayton-Pedersen, 1999; Rendón & Hope, 1996). Economic arguments revolve around the notion that populations historically excluded from higher education must be educated in order to strengthen the nation's economy. In addition, all students need to be able to interact with diverse populations in order to participate in an increasingly global economy. Meanwhile, demographic arguments stem from the supposition that the presence of an increasingly diverse student body requires the creation of curricula and environments that reflect the current student body, and by extension, the diversity of the nation.

This chapter, which focuses on fostering inclusive classroom environments, is written from the perspective that inclusion is a critical component of an education through which students "develop independence in thought and action, …prepare…to be actors and not passive receptors of received ideas and notions, and…dare to dream about creating a more human and just social order" (Jackson & Solís, 1995, p. 7). We believe inclusion is about much more than access or marginal curricular changes. In fact, it is a realization that resides deeply in epistemological questions about who and what we are as a nation and as institutions of higher education and how we as educators, administrators, and members of society, live our lives (Gabelnick, 1997). The type of inclusion we envision requires moving beyond valuing and celebrating difference to enabling transformative action. This action requires addressing issues at a structural level and refusing to engage in all too familiar, faddish, quick fix, surface-level solutions in response to "the challenges of diversity." It is not diversity that is a challenge; "rather, the problem is directly related to the responses of the dominant culture to...[diversity]—responses that function to perpetuate social, political, and economic inequality" (Darder, 1997, p. 342). Hence, we view true inclusion as requiring the courage to confront higher education at the core, engaging the politics of knowledge and the historically defined structures that continue to privilege the elite at the expense of the masses.

Creating inclusive classrooms begins with recognizing that neither classrooms nor knowledge are apolitical (Hogue, Parker, & Miller, 1998). "While [all] knowledge and theories are generated from the standpoint of particular interests, location[s], and life experiences, we have been [erroneously] schooled to believe that knowledge is objective, neutral and separate from the knower" (Bensimon, 1994, p. 23). By recognizing this reality, we have the opportunity to begin creating and nurturing environments where multiple forms of knowledge, identities, locations, and ways of knowing hold credence. As a result, we provide students with validating experiences (Rendón, 1994) and with the skills to make sense of the world around them. These encounters with existing knowledge in inclusive environments allow students to create knowledge (Berry, 1998) and to become actors in shaping a shared future rather than recipients of a fragmented past.

As we engage in this work, it is important to recognize that this is not a process of implementing a predetermined recipe for teaching that somehow creates a liberatory and culturally democratic classroom environment (Darder, 1997; Freire, 1970/2000; Sleeter & McLaren, 1995). Rather, this process is shaped by the way in which we, as educators, engage the world in relationship to our own lives and the lives of our students. Regardless of the type of material we bring into the classroom, in the final analysis, impact is defined by the way we engage our students. Hence, "prior to any engagement with instrumental questions of practice, [we] must delve rigorously into those specific theoretical issues that are fundamental to the establishment of a culturally democratic foundation" (Darder, 1997, p. 331) and necessary for the creation of inclusive classrooms.

Reflexivity

The move toward inclusion can be exciting and fulfilling, but also difficult, painful, and frustrating. For some it is as though this work "attacks received wisdom, wrenches internalized values, and contests assumptions held so deeply that to challenge them feels as if one is fighting nature" (Freidman, 1995, p. 2). For others, it is both a joyous "act of resistance" and "complex, enigmatic, and even personally painful" (Wald, 1997, p.125), illustrating the need for deep personal work in moving toward greater multicultural awareness and inclusiveness. As Palmer (1998) suggests, "the most practical thing we can achieve in any kind of work is insight into what is happening inside us as we do it" (p. 5). For indeed, "nothing happens in the 'real' world unless it happens in the images of our heads" (Anzaldúa, 1999, p. 109).

As a facilitator and instructor of multicultural education courses, Gorski (2000) writes about his experience undertaking a process of self-reflection concerning racial identity. In "Narrative on Whiteness and Multicultural Education," he admits his failure, until recently, to examine multicultural issues introspectively:

> This is the ultimate luxury of whiteness: the ability to see myself as neutral and thus excuse myself from any responsibility for addressing racial issues in education, society in general, and most importantly, myself. Even as a facilitator and instructor of Multicultural Education courses and workshops, I was able to avoid addressing my own issues by assuming either the role of advocate or the role of cultural theorist. Being was easier that way—succumbing to the pressure of academia, which, as an institution, is terrified of self-examination, and so discourages it through insisting on the scientific method and objectivity. (p. 2)

He goes on to say,

> This experience reminded me that, while Multicultural Education is partially about addressing issues on a societal level or in the education system overall, my process for being a truly effective multicultural educator had to begin with a renewed dedication to address the "self" half of my responsibility duality. I had to immerse myself in a systematic process of examining how my experience as a White person informed my teaching and facilitating as well as the lenses through which I saw my students. (p. 3)

In other words, Gorski suggests the necessity of exploring the duality of identity, of exploring the self as an individual vis-à-vis the self as located within the structural context of society.

As we begin to take responsibility for the transformation of self, we must recognize that our beliefs and worldviews have been shaped through interactions and experiences in a society of unequal power relations. Unfortunately, our educational institutions mirror the same systems of power and oppression. As recipients of an education from these institutions, we have received erroneous information, distorted images, and incomplete histories of various groups. For instance, how many of us were ever taught that Iroquois Indians helped shape the origins of democracy in America or that Black feminists played a significant role in the American women's movement? How many of us understand that race is socially constructed yet has very real political and cultural implications, or have ever considered America as a class-based society? The failure of educational institutions to provide a complete story renders our vision of the world inaccurate, making the histories and experiences of marginalized groups invisible. Furthermore, the reality is that most of us still live in segregated worlds and do not have the experience of a truly multicultural society. Therefore, we come to accept a dominant, universal standard that stands as the norm by which others are judged. Feminist scholar and writer bell hooks (1993) notes,

> Most of us were taught in classrooms where styles of teaching reflected the notion of a single norm of thought and experience, which we were encouraged to believe was a universal norm....Most of us learned to teach emulating this model. (p. 91)

Further, her own experience demonstrates how this universal standard is enacted and perpetuated in the classroom:

> When I first entered the multicultural, multiethnic classroom setting, I was unprepared. I did not know how to cope effectively with so much "difference." I had not really been compelled to work within an inclusive setting—one that is truly diverse—and I lacked the necessary skills. This is the case with most educators. It

is difficult for many educators in the United States to conceptualize how the classroom will look when they are confronted with the demographics, which indicate that "whiteness" may cease to be the norm ethnicity [sic] in the classroom settings on all levels. Hence, educators are poorly prepared when we actually confront diversity. This is why so many of us stubbornly cling to old patterns. (p. 94-95)

Unfortunately, we continue to be denied access to information that can mend our fragmented knowledge. The combination of deeply embedded, personal knowledge and the narrowness and partiality of information we receive creates a disconnect between what we actually know and what we believe we know. Furthermore, any realization that our knowledge is biased and inaccurate often leads to feelings of guilt, as we must face the fact that we have all been complicit in systems of marginalization, oppression, and exclusion. Listen to the voice of a White teacher whose experiences with one of his students causes him to confront his own racism:

> I learned from Akmir's reading techniques how to unlearn habits of mine that let such racism in books pass unexamined. Before knowing him, I was not attuned to many of the nuances of racist implication because I was not the victim of racism. I did not suffer through every offensive phrase I encountered when reading, nor did I experience rage when racism was cloaked in the authority of tradition or the language of excellence. The lack of that sensitivity bothered me, and I had to unlearn this insensitivity to biased yet traditional ways of speaking and writing. In addition, I had to learn now to choose my own language and learn to make the avoidance of racist reference habit. I had to think very carefully about talking about "dark intents" and "black deeds," to avoid using comparisons like "civilized/primitive" and "sophisticated/unsophisticated;" and to eliminate characterizations like "disadvantaged" and "deprived." I had to learn to think from the perspective of someone who had not learned racist language, and that experience has been an important part of my growth and development. Akmir's insistence upon the details of racism reference influenced how I read, speak, and write in much the same way that current feminist writing is influencing me. For me it was a matter of unlearning what could be called habits of inclusion and exclusion. (Kohl, 1991, p. 32)

As educators and especially as researchers, we are often trained to believe that acquiring data on something equates with knowing. However, as the aforementioned narratives suggest, having information on societal groups does not mean that we understand the lived experiences of others. Instead, an understanding of lived experiences requires an investment of time and energy in dialogue with others and in understanding ourselves. Furthermore, this process also requires recognizing that as we come to know others, our knowing is different from the knowledge of those living within the context we seek to know, as we are situated outside that context (Darder, 1997).

Classroom Dynamics

By the very nature of the academy, we, as educators, hold power and authority in the classroom, and power differentials affect the way in which students interact, communicate, engage with the material, and challenge classroom presumptions. In addition, the power imbalance between faculty and students may be particularly pronounced in classrooms where issues of race, class, gender, and sexuality are part of the discourse (Higginbotham, 1996). In understanding power in the classroom, the examination of our own positionality is an important piece when considering what influences classroom dynamics and students' responses to engaging issues of diversity (Higginbotham, 1996). While this may mean different things for individual faculty members depending on group membership(s), the task at hand is to create a classroom environment where students feel safe struggling with difficult issues that challenge their assumptions and beliefs. As educators, we must be willing to share aspects of our own experiences and personal investment in the subject matter, particularly those issues that directly confront issues of race, gender, class, and sexuality. As an example of this, Lipsitz (1997) articulates his commitment to the frequently challenging engagement of issues of social class in the classroom, saying:

> I hope to show that identities of race and gender always intersect with class, that unlikely coalitions across identity categories have succeeded in the past, but only when people honestly acknowledged the things that divided them and created actual practices and structures of inclusion rather than just abstract calls for unity. (p. 20)

As students connect with us on various issues, they will feel more liberated to express their feelings and perspectives. Furthermore, students will realize that both faculty and their peers struggle with the complexity of social issues. This will not only restructure the power dynamics in the classroom, but will also help students develop their ideas and belief systems. Reflecting on her experience teaching diverse students, Vacarr (2001) offers the following perspective:

> In the diverse classroom, many of us are unprepared for the discoveries that await us. It is our willingness to step out of the role of the Super Teacher, to reveal our own ignorance, and to engage our students in exploring transformative possibilities that invites the students to do the same. (p. 292)

One of the most challenging ways that students exercise power in the classroom is through resistance. While our instinct may be to ignore resistance, it is critical to recognize and address different manifestations of resistance in the classroom (Higginbotham, 1996). Whether students display resistance by being vocal, silent, or absent, it is important to treat all acts of resistance as a legitimate strategy in the process of learning. We cause the greatest harm when resistance is either ignored or challenged in a way that de-legitimizes the experience of the individual. As students engage in difficult and emotional topics, we must make an effort to create truly liberating classrooms where dissent is not viewed as negative, but is taken as an opportunity to learn from diverse perspectives. We should also be aware of the ways in which students' own positionality and ways of knowing may cause resistance and influence their approach to learning new perspectives. Furthermore, we must establish environments where students do not try to avoid conflict and difference of opinion. It is exactly at the intersection of difference where the greatest amount of learning takes place, and opinions and attitudes change. Exemplifying this practice, McNaron (1997) describes how she, as an openly lesbian faculty member, engages students saying:

> Teaching as a publicly declared lesbian scholar has allowed me tremendous opportunities to challenge lesbian or gay and also heterosexual students in my classes. I no longer worry about being surprised by students' questions

regarding possibly coded homoerotic energy in literary works. In responding to them, I try to remember how terrified I was in the past so that I do not repress whatever it may be that motivates their discomfort. However, I also am unwilling to stop telling students the truth. (p. 34)

This narrative speaks to the need for us, as educators, to model for our students a practice of interrogating difference, welcoming conflict, and creating a dialogue of respect that is based in a sense of humanity. This is admittedly difficult, as most of us have been socialized in a way that makes us fearful of difference. This fear of difference makes it even more important that we model this behavior for students. Many of us, as well as our students, are told in childhood that if we do not have something nice to say about someone, then we should not say anything at all. As children who are curious about the differences we see, we are told not to gaze at others because the "oppositional gaze"[2] is dangerous and discomforting. The White child looking at a Black man is told to stop staring. We silence our young and replace their natural and innocent questioning with fear and contempt. Furthermore, we accept the dominant cultural ways of being as the only ways to be. White, middle-class, male, heterosexual, able-bodied individuals establish the norm and everything in society conforms to that ideal. In our youth, we are socialized to accept this standard, unquestioningly. However, when students enter college, we hope for the interrogation and questioning that would help facilitate discussions about difference more freely. We ask them to relearn what they knew all along, and in the process of facilitating that learning, we find ourselves equally unprepared because, we too, have forgotten what it means to look honestly at a person who is different from ourselves and not feel guilty while we are "looking."

Engaging Principles in Practice

As we have discussed in this chapter, the first realization of working to create inclusive classrooms, and ultimately an inclusive society, is that the work is both personally and professionally challenging. To engage in the work of creating inclusive classrooms, we must continually critique and interrogate ourselves, our scholarship, our pedagogy, and our curricula. What follows are some heuristic tools that we hope readers will find useful in seeking to create and re-create the meaning of inclusiveness in their classrooms.

As a continuous process, Figure 1 illustrates how this work is often embarked upon from multiple points of entry, such as through our scholarship, pedagogy, curricula, or exploration of self. While these entry points are varied, it is important to note that it is when we connect what we do externally with what we experience internally that the process of transformation begins. A dialectical relationship always exists between our work—no matter what the focus or emphasis—and who we are as human beings.

Thus, our work begins with a cognizance and recognition of who we are and where that situates us in society, in the institution where we teach, and in our classrooms (Cannon, 1990). For example, whether we are female, male, working class, upper class, Native American, White, Catholic, Muslim, gay, or straight, these pieces of our identities serve to situate us in society. Next, we must ask how our multiple identities shape our understanding of the world. How has our location within social and economic power relations across race, class, gender, and sexuality informed our worldview? These are questions that can also be asked of students as they engage in their own learning. As we begin to ask these questions and challenge our assumptions, we must consider whether our perspectives foster true inclusiveness and "interrupt the normal hierarchies of society"(Cannon, 1990, p. 126) or whether they merely serve to maintain the status quo.

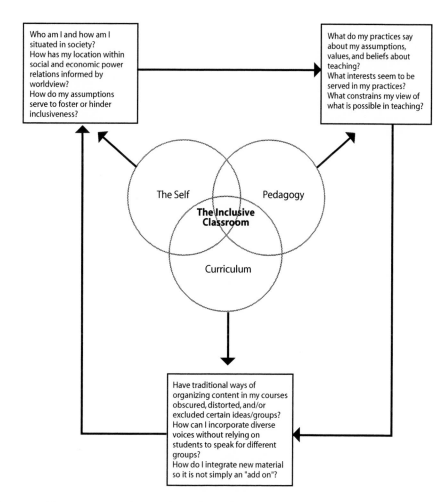

Figure 1. The process of creating an inclusive classroom

In addition to the work on the self, pedagogy and the way we structure courses play a major role in whether classroom interactions mimic and reproduce our current social structure or whether they are environments that become truly inclusive (Cannon, 1990). Engaging this issue, Smyth (1992) posits some valuable questions that allow us to make explicit to ourselves, the assumptions underlying our pedagogical practices:

- What do my practices say about my assumptions, values, and beliefs about teaching?
- Where did these ideas come from?
- What social practices are expressed in these ideas?
- What causes me to maintain my theories? What views of power do they embody?
- Whose interests seem to be served in my practices?
- What constrains my view of what is possible in teaching?

As the social structure of the classroom defines how power is distributed within the classroom, we must also consider who is in the classroom (in terms of race, class, gender, sexuality, or other characteristics), how the classroom is organized physically, and how we fit into the power structure of the classroom. From this analysis, the most effective teaching strategies should be considered (Cannon, 1990).

Fundamental to effective pedagogy in an inclusive classroom are assumptions about teaching and learning and expectations of students. If we view our role as differentiating between students whom we perceive as having aptitude from those we perceive as not having aptitude, our classroom approach will focus on strategies for identifying students to encourage and students to discourage. If we believe that all students can learn, then our approach must be establishing conditions under which learning can take place. If we believe that in order to facilitate student success we must lower expectations, then we will see diversity and excellence as being in conflict. Contrary to this view, we know today that inclusiveness must be created in an environment with high expectations, belief in students' capacity to succeed, and using supportive structures to facilitate learning. Using collaborative learning, peer groups, multiple strategies for teaching, and providing a supportive validating environment are all important elements in this process. As our pedagogy begins to change, further questions to consider throughout this process include assessing our own strengths and limitations in relation to new content and ways of engaging students (Schmitz, 1999). Moreover, we should begin to ask how we will handle difficult and controversial subjects in the classroom and how we will engage assessment of student learning in light of other changes we have implemented in our classrooms (Schmitz, 1999).

The third element for creating inclusive classrooms, following "self" and "pedagogy," is the curriculum. What is contained in curricula is traditionally viewed as "truth" arrived at through objective scientific processes (Garcia & Smith, 1996). However, the truth is that no knowledge or curricula are apolitical, and much of what is used in curricula today is shaped by biases, omissions, and stereotypes (Garcia & Smith). Altering the curriculum is not simply a matter of adding a book or reading to an existing curriculum; nor is it a matter of adding materials so that students will more easily identify with the subject under study. We have to ask about the issues, methodologies, and content being taught and examine these areas from the perspective of educating a diverse group of students in the relevant subject matter. To begin the process of curriculum transformation, Schmitz (1999) offers a valuable set of questions. The questions she posits include:

- Have traditional ways of organizing content in this course obscured, distorted, or excluded certain ideas or groups?
- What new research is available that addresses past distortions and exclusions?
- How will the course change if I include this new research?
- How can I incorporate diverse voices without relying on students to speak for different groups?
- How might a change in this syllabus affect its relation to the rest of the curriculum?
- If the course topics remain the same, what new research, examples, and writings can illustrate these topics?
- How do I integrate new material so that it is not simply an "add-on"?

This process of critiquing our own values and beliefs and how they translate into the type of pedagogy and curriculum we employ, which in turn determines the type of classroom environment we create, is an ongoing process. Figure 2 seeks to capture this process, which speaks to who we are and how we live our lives, thus requiring that we continuously look inward and seek to better understand ourselves, ultimately allowing us to better understand others.

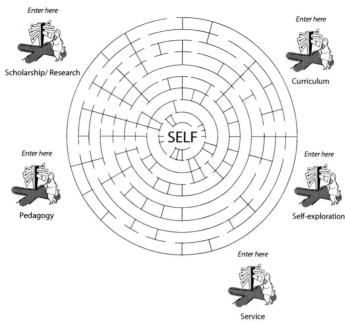

Figure 2. The maze to transformation.

Indicators of Success

Although there is no prescribed formula for creating inclusive classrooms, the notion of inclusivity does not have to remain an elusive one. We are able to provide some "indicators of success" to serve as a guide on the journey toward inclusiveness. As evidence of progress, these indicators do not presuppose completion of one's work; rather, they are meant to encourage continued growth. In addition, the following list is not meant to be exhaustive; instead, it provides some common characteristics that will be evidenced in the inclusive classroom.

- There is a balance of power and equity in the classroom evidenced by all students contributing to class discussions.
- Voices of dissent are not silenced. The classroom environment welcomes a spirit of questioning, critique, and interrogation.
- Students are encouraged to present new ideas and make suggestions with regard to diversifying course curriculum and content.
- A diversity of voices, perspectives, and scholarship are represented in course content and curriculum, and these perspectives are integrally connected to the learning goals and objectives of the course.
- Course material and content evoke emotional responses, as students find their assumptions of the world being challenged.
- Classroom discussions permit the expression of emotions and personal experiences. The classroom is not limited to "intellectual objectivity," but instead is regarded as a space where students can deeply interrogate their own beliefs, assumptions, feelings, and experiences within the context of subject matter.
- Varied instructional styles are used to reflect different ways of learning.

- Students and faculty view conflict as an opportunity for learning, rather than a disruption to the learning process.
- Faculty are comfortable relinquishing their position of power and expertise in the classroom and acknowledge their own development in the process toward greater inclusiveness.

Finally, it is important to understand that there is no single definition of, or approach to, creating inclusive classrooms. Each individual enters the process from a different vantage point, and each class, characterized by a unique group of students and diverse subject matter, will require appropriate modifications. The inclusive classroom is not any one thing; it is a culmination of all things required of a more just society where education truly becomes "the practice of freedom."

Conclusion

In offering a discussion of what we view as critical principles for fostering inclusiveness, we have sought to argue that creating inclusiveness in higher education requires grounding our work in a historically specific understanding of America, higher education, and the experiences of our students. We must understand the context and specificity of different experiences. We must be willing to challenge our own values, beliefs, and assumptions as we work to make sense of our world for ourselves and for our students. We must struggle with making our institution's "webs of significance" explicit (Geertz, 1977) so that we have a more holistic perspective of reality. We must challenge the broken paradoxes of higher education—those separating the head from the heart, facts from feelings, theory from practice, and teaching from learning (Palmer, 1998). We must interrogate our own position within the classroom, our institutions, and the larger society. Lastly, we believe this work should be grounded in a commitment to social justice and a love for humanity, as the struggle to create inclusive institutions of higher education and indeed a more inclusive society continues.

Notes

[1] As this chapter was authored collaboratively, the authors are listed in alphabetical order.
[2] The phrase "oppositional gaze" is borrowed from bell hooks' *The Oppositional Gaze: Black Female Spectators* (1996), which describes the politicization of "looking" relations between Blacks and Whites.

References

Anzaldùa, G. (1999). *Borderlands/La frontera: The new mestiza* (2nd ed.). San Francisco: aunt lute books.

Bensimon, E. (1994). Bilingual cash machines, multicultural campuses, and communities of difference. *Innovative Higher Education, 19*(1), 23-32.

Berry, K. S. (1998). Nurturing the imagination of resistance: Young adults as creators of knowledge. In J. L. Kincheloe, & S. R. Steinberg (Eds.), *Unauthorized methods: Strategies for critical teaching* (pp. 43-55). New York: Routledge.

Border, L. B., & Chism, N. V. (1992). *Teaching for diversity.* (New Directions for Teaching and Learning No. 49). San Francisco: Jossey-Bass.

Cannon, L.W. (1990). Fostering positive race, class, and gender dynamics in the classroom. *Women's Studies Quarterly, 18*(1/2), 86-94.

Darder, A. (1997). Creating the conditions for cultural democracy in the classroom. In A. Darder, R.D. Torres, & H. Gutìerrez (Eds.), *Latinos and education: A critical reader* (pp. 331-350). New York: Routledge.

Dines, G. (1994). What's left of multiculturalism?: Race, class and gender in the classroom. *Race, Sex & Class, 1*(2), 23-34.

Friedman, E. G. (1996). Received ideas and curriculum transformation. In E. G. Friedman, W. K. Kolmar, C. B. Flint, & P. Rothenberg (Eds.), *Creating an inclusive college curriculum: A teaching sourcebook from the New Jersey Project* (pp. 1-9). New York: Teachers College Press.

Freire, P. (2000). *Pedagogy of the oppressed*. New York: Continuum. (Original work published 1970)

Gabelnick, F. (1997). Educating a committed citizenry. *Change, 29*, 30-35.

Garcia, M., & Smith, D. G. (1996). Reflecting inclusiveness in the college curriculum. In L. I. Rendón, & R. O. Hope (Eds.), *Educating a new majority: Transforming America's educational system for diversity* (pp. 265-288). San Francisco: Jossey-Bass.

Geertz, C. (1977). *The interpretation of cultures*. Scranton, PA: Basic Books.

Gorski, P. (2000, Spring). Narrative of whiteness and multicultural education. *Electronic Magazine of Multicultural Education, 2*(1). Retrieved April 15, 2001, from http://www.eastern.edu/publications/emme/2000spring/

Higginbotham, E. (1996). Getting all students to listen: Analyzing and coping with student resistance. *The American Behavioral Scientist, 40*(2), 203-211.

hooks, b. (1993). Transformative pedagogy and multiculturalism. In T. Perry, & J. W. Fraser (Eds.), *Freedom's plow: Teaching in the multicultural classroom* (pp. 91-97). New York: Routledge.

Hogue, C., Parker, K., & Miller, M. (1998). Talking the walk: Ethical pedagogy in the multicultural classroom. *Feminist Teacher, 12*(2), 89-106.

Hurtado, S., Milem, J., Clayton-Pederson, A., & Allen, W. (1999). *Enacting diverse learning environments: Improving the climate for racial/ethnic diversity in higher education*. (ASHE-ERIC Higher Education Report No. 26). Washington, DC: The George Washington University, Graduate School of Education and Human Development.

Jackson, S., & Solís, J. (Eds.). (1995). *Beyond comfort zones in multiculturalism: Confronting the politics of privilege*. Westport, CT: Bergin & Garvey.

Kohl, H. (1991). *I won't learn from you! The role of assent in learning*. Minneapolis, MN: Milkweed Editions.

Lipsitz, G. (1997). Class and consciousness: Teaching about social class. In A. Kumar (Ed.), *Class issues: Pedagogy, cultural studies, and the public sphere* (pp. 9-21). New York: New York University Press.

McNaron, T. A. (1997). *Poisoned ivy: Lesbian and gay academics confronting homophobia*. Philadelphia: Temple University Press.

Palmer, P. J. (1998). *The courage to teach: Exploring the inner landscape of a teacher's life*. San Francisco: Jossey-Bass.

Rendón, L. I, (1994). Validating culturally diverse students: Toward a new model of learning in student development. *Innovative Higher Education, 19*(1), 33-50.

Rendón, L. I., & Hope, R. O. (Eds.). (1996). *Educating a new majority*. San Francisco: Jossey-Bass.

Schmitz, B. (1999). Transforming a course. *CIDR Teaching and Learning Bulletin, 2*(4), 1.

Sleeter, C. E., & McLaren, P.L. (1995). Introduction: Exploring connections to build a critical multiculturalism. In C. E. Sleeter, & P. L. McLaren (Eds.), *Multicultural education, critical pedagogy, and the politics of difference* (pp. 5-28). New York: State University of New York Press.

Smyth, J. (1992). Teachers' work and the politics of reflection. *American Educational Research Journal, 29*(2), 267-300.

Vacarr, B. (2001). Moving beyond polite correctness: Practicing mindfulness in the diverse classroom. *Harvard Educational Review, 71*(2), 285-295.

Wald, A. (1997). A pedagogy of unlearning: Teaching the specificity of U.S. Marxism. In A. Kumar (Ed.), *Class issues: Pedagogy, cultural studies, and the public sphere* (pp.125-147). New York: New York University Press.

Chapter 5

Fostering Positive Intergroup Relations in the First Year of College

*Jesús Treviño
and Kris Ewing*

As college and university campuses become more diverse, one of the most important challenges will be fostering positive intergroup relations and welcoming, supportive campus climates. Unfortunately, institutions of higher learning continue to experience incidents that create negative campus climates such as cross-cultural misunderstandings, intergroup conflict, threats to free speech, incidents of hate speech, and hate crimes. In addition, many campuses have dealt with acts of insensitivity targeting Jews, Muslims, Hispanics, Asian Americans, women, lesbian/gay/bisexual/transgender/queer (LGBTQ) students, African Americans, Native Americans, and others. Such incidents contribute to harsh, unsupportive campus climates, which are detrimental to the retention of students of color (Hurtado, Milem, Clayton-Pederson, & Allen, 1999). Thus, it is important for colleges and universities to invest in improving their campus climates for diversity and promote positive intergroup relations early on as students experience the first year of college.

In this chapter, the authors propose that issues of campus climate and concerns about student retention can be addressed most successfully by engaging first-year students of color in both intragroup and intergroup contact and interaction. Intragroup interaction is defined as experiences and contact with members of the same group (Treviño, 1992). Intragroup interaction might include activities and services that provide cultural, social, psychological, and emotional support for minority students. Intergroup interaction, on the other hand, is contact with members from other groups (Zuniga & Nagda, 1993). Such interaction might include programs and activities that allow students of color to meet students from other groups, promote cross-cultural education, address intergroup misperceptions (e.g., stereotyping, myths), and improve relations between groups (Vasques Scalera, 1999). Both processes are crucial for achieving a multiplicity of outcomes including increased retention, leadership development, improved cross-cultural understanding, reduced intergroup conflict, civic engagement, and a positive campus climate for diversity (Hurtado et al., 1999; Vasques Scalera).

This chapter explores the value of intragroup involvement for students of color and examines some of the issues that impede both intragroup and intergroup interaction. The concept of structured interaction is introduced as a solution to the barriers to intergroup interaction and as a strategy for promoting positive intergroup relations. Finally, promising practices related to the intergroup intervention are presented. Here, two model centers that promote intergroup interaction and address issues related to campus climate are discussed.

Engaging First-Year Students of Color: The Value of Involvement

Research on college students has demonstrated that, upon entering college, students face a variety of developmental and practical tasks. Developmentally, students have to work through and manage a variety of stages related to both personal (Chickering, 1978) and social identity development (Ponterotto, Casas, Suzuki, & Alexander, 1995; Tajfel, 1978). From a practical perspective, new students are challenged to acquire a significant amount of practical knowledge and skills, particularly during the first year that will maximize their chances of survival and success in college (Padilla, 1999). Although there are a number of factors that affect student success, involvement plays a major role. Involvement, defined as the amount of psychological and physical energy that a student invests in her or his collegiate experience (Astin, 1984), has been found to be highly correlated with a number of student outcomes including persistence, retention, and graduation (Astin, 1982; Tinto, 1975); leadership development (Schuh & Laverty, 1983); the development of civic responsibility (Feldman & Newcomb, 1969); the development of social and interpersonal skills (Berman, 1978); and the development of social and intellectual confidence (Astin, 1977). Thus, it is important for new college students to establish new relationships with friends, faculty, and staff in order to succeed in college.

Given the value of student involvement, most student affairs professionals stress the importance and benefits of getting involved, particularly in first-year experience programs and in student organizations and activities. During orientation, new students are introduced to myriad student organizations, programs, and activities with plenty of opportunities for involvement. On some campuses, there are literally hundreds of organizations from which to choose, each having diverse objectives and sponsoring a multiplicity of activities. Fraternities and sororities, political clubs, religious groups, academic organizations, sports clubs, environmental groups, and community service clubs are just some of the many options available to students.

One involvement option for African-American, Asian-American, Native-American, and Hispanic college students are student groups and activities that are organized around race and ethnicity. Examples of these include the Black African Coalition, Hispanic Business Student Association, Korean Student Club, American Indian Council, National Society of Black Engineers, and Asian/Pacific American Students Coalition. The growth and proliferation of such organizations is directly connected to demographic changes in the college-going student population. Thus, as the number of ethnic/racial minorities increases on college campuses, membership in ethnic or race-themed student organizations increases as well (Treviño, 1992).

Researchers have found that ethnic or race-themed student groups and activities contribute positively to the collegiate experience of students of color. For example, some studies suggest that these student organizations serve to protect students of color from alienating and harsh campus climates (Berol, Camper, Pigott, Nadolsky, & Sarris, 1983). In addition, these organizations are sources of social support and provide needed services for students of color (Astin, Treviño, & Wingard, 1991). Ethnic or race-themed student organizations are also perceived as making cultural contributions to students by providing opportunities for students of color to mix with students of similar values and backgrounds. For example, Allen (1985) argued that African-American student organizations contribute to Black students' integration into college and to their overall satisfaction with campus social life.

Moreover, ethnic or race-themed student organizations make contributions to campus by helping recruit and retain students of color (Carr & Chittum, 1979; Nieto, 1986) and by providing social and academic support to their members (Allen, 1985; LeCounte, 1987). Some studies also suggest that a correlation exists between students' involvement in ethnic-specific groups and an increased interest in leadership development activities (Treviño, 1992). In sum, it is clear that ethnic/racial involvement opportunities can be beneficial to the growth and development of first-year students of color.

The Contradictions of Involvement

Despite research suggesting the positive effects of participation in ethnic-specific student activities, it is important to note that first-year students of color may receive contradictory messages from college personnel, faculty, and peers about the importance of participating in intragroup student organizations and activities. On the one hand, most first-year students are strongly encouraged to get involved in student groups and activities on campus (Pascarella & Terenzini, 1991). However, students who make the decision to get involved in ethnic or race-themed student organizations and activities may receive the message, from both peers and college staff, that they are segregating themselves (Chen, 2001; Traub, 1999). Thus, while getting involved in predominantly White student organizations such as Greek fraternities and sororities is often viewed as a positive, worthwhile experience, participating in ethnic and race-based organizations may be interpreted as a negative form of self-segregation or balkanization (American Association of Colleges & Universities, 1995; D'Souza, 1991; Hurtado et al., 1999; Tatum, 1997).

What constitutes "positive" or "negative" involvement is often a matter of perception (Hurtado et al., 1999). Whereas some perceive participating in race- or ethnic-specific activities as a negative form of involvement that fosters segregation and isolation, others may view this form of involvement as helpful, because many of these activities and organizations promote cultural awareness on campus and act as social and cultural support networks that protect minority students should they experience discrimination or insensitivity to their culture, religion, or lifestyle (Astin et al., 1991; Chavez, 1982; Gordon & Treadwell, 1992; Loo & Rolison, 1986). Consequently, first-year students of color often receive mixed messages about what should be the ideal form of involvement.

Several difficulties are inherent in the way the self-segregation debate is framed. The first is that the language and definitions employed to frame the quandary are often problematic. As indicated above, what some might consider to be self-imposed isolation or segregation, others may perceive as a valuable form of networking and social support. Second, the debate is often conceptualized as an either/or issue: segregation along racial or ethnic lines as opposed to mixed-group interactions. In short, either students voluntarily segregate in a race/ethnic specific organization, or they choose to interact in diverse, mixed-group settings. What is rarely proposed is that both forms of involvement can have positive and meaningful outcomes. In other words, campus communities may be slow to recognize that students need both involvement opportunities that provide social and cultural support and promote contact and dialogue with students from diverse groups. In fact, both forms of involvement can, and should, co-exist on a college campus, and both can be beneficial to first-year students of color. Stated differently, first-year students of color should have the option and be encouraged to participate in both race-specific or ethnic activities and initiatives (intragroup involvement) and activities that promote meaningful contact and interactions among different groups (intergroup involvement).

Structured Intergroup Interaction and Involvement

Most campuses have opportunities for first-year students of color to get involved in ethnic or race-themed activities and programs. In fact, many colleges and universities have minority or multicultural support centers that strive to meet the needs of first-year students of color via race-specific or ethnic student organizations, programs, and services. The challenge for institutions of higher education, however, is to support the involvement of students of color in ethnic-specific activities while at the same time creating and sustaining purposeful, structured intergroup interaction between and among students of color and other students on campus. Meaningful and structured intergroup interaction among students is severely lacking at our colleges and universities (Schoem & Hurtado, 2001). Students have very few programmatic and "safe" opportunities (i.e., being able to ask questions without getting challenged) to interact with members of groups to which they do not belong (Musil, García, Moses, & Smith, 1995). This limits opportunities for students to understand each other and the potential for colleges to help students achieve self and group identity, greater open-mindedness, a decrease in prejudice and stereotyping, a willingness to take action against discrimination, greater civic engagement, and other important outcomes necessary to live and work in a democratic and diverse society.

The Dynamics of Intergroup Interaction on College Campuses

One of the assumptions that colleges and universities have made related to campus diversity is that bringing together large numbers of students, faculty, and staff from a multiplicity of backgrounds will in and of itself lead to positive intergroup interaction, cultural sharing, and intergroup harmony. Many examples from history suggest that this belief is false (Winkelman, 1993). In fact, the opposite is likely to occur. Cross-cultural conflict, misunderstandings, and intergroup tension are usually the outcomes of diverse groups that live and work in close proximity to each other. Several explanations for this phenomenon are possible. First, individuals are not easily persuaded to participate in and with other groups outside their culture of origin. People are motivated to stay within their own groups. As indicated earlier, some groups on college campuses provide students with a sense of safety and security from harsh campus climates (Hurtado, 1990), and culture-specific groups are likely to fall into this category. Second, when individuals from diverse backgrounds come in contact with each other, their different customs, traditions, languages, values, and world views can clash, causing conflict and misunderstandings. In addition, intergroup processes such as stereotyping, in-group favoritism, anxiety, and intergroup conflict impede groups from interacting, cooperating, and understanding each other (Stephan & Stephan, 1996).

These realities give rise to several implications. First, the increasing number of first-year students of color arriving on campus suggest that intergroup conflict and cross-cultural tensions may intensify as institutions become more diverse. Thus, there is a need to develop strategies to decrease conflict and create greater understanding between and among different groups. Second, interaction between individuals and groups from diverse backgrounds does not always occur naturally, and deliberate efforts should be made to structure this kind of involvement so that it will be meaningful and will address the difficult issues related to diversity (Hurtado, Dey, & Treviño, 1994).

Finally, when intergroup interaction is structured, diversity becomes an asset as colleges and universities harness the power of diverse groups (i.e., languages, cultures, customs, perspectives, talents, skills) in achieving educational outcomes. The outcomes associated with intergroup interaction are beneficial for all students, but in particular for first-year students of color (Schoem & Hurtado, 2001).

Structured Intergroup Interaction Initiatives on College Campuses

During the last decade, a few colleges and universities have started to demonstrate an interest in promoting structured intergroup interaction and involvement among diverse student groups. The University of Michigan, for example, has sponsored a student program to foster intergroup dialogue and learning for well over a decade. This intergroup dialogue program brings different groups together to share in learning about each other's culture. One dialogue may bring together African Americans in structured dialogue with Whites. Another dialogue may combine Latinos and Whites, and still another dialogue may occur between heterosexuals and members of the LGBTQ community, as well as many other combinations of groups coming together for intergroup discussions and learning. Students receive academic credit for what is essentially a course in the form of intergroup dialogues. The University of Massachusetts; University of Washington; California State University, Long Beach; University of Maryland; University of Illinois; and a number of other institutions have implemented intergroup dialogue programs based on the Michigan model. Other institutions are experimenting with different forms of structured intergroup involvement including retreats and story circles (i.e., intergroup interaction using stories as the impetus for working through issues of diversity). These include Santa Ana Community College and Emory University.

Several institutions of higher education have taken a step beyond intergroup dialogue programs and have created entire centers devoted primarily to the creation and promotion of structured intergroup interaction activities and programs. These are entities that are responsible for creating opportunities for first-year students of color, as well as other students representing a multiplicity of groups, to come together and learn from each other in an intergroup context. Examples include the Intergroup Relations Center at Arizona State University; the Center on Diversity and Community at the University of Oregon; the Intergroup Relations Center at California State University, Sacramento; the Student Intercultural Learning Center at the University of Maryland; the Center for Multicultural Excellence at the University of Denver; and the Center for American and World Cultures at Miami University of Ohio.

The Intergroup Relations Center at Arizona State University

Arizona State University has both a Multicultural Student Center (MSC) and an Intergroup Relations Center (IRC). The MSC is responsible for providing a variety of services primarily for students of color in the areas of academic, social, and cultural support. The MSC staff encourages first-year students of color to participate in a variety of ethnic/racial student groups on campus and in initiatives that support their academic success. The Intergroup Relations Center, on the other hand, is a comprehensive, multipurpose, inclusive, fully staffed and funded, action-oriented center that reports to the Office of the Executive Vice President and Provost of the University. The Center works with faculty, staff, and students to create structured intergroup interaction activities and to improve intergroup relations and the campus climate for diversity. The IRC consists of six staff members charged with working on intergroup issues related to race and ethnicity, sexual orientation, gender, nationality, disability status, religion, socioeconomic status, and other group dimensions. Moreover, the staff of the IRC undertake intergroup relations training and education, intergroup conflict de-escalation (both in and out of the classroom), community building between and among different groups, and intergroup relations research; consult on issues of diversity; collect educational resources on diversity; and advocate in relation to issues of diversity.

Since its inception seven years ago, the staff of the IRC has provided and organized numerous initiatives designed to bring different groups together to work on issues of diversity. These have included approximately 600 diversity workshops for faculty, staff, and students; two "Campus Climate for Diversity" summits designed to bring together the ASU community to examine and find solutions to diversity-related concerns; four annual conferences for ASU faculty and teaching assistants focusing on diversity in the classroom; and four faculty diversity training institutes. They have also administered a 400-student intergroup dialogue program each year, based on the University of Michigan model (Treviño, 2001); three retreats for women designed to create social consciousness among ASU women; five intergroup relations training retreats (80 participants per retreat) for students; a women's program that uses story circles for examining and learning about diversity; and a staff intergroup dialogue program. IRC staff work with the Multicultural Student Center to include students of color in their programs, particularly first-year students of color. Thus, at ASU, first-year students of color participate in both ethnic-specific (intragroup) activities and organizations as well as in structured intergroup activities.

The Center for Multicultural Excellence at the University of Denver

The University of Denver (UD) employs a hybrid model, one that combines the best of both a "Multicultural Student Center" and an "Intergroup Relations Center." Known as the Center for Multicultural Excellence (CME), this Center focuses on addressing issues related to race and ethnicity and on providing support services for students, staff, and faculty of color. The Center also organizes structured intergroup contact among African-American, Hispanic, LGBTQ, and international students; students from diverse religious backgrounds; and other groups at UD. All activities of the CME reconceptualize diversity as an asset that contributes to the quality of the University. Furthermore, their positive approach helps to counter the negative stigma (e.g., segregation, quotas, underprepared students) that many ethnic-specific programs and offices carry on college campuses. The work of the CME is very much grounded in Rendón's (1994) framework of validation and in research on student success (Padilla, 1999). More specifically, the terms and language employed to refer to first-year students of color are validating and include "scholars of color," "excellence," "academically talented," and "gifted." In addition, the CME staff organizes and supports structured interaction programs and activities for students, including first-year students of color. These are designed to structure contact and interaction between students belonging to different groups. Some of these include community of color circles (i.e., interaction between students of color), intergroup dialogues, and intergroup relations training retreats. The work of the CME also includes intergroup relations training for all students examining racism, heterosexism, sexism, classism, ableism, and other dimensions of intergroup relations.

Although it is important to acknowledge that other universities are using different models, the two initiatives described above are unique in that they represent opposite ends of a spectrum. That is, one model (i.e., Arizona State University) has both a unit for ethnically and racially diverse students and a separate center for all students. At the other end of the spectrum is a model (i.e., University of Denver) that combines many different groups into one office.

Conclusion

Colleges and universities need to work toward improving their campus climates for diversity, particularly if they want to recruit and retain students of color. This is especially true for first-year students of color. In this chapter, the authors propose that the involvement of first-year students of color in both intragroup and intergroup activities is healthy and necessary for both individual and group identity development. With respect to the latter, more colleges and universities are beginning to invest in intergroup interaction activities that bring together students from diverse backgrounds to learn about each other.

Certainly, the recent Supreme Court decision on affirmative action validates and highlights the importance of having a diverse student body and the positive learning that occurs when students interact with each other (Gurin, Nagad, & Lopez, 2003). A significant body of research supports the importance of involvement in both intergroup student initiatives and ethnic or race-themed organizations and activities (Hurtado et al., 1994). A new challenge for first-year programs is developing creative and meaningful ways to encourage students of color to get involved in organizations and activities that are specifically targeted at their racial or ethnic background and in those that bring students of color into contact with students from other cultural backgrounds. Consequently, fostering positive intergroup relations between minority and majority students is an important challenge that merits careful attention from first-year educators.

References

Allen, W. R. (1985). Black student, white campus: Structural, interpersonal, and psychological correlates of success. *Journal of Negro Education, 54*(2), 134-137.

American Association of Colleges and Universities (1995). *The drama of diversity and democracy: Higher education and American commitments.* Washington, DC: Author.

Astin, A. W. (1977). *Four critical years: Effects of college on beliefs, attitudes, and knowledge.* San Francisco: Jossey-Bass.

Astin, A. W. (1982). *Minorities in American higher education: Recent trends, current prospects, and recommendations.* San Francisco: Jossey-Bass.

Astin, A. W. (1984). Student involvement: A developmental theory for higher education. *Journal of College Student Personnel, 25*(4), 297-308.

Astin, A. W., Treviño, J. G., & Wingard, T. L. (1991). *The UCLA campus climate for diversity: Findings from a campuswide survey conducted for the Chancellor's Council on Diversity.* University of California, Los Angeles: Higher Education Research Institute.

Berman, W. F. (1978). Student activities and student development. *NASPA Journal, 16*(2), 52-54.

Berol, B., Camper, D., Pigott, C., Nadolsky, R., & Sarris, M. (1983, March). Separate tables: Why White and Black students chose to segregate. *Newsweek on Campus,* 4-11.

Carr, P. J., & Chittum, C. (1979). *A study to identify non-academic factors which may positively influence the recruitment of other race students at Virginia's state supported institutions of higher education: A final report.* Washington, DC: National Institute of Education (ERIC Document Reproduction Service No. ED 187 166)

Chavez, E. (1982, August). Minority student involvement in student activities. *The Bulletin of the Association of College Unions-International,* 15-16.

Chen, J. (2001). Sticking together: Is there self-segregation at Yale? *The Yale Herald.* Retrieved May 3, 2003 from, http://www.yaleherald.com/article.php?Article=799

Chickering, A. W. (1978). *Education and identity.* San Francisco: Jossey-Bass.

D'Souza, D. (1991). *Illiberal Education: The politics of race and sex on campus.* New York: Free Press.

Feldman, K. A., & Newcomb, T. M. (1969). *The impact of college on students.* (Vol. 1). San Francisco: Jossey-Bass.

Gordon, L., & Treadwell, D. (1992, January 24). On race relations, colleges are learning hard lessons. *The Los Angeles Times*, pp. A1, A16, A17.

Gurin, P. , Nagad, B.A., & Lopez, G.E. (in press). The benefits of diversity in education for democratic citizenship. *Journal of Social Issues.*

Hurtado, S. (1990). *Campus racial climates and educational outcomes.* University of California, Los Angeles: Unpublished doctoral dissertation.

Hurtado, S., Dey, E., & Treviño, J. (1994). *Exclusion or self-segregation? Interaction across racial/ethnic groups on college campuses.* Paper presented at the annual conference of the American Educational Research Association, New Orleans, Louisiana.

Hurtado, S., Milem, J., Clayton-Pederson, A., & Allen, W. (1999). *Enacting diverse learning environments: Improving the climate for racial/ethnic diversity in higher education* (ASHE-ERIC Higher Education Report Vol. 26, No. 8). Washington, DC: The George Washington University, Graduate School of Education and Human Development.

LeCounte, D. W. (1987). American Indian students in college. In D. J. Wright (Ed.), *Responding to the needs of today's minority students* (New Directions for Student Services No. 38) (pp. 65-79). San Francisco: Jossey-Bass.

Loo, C. M., & Rolison, G. (1986). Alienation of ethnic minority students at a predominantly White university. *Journal of Higher Education, 57*(1), 58-77.

Musil, C.T., García, M., Moses, Y. T., & Smith, D. G. (1995). *Diversity in higher education: A work in progress.* Washington, DC: American Association of Colleges and Universities.

Nieto, J. (1986). *Addressing ethnic underrepresentation at San Diego State University.* San Diego State University: Core Student Affirmative Action.

Padilla, R. V. (1999). College student retention: Focus on success. *Journal of College Student Retention, Research, Theory & Practice, 1*(2), 131-145.

Pascarella, E. T., & Terenzini, P. T. (1991). *How college affects students: Findings and insights from twenty years of research.* San Francisco: Jossey-Bass.

Ponterotto, J. G., Casas, J. M., Suzuki, L. A., & Alexander, C. M. (1995). *Handbook of multicultural counseling.* Thousand Oaks, CA: Sage Publishing.

Rendón, L. I. (1994). Validating culturally diverse students: Toward a new model of learning and student development. *Innovative Higher Education, 19*(1), 33-51.

Schoem, D., & Hurtado, S. (2001). *Intergroup Dialogue: Deliberative democracy in school, college, community, and workplace.* Ann Arbor: University of Michigan Press.

Schuh, J. H., & Laverty, M. (1983). The perceived long term effect of holding a significant leadership position. *Journal of College Student Personnel, 24*(10), 28-32.

Stephan, W. G., & Stephan, C. W. (1996). *Intergroup relations.* Boulder, CO: Westview Press.

Tajfel, H. (1978). *Differentiation between social groups: Studies in the social psychology of intergroup relations.* (European Monographs in Social Psychology No. 44). London: Academic Press.

Tatum, B. D. (1997). *Why are all the Black kids sitting together in the cafeteria.* New York: Basic Books.

Tinto, V. (1975). Dropout from higher education: A theoretical synthesis of recent research. *Review of Educational Research, 45*(1), 89-125.

Traub, J. (1999, May 2). The Class of Prop. 209. *The New York Times,* p. 44.

Treviño, J. (1992*). Participation in ethnic/racial student organizations.* University of California, Los Angeles: Unpublished doctoral dissertation.

Treviño, J. G. (2001). Voices of Discovery: Intergroup Dialogues at Arizona State University. In D. Schoem & S. Hurtado (Eds.), *Intergroup Dialogue: Deliberative Democracy in School, College, Community, and Workplace* (pp. 87-98). Ann Arbor: University of Michigan Press.

Vasques Scalera, C. M. (1999). *Democracy, diversity, and dialogue: Education for critical multicultural citizenship.* Unpublished doctoral dissertation, University of Michigan.

Winkelman, M. (1993). *Ethnic relations in the U.S.: A sociohistorical cultural systems approach.* San Francisco, CA: West Publishing.

Zuniga, X., & Nagda, B. A. (1993*).* Dialogue groups: An innovative approach to multicultural learning. In D. Schoem et al. (Eds.), *Multicultural teaching at the university* (pp. 233-248). Westport, CT: Praeger.

Chapter 6

Academic and Social Integration: A Key to First-Year Success for Students of Color

James A. Anderson

A significant body of research has emerged in the last two decades describing why students stay in college and why they leave. Various explanations have been offered about student attrition and persistence, but one thing that is evident, regardless of the view, is that the first year in college represents a critical juncture for students in general and is especially significant for certain populations: students of color, nontraditional students, first-generation college students, low-income students, underprepared students, and those for whom English is a second language.

The importance of retaining students of color in the first college year cannot be overstated. First- to second-year attrition rates are highest for students of color, and these losses ultimately translate into fewer students graduating from college. For example, the attrition rate of African Americans during the first year of college is approximately 63% and 54% for Latinos, compared to 42% for Whites (Rendón & Nora, 1999). Consequently, students of color remain underrepresented in degree attainment. In 2000, they earned 21.8% of all bachelor's degrees awarded, while representing more than 28% of all undergraduates (Harvey, 2002).

Any educator wishing to address the achievement, retention, and socialization of students of color must consider the wide array of research conducted by minority and majority scholars (Braxton, 2000; Cabrera, Castañeda, Nora, & Hengstler, 1992; Cabrera, Nora, & Castañeda, 1993; Nora, 1987; Pascarella & Terenzini, 1991; St. John, Cabrera, Nora, & Asker, 2000), who have explored theories of retention and the impact of financial aid, perceptions of discrimination, and other factors on student persistence. Other researchers (Rendón, 2002; Rendón & Hope, 1994; Terenzini et al., 1994) have examined the transition to college, the influence of validation on low-income students, and theoretical considerations in the study of minority student retention. Hurtado (1992) and Chang (2001) provide important research regarding campus climate and the impact of diversity on students. Other researchers examining diversity and multicultural issues include Banks (1991), Smith (1989), Stage (1989), and Tierney (1992). Related to this body of research is Tatum's (1992) exploration of racial identity theory. Other researchers have focused on issues related to learning and success. For example, Darder (1991) addresses cultural democracy as it relates to teaching and learning in the classroom. Astin's (1985) involvement theory guides us in understanding how students become engaged in college, and Nettles, Theony, and Grosman (1986) provide a conceptual understanding about college achievement.

Perhaps the most widely used model of student retention is Tinto's (1993; 1997) theory of student departure, which stresses the importance of academic and social integration and involvement for students in their first year. The National Study of Student Support Services (Chaney, Muraskin, Cahalan, & Rak, 1997) reinforces Tinto's work but focuses on first-generation and low-income students. Another powerful source of evidence on the importance of the first year has been the work and research emerging from the National Resource Center for The First-Year Experience and Students in Transition, housed at the University of South Carolina.

The National Resource Center produces an academic journal and hosts a conference series that have served as forums for disseminating important research findings about the performance and retention of students of color in their first year in college. This work serves to develop greater levels of understanding and appreciation by administrators and faculty members of the differences and similarities within and among racial and cultural groups. The articles and presentations have focused on various sub-populations including:

- African-American students (Gold, Deming, & Stone, 1992; Hargrove & Sedlacek, 1997; Kim & Sedlacek, 1996; McAdams & Foster, 1998)
- Honor students of color (Noledon & Sedlacek, 1996)
- Hispanic students (Buck, 1985)

Other publications focusing on students of color in their first year of college include:

- Native-American students (Benjamin, 1993; Leap, 1988)
- Hispanic and African-American students (Charbonneau & John-Steiner, 1988; Hurtado, Carter, & Spuler, 1994; Treisman, 1992)

Many institutions continue to grapple with lingering questions, such as to what extent is persistence due to institutional factors rather than student factors? An examination of the substantive research of the past two decades can assist institutions in evaluating the current efficacy of their first-year efforts for students of color and identifying predictors of success for these students. Moreover, the research can point to overarching themes and commonalities that can suggest how campus-based programs and activities can be linked to enhance productivity. When this occurs, institutions can begin to identify the emergence of models that link theory, research, and practice.

Challenges to Academic and Social Integration

During their initial adaptation to the college culture, students face a plethora of challenges. They must make practical adjustments like registering for classes, locating buildings, and procuring books and student IDs. However, the most significant challenge is associated with developing responsibility for learning and academic success. For many first-year students, the college classroom is a rewarding experience; for others, it becomes a source of dissonance. In either case, students attempt to identify anchors that, over time, help them find meaning in the first college year. When anchors emerge as effective mechanisms, they contribute to academic and social adjustment, and ultimately, establish a comfort zone for the student. Students can also select anchors that satisfy certain social and psychological needs or promote affiliation with certain groups, yet these mechanisms may not lead to academic success. Some students may need to delay their participation in student organizations, campus Greek life, or athletics until they establish an academic foothold at the institution. First-year students cannot lose sight of their ultimate challenge, which is to persist toward goal completion (i.e., diploma, certificate, transfer, work).

Students in general come to college with varied expectations about the appropriate pathways to effective learning and success. Students who exhibit varied learning styles may respond to the same course content and instruction in different ways. Anderson and Adams (1992) detail the characteristics of relational learning styles that tend to be more characteristic of students of color. These students, when exposed to traditional college classrooms, place an emphasis on affective and reality-based learning, a broad and personal approach to the processing of information, a search for relevance and personal meaning in what is taught, and a need for qualitative feedback. Moreover, these same students understand that certain tools (i.e., motivational, academic, and cognitive) can help them negotiate courses or classrooms that tend to be traditional and more content-centered than student-centered. Where do students acquire these tools? Some were gleaned from prior educational experiences (K-12), cultural origins, and parental and peer influence; from an unexplained acumen about preparing for the unknown; and from the generalized expectancy of success that solidifies after years of positive reinforcement gained from seeing others, like themselves, succeed as a consequence of direct mentoring and encouragement.

For most students of color this vista of knowledge, encouragement, and practice either did not exist, was not reinforced, or if it was present, competed with other practical exigencies of life. Their first college year involves being presented with the same challenges and academic demands as majority students; however, they must also contend with the Eurocentric biases that are often overt and covert, ranging from lower expectations of success for students of color by some campus groups to the selection of content in traditional courses (such as history and literature) that value a White, male perspective and reward students who value that perspective as well. A Eurocentric bias in the classroom does not, by necessity, represent a negative or harmful intent. For many faculty, it is simply the byproduct of their graduate and professional academic training. This bias becomes harmful to students when it reflects a "lack of inclusiveness" in the college curriculum. This bias often is not obvious to an entering student or an unsophisticated scholar. For students of color, bias can occur in the curriculum when they do not see themselves represented in curricular materials, when multicultural materials are addressed as an "add on" to traditional course content, or when personal growth and self-esteem are not affected in positive ways (Bensimon, 1994; Chavez, O'Donnnel, & Gallegos, 1994; Lopez, 1993; Schmitz, 1992; Stake & Gerner, 1987).

As a result of such concerns, cultural pluralism has become a more significant aspect in the planning of curricular initiatives at many institutions. The Cultural Legacies project (Schneider, 1991), sponsored by the Association of American Colleges and Universities, offers a blueprint for connecting inclusiveness to the traditional curriculum. It emphasizes:

- Rethinking what students should know about Western traditions
- Redefining core knowledge to include the study of U.S. pluralism and other parts of the world

- Paying more attention to defining the kind and level of skills students are expected to acquire in specific courses and to the pedagogies that accomplish skill-related goals
- Changing the way faculty members think about their role in the teaching/learning equation

Although the research findings are still emerging, initial indicators suggest that when first-year students of color are exposed to a relevant, global, and inclusive curriculum we increase their ability (a) to adjust academically and socially to the challenges of college, (b) to find a place for themselves (and others like them) within the academy, (c) to maximize their learning potential, (d) to progress toward degree completion, and (e) to develop a strong sense of academic self-esteem that is linked with the expectation of success. However, most two- and four-year institutions have not fully developed the intentional curricular and co-curricular changes needed to achieve these outcomes. Moreover, the problems of non-inclusion are magnified when students of color represent an obvious minority on a majority campus (Eimers & Pike, 1997; Steward, Jackson, & Jackson, 1990; Thompson & Fretz, 1991).

African-American and Hispanic students at predominantly majority institutions are often expected to rely on majority students and faculty in making their adjustments to campus life. Historically, this has been a difficult task even for students of color who come to college with a knowledge base and set of behaviors that strongly identify with a Eurocentric frame of reference. For example, students of color who have been identified as "gifted" relative to conventional standards (i.e., SAT scores, grade point average, class rank) experience the pressures of rejection and isolation from both their majority and non-majority peers during their first year in college (Fries-Britt, 1997; Steele, 1995). Academically talented students of color face the difficult task of balancing a dual identity with significant academic and social consequences. They may suppress their abilities to perform in order to conform to the stereotype of being a member of a racial group who, for some in the campus community, is not expected to achieve because he or she is perceived to lack motivation, talent, or intellect. Alternately, if they perform well, they risk isolation and ridicule because they are perceived to be "acting White." Another way to explain the challenges of dual identity is to propose that students of color have to adopt different interaction styles when interacting in an all-White or predominantly White environment (Loo & Rolison, 1986; Willie, 1981). These students might experience a two-world existence within which two or more different interaction styles are required and for which several comfort levels are experienced. A range of variables need to be examined to shed light on the adoption of interaction styles both in cross-race and within-race comparisons.

Steele (1999) hypothesized that, when academically talented African-American students do not perform as well as their White counterparts, their performance is not due to lack of preparedness or ability but rather to the existence of a "stereotype threat." He defined this as the perception of being seen in light of negative stereotypes or the concern of doing anything that might inadvertently confirm such stereotypes. The continued stress and pain associated with stereotype threat may cause some students to develop a negative coping strategy; that is, they begin to care less about academic situations and events, leading to low performance. Steele hypothesized that students must care about the event or activity to be upset at the prospect of being stereotyped. Therefore, high-achieving African-American students may stop trying to excel academically (i.e., cease to care about the activity) in order to protect themselves from stereotype threat.

Findings from several studies revealed that once the threat of stereotype was removed from various testing situations, disparities in performance among African-American and White students no longer existed (Steele).

Gibbs (1974) cited numerous studies in which African-American students suffer from a series of identity problems resulting from culture conflict. Through a review of case records of African-American students experiencing ethnic or cultural conflicts, Gibbs identified four modes of adaptation to the college and university environments: withdrawal, separation, assimilation, and affirmation. Withdrawal is characterized by feelings of hopelessness, loneliness, and alienation. The student chooses to avoid contact with the conflict by typically withdrawing from all social and academic activities. Students experiencing the separation mode are often perceived as militant. Hostility, anger, and anti-White behavior characterize this mode of adaptation. Assimilation is characterized by the desire for acceptance and approval from the prevailing dominant culture. Assimilated students usually have little contact with other African-American students. Finally, affirmation is characterized by African-American students' self-acceptance and affirmation of who they are. They are open to learning about other cultural and ethnic groups, and they are highly motivated to achieve their goals. Gibbs concluded that the student's motivation, peer relationships, faculty relationships, emotional well-being, and many other intangible factors contribute to the student of color's ultimate transition to the college setting, regardless of the mode of adaptation observed.

Loo and Rolison (1986) studied the alienation of students of color at predominantly White institutions to address the problems of social discomfort that these students experienced. The objective was to assess the extent and nature of sociocultural alienation and academic satisfaction among students of color, then determine whether the alienation and satisfaction of these students differed significantly from that of White students. Finally, the researchers assessed similarities and differences in the attitudes of White students and students of color. The sociocultural alienation of students of color was significantly greater than that of White students. A majority of both students of color and White students (70%) believed that students of color faced greater sociocultural difficulties on campus than did White students. Two major reasons cited for this belief were (a) the cultural dominance of White, middle-class values on campus that pressured students of color to acquire these values and to reject their own and (b) ethnic isolation resulting from African Americans being a small proportion of the student body. Suen (1983) found that African-American students had greater feelings of alienation than their White counterparts, due in large part to their significantly higher levels of social estrangement. He found that African-American students consistently scored higher than their White counterparts on test scales that measured feelings of meaninglessness, social estrangement, and powerlessness.

While the academic literature offers some important suggestions about strategies that promote success, it is the close examination of successful programs for students of color that yield more detailed information about their transition in the first year.

Committing to Strategic Initiatives to Retain Students of Color

Institutional decisions about investing in retention strategies for majority and non-majority students are a direct correlate of how decision-makers account for enrollment and persistence trends. For example, the following five assertions appear in the literature and inform campus programming efforts:

- Academic preparedness for college is one of the main factors accounting for the persistence of students of color (Tinto, 1997).
- Successful retention of non-majority students involves severing ties early with parents, past communities, and reference groups that impede personal and social adjustment (Tinto, 1993).
- Prejudice and discrimination are unique to minorities and have a direct impact on their persistence in college (Hurtado, 1992, 1994; Hurtado et al., 1996).
- Academic and social integration are critical to the retention of students of color in the first year (Cabrera et al., 1993; Pascarella & Terenzini, 1991).
- Upon entering college, students of color need to become part of identity groups that promote academic and cognitive development (Steele, 1995).

Although these assertions can be viewed as part of a general student adjustment model, they clearly represent separate domains. As mentioned earlier, charting the characteristics of successful programs for first-year students of color might be a strategic approach since it allows for inter-institutional comparisons. Using that strategy yields the following findings:

- *The early development of a sense of community is important.* It can begin with a summer bridge program or early in the first college year. The key activities for creating community include promoting positive relationships, introducing students to the expectations and demands of college, providing intrusive academic advising, and enabling students to gain needed academic skills.
- *Despite the claims of anti-affirmative action advocates, "race-specific" retention programs and learning communities are highly successful when they are well structured.* Among the benefits are (a) a community of high-ability students to whom other students of color can connect, (b) a localizing of academic supports and financial resources, (c) the presence of faculty and staff who are well trained and who are aware of the needs and abilities of the students, (d) structured tasks and activities that promote academic and social integration and cognitive development, and (e) the opportunity to develop a dual identity that is associated with being talented and (rather than versus) a member of one's racial or cultural community.
- *Students of color do experience success in their first-year courses.* This success may occur for several reasons including thematically linked courses; strong academic supports; the use of small, dynamic discussion groups; and the presence of effective instructors and tutors. The development of targeted academic and cognitive skills (i.e., critical discourse and thinking, problem solving, active learning) is a priority.

Although the increased presence of diverse groups on college campuses is hailed as a necessity for the improved persistence of students of color, scant evidence exists that such diversity has a primary impact on retention. The successful persistence of students of color is directly linked to structures, tasks and activities, resource development, and planning efforts that are proven entities.

Strategic initiatives are important because they can serve as broad, overarching themes that alert campus communities to what is important and valued, to the emergence of a new or redesigned vision, and to the prospect that resources will be redirected to support the initiatives. In terms of strategic (success) initiatives for students of color, the following could serve as examples:

- A three-year faculty development initiative that upgrades the instructional competencies of faculty in first-year courses, especially those who serve higher percentages of students of color
- The incorporation of well-trained peer mentors in curricular and co-curricular support programs for students of color
- Grants to departments/programs that develop creative activities/strategies that support students of color in the first year

The initiative should be flexible enough that it respects and accounts for department/program individuality, while maintaining the overall integrity of the initiative. Thus, peer-mentoring activities may vary across three different departments but still address the basic objectives of the initiative. Thus, the power of strategic initiatives is not in their existence, but in their translation into department and program projects and activities, especially those that promote social and academic integration. Examples of two initiatives focused on academic integration are outlined below.

Including the Academic Voice of Diverse Students

Smoke and Haas (1995) describe a significant programmatic effort that allowed students from nontraditional backgrounds to recognize the value of their own knowledge and experience as they constructed academic voices within a traditional discipline. Their clients were primarily low-income, first-generation, developmental students of color who participated in a basic writing course linked to a United States history course at Hunter College, CUNY.

Starting from the premise that their students did not know how to use their knowledge and experiences in the academic world, the authors developed an academic discourse community in which students and faculty used shared language and respect to promote the validity of the "student voice" and knowledge base, while showing them how to integrate both into their academic work. The linked writing course was diametrically different from those developmental and ESL writing courses that used disconnected topics or overemphasized the mechanics of good grammar and usage while divorcing the learner from the topic.

The authors presented the material in a variety of formats thus recognizing students'í different learning styles and enabling more students to comprehend challenging material. Writing about history helped the students focus on their own lives and on their future. Students reported that they empathized with historical figures with whom they could identify. By linking classes, students were able to approach new and more demanding material, while including their own voices and ideas.

Approximately 90% of the students in the linked courses passed both courses, as well as the state-mandated writing test (CUNY WAT). A significant ancillary effect was the alliances formed among students who were racially and culturally different.

Empowering Students of Color in Math and Science

Triesman (1992) sought to develop a sense of identity, empowerment, and student success among African-American and Hispanic college students who were experiencing difficulty in mathematics, especially calculus and pre-calculus. He noted that many successful Asian students formed and participated in a networked social system soon after they began college. Within these groupings social status was increased by one's ability to help others.

Borrowing from the Asian student model of peer-group work and encouragement, Triesman built his Mathematics Workshop Program around three strategic principles: (a) involve less successful students in more demanding groups, (b) allow students to discuss homework, and (c) allow students to work in collaborative small groups. Triesman served only as a coach. The program was highly successful as the percentage of students who received a "D"î or "F" in the course was reduced from 60% to 4%. This effort has been replicated at numerous institutions.

As was the case with linked courses at Hunter College, the program's success hinged on the use of interactive student group work. Students did not refrain from attempting answers and solutions in "their own voice," because they had a higher level of preparedness; they knew the group was fair; and they learned to enjoy the challenge of demanding work. Early success in mathematics translated into early entry into an academic major and degree program.

Practical Approaches to Academic and Social Integration

College and university campuses are complex social systems that have a tendency to change slowly. Yet change is necessary if we are to ensure the success of students of color. To promote institutional change effectively, decision-makers must commit to initiatives reflecting the "best"îresearch, models, and practices. Although a wide range of beneficial practices have been suggested, a few consistently appear in the literature associated with retention, diversity, first-year success, teaching effectiveness, and student engagement. Such practices have a positive impact across different programs and institutional types and, thus, appear more reliable and valid. One example of this kind of practice is the enhancement of student-student and student-faculty interactions both in and out of class.

While a wealth of knowledge is available to guide the self-examinations of institutions, it is a commitment to action items that represents the most significant challenge. The following recommendations emphasize the importance of academic and social integration in the development of structures, policies, and practices that foster excellence among students of color in the first year.

Social Integration

1. Institutions should encourage first-year students of color to participate in campus activities and support programs that promote (a) increased social involvement with peers, (b) informal social interactions with faculty, (c) greater use of support services, and (d) participation in racially focused cultural activities that are associated with positive outcomes. Peer-to-peer social activities should emphasize characteristics of cooperative learning and engagement and should be structured in a way that allows for an assessment of their quality and effectiveness. Informed interactions with faculty should reach beyond simple social exchanges and emphasize attainable outcomes for students such as facilitating insight into linking academic and career pathways, or addressing student anxieties about unforeseen challenges.

2. Campus administrators and decision-makers should create an empowering environment that allows students of color to have positive attitudes toward their ethnic identity and to identify and bond with the broader campus community. For example, each spring campuses make well-meaning, but sometimes awkward, attempts to celebrate Black History Month through varied activities. Yet, the celebrations often

do not impact the broader campus community, nor do students of color see consistent evidence that their culture and ethnic identity are valued in ways that would empower them. The marking of Black History Month, Hispanic Heritage Month, or similar cultural celebrations will be more meaningful if faculty in first-year seminars, composition courses, and general education courses engage first-year students in discussions of the social, political, cultural, or historical outcomes associated with their own indigenous ethnic groups and those of different racial or ethnic groups. This approach could also emphasize active learning, critical discourse, and analytical communication, thus linking social integration with learning outcomes.

3. Student development administrators and staff should create campus-based student development models that take into account the experiences and unique needs of students of color. For example, campus programs focusing on student leadership development could emphasize outcomes associated with diversity and globalism, since these outcomes are often associated with 21st century leadership competencies. Examples of such outcomes include:

- Developing a common vocabulary, including redefining terms like "authority" and "leadership"
- Knowing how to draw from their own cultural contexts and those of others
- Becoming well versed in the different kinds of "isms" and "centrisms"
- Developing a sense of social ethics and social responsibility
- Being willing to tolerate different types of stress and ambiguity

4. Faculty can learn to use communication modes in first-year courses that promote equity and civility in the classroom (Sanders & Wiseman, 1994). Many instructors assume that students respect the differences they confront in the classroom and tolerate learning styles and worldviews different from their own. This is not always the case. When this does not happen, instructors and students share a responsibility to ensure that differences do not become a catalyst for inequality, harm, and dissension. Tiberius and Billson (1991) suggest several ways that this responsibility can be shared:

- By setting the tone for openness and mutual responsibility early
- By acknowledging feelings about differences and creating a safe climate for discussion
- By not insisting on a "politically correct" position, but rather, by helping students explore all sides of a position
- By not allowing inappropriate or harmful comments to pass unnoticed, but instead, exploring the sources of such verbalizations and capitalizing on teachable moments

Academic Integration

1. Institutions should engage in a correlational analysis of major performance measures associated with students of color at entry with evaluation measures of academic and social integration (see Fleming & Morning, 1998). For example, most institutions collect data on new students that examine first- to second-year retention, movement into the major, or course-taking patterns. Examining this data relative to other assessments, such as pre-post assessments of college adjustment,

learning style assessments, indicators of cognitive or higher-order competency gains, and measures of academic self-confidence may help explain retention data and academic progress.

2. Mechanisms should exist that introduce students of color to the necessary coping strategies to persist and use faculty and peer mentors as primary support systems. At North Carolina State University, two first-year programs (i. e., Transition Program and First Year College) focus on the integration of students of color into the campus culture. They both use well-trained advisors and mentors, and each group is charged with developing information and activities about needed coping strategies. One strategy that is emphasized is "student responsibility for learning." Students engage in conversations and activities about becoming actively involved in their education; cultivating effective attitudes, behaviors, and skills for thinking and learning; and engaging fully in academic discourse. Both programs rely on dynamic small-group interactions that emphasize cooperative learning.

3. Students of color should participate in first-year seminars with students who reflect a range of backgrounds, perspectives, and skill levels. This is not to suggest that they cannot also participate in formal and informal groupings that might be race- or culture-specific. However, their most significant growth and maturity will emerge from interactions that involve diversity. Faculty can ensure positive interactions in the seminar by adding race and culture to course content, and by promoting cooperative, not competitive, learning activities. Positive student-student and student-faculty interactions should exist both in and out of the classroom.

4. The institution should provide ways for students of color to report and seek redress for negative experiences. This will involve the presence of both formal and informal grievance procedures.

It is imperative that campus decision-makers commit to the creation of empowering environments where students of color can develop positive attitudes toward their ethnic identity, identify with the broader campus environment, become responsible learners, have available support systems, and acquire the necessary coping strategies to persist. Administrators and faculty should employ strategies to deal effectively with institutional barriers that prevent the implementation of empowerment strategies and discourage social and academic integration. When all of this occurs, students of color will capitalize on the ingredients that create positive and empowering learning environments.

References

Anderson, J. A., & Adams, M. (1992). Acknowledging the learning styles of diverse populations: Implications for the college classroom. In L. L. B. Border, & N. V. N. Chism (Eds.), *Teaching for diversity.* (New Directions for Teaching and Learning No. 49). (pp. 19-33). San Francisco: Jossey-Bass.

Astin, A. W. (1985). *Achieving educational excellence.* San Francisco: Jossey-Bass.

Banks, J. (1991 Spring). Multicultural literacy and curriculum reform. *Educational Horizons Quarterly Journal,* 135-140.

Benjamin, D. P. (1993). A focus on American Indian college persistence. *Journal of American Indian College Persistence, 32*(2), 24-40.

Bensimon, E. (Ed.). (1994). *Multicultural teaching and learning: Strategies for change in higher education.* University Park: Pennsylvania State University.

Braxton, J. M. (2000). *Reworking the student departure puzzle.* Nashville, TN: Vanderbilt University Press.

Buck, C. (1985). *Summer bridge: A residential learning experience for high-risk freshmen at the University of California, San Diego.* Paper presented at the Fourth Annual National Conference on the Freshman Year Experience, Columbia, SC.

Cabrera, A. F., Castañeda, M. B., Nora, A., & Hengstler, D. (1992). The convergence between two theories of college persistence. *The Journal of Higher Education, 63,* 143-164.

Cabrera, A. F., Nora, A., & Castañeda, M. B. (1993). College persistence: Structural modeling of an integrated model of student retention. *Journal of Higher Education, 64,* 123-139.

Chaney, B., Muraskin, L., Cahalan, M., & Rak, R. (1997). Third-year longitudinal study results and program implementation update, National Study of Student Support Services. Washington, DC: U.S. Department of Education.

Chang, M. J. (2001). Is it more than getting along? The broader educational implications of reducing students' racial biases. *Journal of College Student Development, 42*(2), 93-105.

Charbonneau, M., & John-Steiner, V. (1988). Patterns of experience and the language of mathematics. In R. Cocking & J. Mestre (Eds.), *Linguistic and cultural influence on learning mathematics.* Hillsdale, NJ: Earlbaum.

Chavez, R. C., O'Donnell, J., & Gallegos, R. L. (1994, April). *Pre-service students' perspectives on "dilemmas" in a multicultural education course.* Paper presented at the annual meeting of the American Educational Research Association, New Orleans, LA.

Darder, A. (1991). Creating the conditions for cultural democracy in the classroom. In *Culture and power in the classroom* (pp. 99-128). Westport, CT: Greenwood Publishing.

Eimers, M., & Pike, G. (1997). Minority and non-minority adjustment to college: Differences or similarities? *Research in Higher Education, 38,* 77-97.

Fleming, J., & Morning, C. V. (1998). Correlates of the SAT in Minority Engineering Students. *Journal of Higher Education, 69*(1).

Fries-Britt, S. (1997). Identifying and supporting gifted African-American men. In M. Cuyjet (Ed.), *Helping African-American men succeed in college.* (New Directions for Student Services No. 80). San Francisco: Jossey-Bass.

Gibbs, J. (1974). Patterns of adaptation among Black students at a predominantly White university: Selected case studies. *American Journal of Orthopsychiatry, 44,* 728-740.

Gold, M., Deming, M. P., & Stone, K. (1992). The bridge: A summer enrichment program to retain African-American collegians. *Journal of The Freshman Year Experience, 4*(2), 101-117.

Hargrove, B. K., & Sedlacek, W. E. (1997). Counseling interests among entering Black freshmen over a ten-year period. *Journal of the Freshman Year Experience and Students in Transition, 9*(2), 83-98.

Harvey, W. (2002). *Minorities in higher education 2001-02: Nineteenth annual status report.* Washington, DC: American Council on Education.

Hurtado, S. (1992). The campus racial climate: Contexts of conflict. *Journal of Higher Education, 63*(5), 539-569.

Hurtado, S. (1994). The institutional climate for talented Latino students. *Research in Higher Education, 35,* 21-41.

Hurtado, S., Carter, D. F., & Spuler, A. (1996). Latino student transition to college: Assessing difficulties and factors in successful college adjustment. *Research of Higher Education, 37*(2), 135-158.

Kim, S. H., & Sedlacek, W. E. (1996). Gender differences among incoming African-American freshmen on academic and social expectations. *Journal of the Freshman Year Experience, 8*(1), 25-37.

Leap, W. (1988). Assumptions and strategies guiding mathematics problem solving by Ute Indian students. In R. Cocking & J. Mestre (Eds.), *Linguistic and cultural influences on learning mathematics.* Hillsdale, NJ: Erlbaum.

Loo, C., & Rolison, G. (1986). Alienation of ethnic minority students in a predominantly White university. *Journal of Higher Education, 57,* 58-77.

Lopez, G. E. (1993). *The effect of group contact and curriculum on White, Asian American, and African American students' attitudes.* Unpublished doctoral dissertation, University of Michigan.

McAdams, R. R., III, & Foster, W. A. (1998). Promoting the development of high-risk college students through a deliberate psychological-based freshman orientation course. *Journal of the Freshman Year Experience and Students in Transition, 10*(1), 51-72.

Nettles, M., Theony, A., & Gosman, E. (1986). Comparative and predictive analyses of Black and White students' college achievement and experiences. *Journal of Higher Education, 57*(3), 289-328.

Noledon, D. F., & Sedlacek, W. E. (1996). Race differences in attitudes, skills, and behaviors among academically talented students. *Journal of the Freshman Year Experience and Students in Transition, 8*(2), 43-56.

Nora, A. (1987). Determinants of retention among Chicano college students: A structural model. *Research in Higher Education, 26,* 31-51.

Pascarella, E., & Terenzini, P. (1991). *How college affects students.* San Francisco: Jossey-Bass.

Rendón, L. I. (2002). Community college Puente: A validating model of education. *Journal of Educational Policy and Practice, 16*(4), 642-667.

Rendón, L. I., & Hope, R. O. (1994). *Educating a new majority: Transforming America's educational system for diversity.* San Francisco: Jossey Bass.

Rendón, L. I., & Nora, A. (1999). *Student academic progress: Key data trends.* Report prepared for the National Center for Urban Partnerships, Ford Foundation. Tempe, AZ; UPP Assessment Center.

Sanders, J. A., & Wiseman, R. L. (1994). The effects of verbal and nonverbal teacher immediacy on perceived cognitive, affective, and behavioral learning in the multicultural classroom. In K. Feldman & M. B. Paulsen (Eds.), *Teaching and learning in the college classroom* (pp. 623-626). New York: Ginn Press.

Schmitz, B. (1992). *Core curriculum and cultural pluralism.* Washington, DC: Association of American Colleges & Universities.

Schneider, Carol G. (1991, May/June). Engaging cultural legacies: A multidimensional endeavor. *Liberal Education,* 2-7.

Smith, D. (1989). Organizing for diversity: Fundamental issues. *The Challenge of Diversity: Involvement or Alienation in the Academy.* (ASHE-ERIC Report No. 5). Washington, DC: The George Washington University, School of Education and Human Development.

Smoke, T., & Haas, T. (1995, Winter). Ideas in practice: Linking classes to develop students' academic voices. *Journal of Developmental Education, 19*(2), 28-32.

Stage, F. K. (1989). Reciprocal effects between the academic and social integration of college. *Research in Higher Education, 30,* 517-530.

Stake, J. E., & Gerner, M. A. (1987). "The women's studies experience": Personal and professional goals for women and men. *Psychology of Women Quarterly, 11,* 277-284.

Steele, C. M. (1995). Stereotype threat and the intellectual test performance of African Americans. *Journal of Personality and Social Psychology, 69,* 797-811.

Steele, C. (1999). Thin ice: "Stereotype threat" and Black college students. *The Atlantic Monthly, 284*(2), 44-54.

St. John, E. P., Cabrera, A. F., Nora, A., & Asker, E. H. (2000). Economic influences on persistence reconsidered: How can finance research inform the reconceptualization of persistence models? In J. M. Braxton (Ed.), *Reworking the student departure puzzle* (pp. 29-47). Nashville, TN: Vanderbilt University Press.

Steward, R., Jackson, M., & Jackson. J. (1990). Alienation and international styles in a predominantly White environment: A study of successful Black students. *Journal of College Student Development, 31,* 509-515.

Suen, H. (1983). Alienation and attrition of black college students on a predominantly White campus. *Journal of College Student Personnel, 24,* 117-121.

Tatum, B. D. (1992). Talking about race, learning and racism: The application of racial identity development theory in the classroom. *Harvard Educational Review, 62* (1), 1-24.

Terenzini, P., Rendón, L., Upcraft, L., Millar, S., Allison, K., Gregg, P., & Jalomo, R. (1994). The transition to college: Diverse students, diverse stories. *Research in Higher Education, 35,* 57-73.

Thompson, C. E., & Fretz, B. R. (1991). Predicting the adjustment of Black students at predominantly White institutions. *Journal of Higher Education, 62*(4), 437-450.

Tiberius, R. G., & Billson, J. M. (1991). The social context of teaching and learning. In R. J. Menges & M. D. Svinicki (Eds.), *College teaching: From theory to practice.* (New Directions for Teaching and Learning No. 45). San Francisco: Jossey-Bass.

Tierney, W. G. (1992). An anthropological analysis of student participation in college. *Journal of Higher Education, 63*(6), 603-617.

Tinto, V. (1993). *Leaving college: Rethinking the causes and cures of student attrition* (2nd ed.). Chicago, IL: University of Chicago Press.

Tinto, V. (1997). Classrooms as communities: Exploring the educational character of student persistence. *Journal of Higher Education, 68,* 599-623.

Treisman, U. (1992). Studying students studying calculus: A look at the lives of minority mathematics students in college. *The College Mathematics Journal, 23*(5), 362-372.

Willie, C. V. (1981). *The ivory and ebony towers.* Lexington, MA: Heath.

Section 3

Working with Specific Populations

Chapter 7

Enhancing the First-Year Experience of African Americans

Wynetta Y. Lee

The first year of college is among the most exhilarating and memorable events in a young adult's life. Expectations for the future are at the threshold of reality, and new meaning is given to the ideals of "responsibility," "success," and "goal attainment." My first college year was several decades ago, but the memory of that experience is as clear as if it happened yesterday. Like most entering students, I entered college ready to set the academic world on fire—or so I thought. I soon discovered that I was the only combustible material in the academic world. When I entered a large, predominately White institution in the mid-west, I had no idea that I was entering an environment that was unlike any that I had experienced previously. My initial optimism and passion for learning started to fade during the first week of college when I had my first encounter with an institutional staff person.

During the orientation week of my first year, I believed that following directions was the pathway to success, so I went to a first-year advisor for academic advising as instructed. It puzzled me that at this initial meeting my advisor did not ask me anything, nor did she refer to my record. She began our conversation by stating that her calendar was very crowded; she had many other students to see and was pressed for time to meet with her graduate advisor about her own degree requirements. So as a favor to me, she was going to "cut to the chase" and tell me that I should avoid traditional disciplines and elect to major in either home economics or physical education if I wanted to actually graduate. Clearly, her advice came without any knowledge of my academic background or my career aspirations. In short, she did not know me or my history, yet she was deciding my future. Since she was an institutional representative, I felt as though the university was telling me to abandon my intentions of pursuing a science degree. My mind quickly flooded with thoughts of the cognitive calisthenics I had undergone in preparation for college, and I found myself consumed with anger and confusion. I was insulted that my future had been decided without me. Somehow I managed to compose myself enough to respectfully ask why

93

those were my only choices. She replied that her experience suggested that African-American students were most successful in these majors.

During that week, I encountered several other staff members who believed I was an academically underprepared, first-generation, in-state, African-American student who had entered the university through a special program. With the exception of race, I was the opposite of what university staff labeled me. I was an out-of-state student, not on financial aid, and the daughter of a university alumna. However, my background did not matter to the University personnel I initially encountered. I questioned my institutional choice daily as I soon discovered that I did not understand Midwestern Whites, and I had very little in common with the other African-American students on campus. So, I spent the first few months drifting along in a fog of confusion, insecurity, and isolation.

In retrospect, I understand that I was a victim of megagrouping (Anderson, 1995); I was put into a macro category into which many but not all African-American students at the university fit. Staff assumptions about my academic failure nearly became a self-fulfilling prophecy. My early first-year experiences transformed me from a motivated, passionate learner with a history of academic excellence, into a depressed, tuition-paying shell of my former self with no clear goals for the future. My survival during the first year happened much more by accident than by institutional design. Late in my first year at a Big 10 institution, acts of divine intervention provided me with an opportunity to meet some African-American graduate students and staff who steered me to appropriate resources and restored my sense of academic confidence. Unfortunately, my initial first-year experience continues to be the experience of too many African-American students today.

This chapter presents salient information regarding the experiences of African-American first-year students in higher education. A model for reframing practice relative to this population of students is offered for those who are courageous enough to think outside the box. The following sections were developed from both relevant literature and from a synthesis of more than 20 years of professional experience working with and conducting/directing research on African-American college students. Professional experience was gained at both predominately White institutions (PWIs) and at historically black colleges and universities (HBCUs). Similarly, the research reviewed here was conducted at both predominately White institutions and at HBCUs and consisted of both quantitative and qualitative research methods.

Description of the Population

When thinking about African Americans as a group, it is important to distinguish between race and ethnicity; two terms that are often used interchangeably. Ethnic groups share history, culture, values, behaviors, and other qualities that form a foundation for a shared identity. Many of the characteristics of an ethnic group are internal, non-visible descriptors. Racial groups, however, share physical characteristics (i.e., skin color, hair texture, and other physical features), many of which are visibly detectable traits (Banks & McGee Banks, 1997). People can share an ethnic identity, but be members of different races. This distinction between race and ethnicity is important because some students who visibly appear to be U.S.-born African Americans are, in fact, not carbon copies, in terms of culture.

Generally, the ethnic realities of African-American students are grounded in African culture, but infinite variations result from family influence, religion, geographic region, and life experiences. Both native-born and foreign-born students of African descent consist of smaller, identifiable micro-populations each with its own distinct cultural flavor. Each micro-population has customs, behaviors, histories, and language that puts a different face on the core African culture.

Native-born African Americans

As a group, U.S.-born African Americans encompass a range of different cultural realities, and we should avoid making assumptions about a student's ethnic orientation as a result of physical traits, especially during the first year of college. Since students are vulnerable when they face the unknowns of a new environment, they may be easily insulted by those whom they think should know better. Mistakes resulting from faulty assumptions could be costly, damaging students' hopes for positive, productive future encounters.

Foreign-born Students of African Descent

Some students of African descent are foreign-born, coming from Africa, the Caribbean, South America, England, or other countries and are naturalized American citizens, permanent residents, or international students. These students have physical features that mirror native-born students of African descent and often share core elements of African culture. However, for some students their ethnic identity is primarily rooted in the culture of their native country rather than African culture.

Bi-racial Students

There is a growing population of bi-racial students, who have one parent of African descent (native or foreign-born) and one parent of a different race. Most bi-racial students embrace a dual racial identity and are offended when they are expected to choose one race over the other. For these students, choosing one race would, in effect, be choosing one parent over the other. Nevertheless, students most closely identify with the race of the mother. In addition, bi-racial students who live in predominately White neighborhoods tend to have a stronger "White" identity, especially when their mother is White (Robinson, 2001; Robinson & Howard-Hamilton, 2000). (For more information, on multiracial students see chapter 11.)

Other Characteristics

College-going African-American students possess other diverse characteristics. For example, some African-American students are first-generation college students, but others are second- and third-generation college students. Some African-American students come from households with low socioeconomic status, while others come from middle- and upper-income households. Some African-American students come from single-parent households or from the foster care system, but others come from traditional, intact families. Some African-American students are academically underprepared for college, but others are high-achieving students (Freeman, 1999). Clearly, the African-American student population is not a homogeneous group.

Influences on the First-Year Experience

Pre-college Issues

African-American students have higher postsecondary aspirations than any other group, when income is held constant (Freeman, 1998). For thousands of African Americans, the desire for a college education has actually become a reality at colleges and universities across the nation. Although some progress has been made in African-American enrollment and degree attainment in higher education, there is room for improvement (Nettles & Perna, 1997), especially among African-American males who are underrepresented in enrollment and degree completion statistics (National Center for Educational Statistics, 2000).

Given their college aspirations and the variety of educational opportunities available, African-American students should be making better progress in terms of their presence in higher education as measured by traditional indicators, such as enrollment, persistence, progression, and degree-completion rates. Their lack of more pronounced progress is indeed a paradox that makes the quality of the first-year experience particularly important for the African-American student.

Going to college, rather than to work or to the military, is still a difficult decision for African-American students (Freeman, 1998). Issues of curricular content, especially the absence of African-American culture in that content, influence the college decision-making process for African-American students in terms of institutional selection and enrollment. Perceived psychological barriers and "absent voices present the greatest challenge to closing the gap between aspirations and participation in higher education" (Freeman, 1998, p. 190). Additionally, African-American students have too little evidence that they can be academically successful in college. The lack of encouragement by their K-12 teachers leads many African-American students to abandon their aspirations for college. Even high-achieving African-American students often enter college without the confidence they need to be academically successful (Freeman, 1999). Therefore, the absence of African-American authors, culture, or history from course content and the lack of institutional support can result in African-American students choosing to pursue other options such as the military and the unskilled labor market, rather than attend college.

In addition, financial barriers continue to impact college access, exacerbating the gap between aspirations and participation. Admittedly, financial aid alone will not close the gap; however, knowledge about and the acquisition of financial aid would lower this barrier to higher education (Freeman, 1998).

Academic Influences

Institutional choice. A wide variety of colleges and universities operate in the United States. For the sake of discussion, institutional choice will focus on historically Black colleges and universities (HBCUs) and predominately White institutions (PWIs).

HBCUs and PWIs are considerably different in both the concept and approach to "cognitive development" of undergraduate students. Research shows that large numbers of African-American students at PWIs have feelings of discrimination and isolation, which have a negative impact on indicators of academic success, such as persistence, progression, grades, and graduation (Fleming, 1984; Lee 1992; Lee, 1997a; Nettles, Thoeny, Gosman, & Dandridge, 1985). HBCUs, on the other hand, are more student-centered than PWIs. These institutions view the student as a whole person, one undergoing a cognitive, spiritual, emotional, and social transformation (Davis, 1998). More African-American students attend PWIs, but the majority of African-American degrees are awarded at HBCUs (Nettles & Perna, 1997). They have "unique abilities to effectively structure environments that lead to greater achievement outcomes for their students" (Davis, 1998, p. 147), evidenced by income and graduate education attainment. Not only are African Americans successful at HBCUs, White students are also successful at these institutions (Wells-Lawson, 1994).

College preparation. Focus group interviews were held with African-American students at both a PWI and an HBCU (Lee, 1997a). The students were all "successful" students in that they survived the first college year and had been continuously enrolled in college. Students were asked to reflect on and describe their preparation for college. The conversation was lively since many fond memories of "tough," "sweet," and "odd-ball" teachers emerged in the discussion. Students across sessions indicated that educationally they thought they were well-prepared for college until they went to their first college class. Most of the students in each session took "Academic Prep" or "College Prep" courses in high school, which focused on science, math, and language arts (more literature than writing). Although students left high school feeling academically prepared for college, they were not prepared for "college life." An African-American female student illustrates this point:

> *I thought high school was tough. I didn't know I had it so good until I came here. Back in the day I could get assignments done in no time at all. I could write a paper in about half an hour. I could do homework, work after school, hang with my girls, chat with my honey, and still be in bed before 10:00 or 11:00 pm. I always got good grades, too. It ain't even close to that now. It takes me days, not minutes, to write a paper and to do class assignments. It is a full-time job just to keep up with the work. The work here isn't as hard as I thought it would be, but there sure is a lot of work to do. It's as if every professor thinks that you are taking one class—theirs. I wasn't prepared to put all my time and attention into college and have such a narrowly defined life.*

One student, who disclosed that he was a third-generation college student, indicated that he too was not prepared for college. His parents and one grandparent had attended college, and one parent graduated from college. Parental accounts of college and detailed descriptions of what to expect were frequent topics of conversation. However, his parents' version of college and his own college experience were different. His parents attended college when it was a structured environment with many staff monitoring student behavior, while the student experienced infinite freedom without fully understanding the responsibility that came with that freedom. He found himself on academic probation after the first semester and having to live with disappointed parents over the winter holiday. Other students related to this experience and indicated that moving from the structure of home and high school to the immediate freedom of college was a difficult transition that interfered with academic responsibilities in the first year of college.

Some students in this study were familiar with the social side of the institution (e.g., athletic events, concerts, parties, special events prior to enrollment). All of the students agreed that they knew very little about the academic rigor of their institutions prior to enrollment. As a result, students indicated that most of the classes started at a level above their preparation. According to one African-American male student:

> *I went to an all White high school in a small town where there was nothing much to do. I would come to campus so much that people thought I was a student here. The parties were live and the girls looked liked models. I learned my way around campus before I was a senior [in high school]. The first week you come they have you going to a lot of meetings during the day where you listen to a lot of people speak and at night there was always something going on to keep you up late. You didn't have to think much during the first week. The second week...that was a different story. I went to my first class half asleep, because I was tired. When I started to pay attention, I knew that I was in trouble.*

I was in the "intro" math class and it sounded like a foreign language. He didn't start where my [high school] classes ended. The party life I enjoyed here in high school ended after my first week here.

Learning environment. The fit between students' learning preferences and the institutional environment is very important. Too often the incongruence takes its toll on students, resulting in a stressful first-year experience. Some, not all, African Americans enter college with underdeveloped skills for success in the classroom. They tend to be dualistic thinkers, unable to think in complex, analytical ways. Therefore, they do not have a strong ability to identify assumptions, draw implications, or assess perspectives (Lee, 1997a). In addition, as mentioned earlier, African Americans, as a group, are not homogenous in their learning environment preferences (Lee, 1997a). Thus, strategies that treat students as cognitively identical are likely to be ineffective.

Critical thinking. Facione, Facione, and Sanchez (1994) define critical thinking as a non-linear, recursive, human cognitive process that forms a judgment about what to believe or do in a given context. The core set of cognitive skills used in critical thinking include analysis, interpretation, inference, explanation, evaluation, and self-regulation—all of which are essential skills for attaining academic success in college. Some African Americans, in this study, entered college lacking skills for truth seeking, open-mindedness, analytical thinking, systematic work, and maturity by society's standards. Such underdeveloped skills may result in the need to work on "cognitive maturity and epistemic development" (Facione et al., 1994, p. 3).

Conclusions about African-American students' critical-thinking ability should be drawn cautiously when elements of African culture are considered. Critical thinking requires a comfort level with conflict, disagreement, and disharmony. African culture is rooted in inclusion, harmony, and empowerment of all members, and it carries a respect for those in authority. African-American students may bring a lifetime of African culture into the first-year experience, which is counter to the perceived values of academic culture—pursuing contradictory thoughts, challenging ideas, being aggressive, or questioning authority, while learning in a competitive, chaotic environment.

Human Influences

Racism. Bias, bigotry, preconceptions, and prejudice are descriptors of racism, which contribute to feelings of discrimination among African-American students (Fleming 1984; Lee, 1992; Nettles et al., 1985). African-American students enter college fully aware of "race" and how it can potentially affect their academic success. Feelings of discrimination can deter efforts to interact with other students and faculty by prompting students to avoid those who evoke these feelings. This pattern of avoidance in the first year of college contributes to feelings of isolation in the university environment throughout the college career and results in the underachievement of African-American students (Fleming, 1984; Freeman, 1999).

Family. The power of family should not be underestimated when it comes to the success of African-American students. These students often have very strong relationships with parents, grandparents, and siblings. African-American students tend to feel that it is important for them to "make the family proud" and that failure would bring disgrace on them and on their family (Lee, 1997a). This connection to family motivates students to work hard, especially during the first year, but it can also become a source of stress for some students. The influence of family is not restricted to immediate, biological ties, but includes significant others who have been instrumental in the development of the student prior to entering college. Extended family usually includes close friends of the family, such as distant relatives, godparents, or lifelong friends of the students' parents and perhaps a close adult friend of the student from church, school, and civic organizations (Ross, 1998).

Spirituality. Hamilton and Jackson (1998) indicate that spirituality has three major components: (a) a sense of self-awareness, (b) a sense of interconnectedness and wholeness in the self and the world, and (c) a sense of a higher power working within the self and the world. African-American students generally enter college with a sense of spirituality manifested in religious rituals such as attendance at formal church services, prayer, and meditation. Further, they identify with myriad religious traditions (e.g., Protestant, Catholic, Muslim) that serve as a source of direction, stability, and calm in the midst of chaos. Spirituality, as a foundation of faith in a brighter future, gives students hope in hopeless situations. It provides direction and clarity of purpose that is very much needed in the first-year experience.

During focus group interview sessions with first-year students, an African-American male student reflected on the importance of spirituality in his life:

> *I'd probably feel misguided and not really sure what I want to do. I've always been one of those people who kind of knew what I wanted to do, but if I didn't have that [spirituality] I'd probably be like a lost soul walking, just not really knowing what my dreams were going to be or what I wanted to do in life or what kind of person I would want to become. I'd probably feel very lost. Definitely. (Nero, 2001, p. 19).*

Spirituality is an important and particularly sensitive topic for African-American students. Since their sense of spirituality is often passed down from their mother, teasing or joking about it would be the equivalent of insulting the matriarch of the family (Nero, 2001).

Strategies for Enhancing the First-Year Experience

The popular African proverb says, "It takes a village to raise a child," indicating that a community is responsible for the most vulnerable of its members. When applied to higher education, this suggests that all institutional units within a college or university should foster the success of African-American students and others who might be at risk. Both academic and student affairs staff members should address the needs of this population. Strategies to enhance the first-year experience of African-American students should evolve from a collaborative community perspective rather than a territorial program perspective.

However, institutions are complex environments, composed of a community of scholars. Specific areas of responsibility, identifiable relationships, and complex communication patterns exist among its members. Thus, despite efforts to enhance the first-year experience for African-American students, progress remains painfully slow. Many explanations for this condition exist. One reason is a practice of blaming the victim. This line of thinking maintains that students are solely responsible for their success, or failure, in college. Alternately, those who are held accountable for African-American students' higher education achievement, find it difficult to move from studying the problem to resolving the problem. In other words, there is a weak connection between research and practice that adversely affects African-American students. Research and practice should be brought together in new ways so that African-American students will be empowered to acclimate to their new educational environment without sacrificing their cultural identity.

Colleges and universities are institutionally centered in their operations, often by necessity.

Usually too many expected institutional outcomes arise in the face of diminishing resources. However, the successful retention of African-American students requires institutions to become student-centered in their behavior, moving from a model of mass production to customization. Institutions must use diverse strategies for diverse populations rather than a one-size-fits-all approach to service provision and curriculum development.

A logical question is "how can institutions, with finite resources, effectively become student-centered in order to retain African-American students?" Moving from a conceptual understanding to action is no small feat. Boone's (1997) community-based programming (CBP) process offers insights on how this question might be addressed.

CBP is a process that encompasses "a series of interconnected processual tasks...affecting collaboration among the people [and] their leaders...in identifying and seeking resolution of major...issues" (Boone, 1997, p.3). The process, in this case, would lead to a change in university culture as it is a rational, comprehensive approach for resolving a specific issue involving a specific target public. As used here, the issue addressed is the quality of the first-year experience for African-American undergraduate students. The objective would be to provide an environment where African-American students can gain a sense of empowerment, cognitive maturity, and academic confidence in the first year that will help them attain their educational goals.

Student Empowerment Model

The Student Empowerment Model (SEM) is a theoretical model that focuses on the connections between the inputs, educational processes, and outputs (see Figure 1). However, the emphasis for change in the SEM is on the institution, rather than on the student. It is assumed that admission procedures are compatible with institutional policy, resulting in the matriculation of a student population that meets institutional quality measures for success. Thus, institutions are responsible for the students who are admitted and at the very least should ensure that attrition is not institutionally driven. The model proposes an operational strategy for institutional personnel to become acquainted with African-American students (inputs) and to effectively enhance college experiences (educational processes) so that the first-year experience for African-American students will increase their potential to persist until degree completion (outputs). The SEM has at its core African-American students' academic success and the broken lines indicate that the success of these students depends on the success of institutional proactivity in helping them attain their educational goals. The model has three macro processes: (a) institutional preparation, (b) institutional transformation, and (c) institutional assessment.

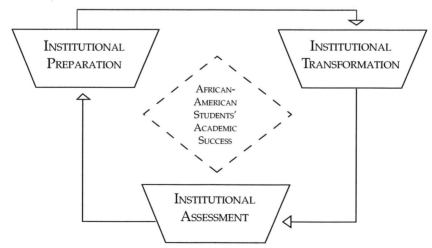

Figure 1. Student empowerment model.

Institutional Preparation

The institutional preparation phase of the process sets the stage for empowering African Americans for success in the first-year experience. The goal is to grow, rather than force, support so that institutional change can be systemic and sustained. The institutional preparation phase of the model involves two sub-processes: institutionalization and environmental analysis.

Institutionalization. Vaughan (1997) defines institutionalization as "the process by which an institution incorporates changes into the structured and often highly formalized system that constitutes the...organization" (p. 48). The institutionalization process requires the organization to make a strong commitment to the success of African-American students that is woven into the fabric of the institution—not merely an add-on activity. Successful institutionalization is best accomplished in what Bolman and Deal (1991) refer to as the human resources frame. The human resources frame focuses on the fit between the institution and students. The institutionalization process holds that people are the most important resource, and the effective interaction among people (across hierarchical, racial, and gender strata) is mutually beneficial to the perpetual existence of the institution and to the success of African-American students.

Leadership, especially on the part of the college president, is important in securing the commitment of those within the village. The president must be a maverick in the institutional preparation process, a visionary leader who is willing to invest institutional resources for the retention of African-American students. Visionary leadership, steeped in idealism that supports the active intermingling of academic excellence and social responsibility, is essential for institutionalizing the value of academic achievement among African-American students.

Environmental analysis. The environmental analysis process involves direct contact with African-American students in order to understand their experiences from their perspective and to gain their recommendations for institutional actions (Nichol, 1997). Thus, institutions would have a deeper understanding of the African-American students they serve. A mixed-methods approach, using both quantitative and qualitative methodologies, provides both breadth and depth in understanding how to retain African-American students in higher education. Such studies tell us not only *what* is happening but they also help us to answer the question of *why* it happens. The environmental analysis process should seek to discover both cognitive and non-cognitive institution- specific issues that threaten the retention of African-American students. These issues are likely to be similar across institutions but will vary in importance among institutions. The environmental analysis process involves ranking issues by priority and confirming these rankings with members of the targeted population (i.e., African-American students). This confirmation process is an essential element in empowerment since it meaningfully involves African-American students in the institution's efforts to enhance the first-year experience for new students.

Institutional Transformation

The institutional transformation process involves changes in the university's environment that would make learning conducive for all students. It transforms the institution from a reactive environment that accidentally retains some African-American students into an environment that is proactive and enhances the academic performance of these students through planned deliberate action. The institutional transformation process involves specific activities, including staff development for front-line institutional personnel, structured connections with faculty, and proactive service provision.

Staff development. Institutional personnel who have the initial contact with African-American students are key actors in the quality of their first-year experience. Staff members such as recruiters, admissions counselors, advisors, faculty who teach first-year courses, residence hall staff, tutors, orientation staff, security officers, and secretaries have the first chance to make the first-year experience a positive one that will make retention in subsequent years a strong possibility. Staff development activities should make these staff competent in their ability to communicate in cross-cultural situations (Hernandez & Isaacs, 1998).

Faculty connections. Connecting with faculty is an essential element of the academic success of African-American students. A faculty mentor should be identified for students as early as possible, preferably one who is in the student's intended major field. Being able to match students and mentors on the basis of race or gender should be considered a luxury rather than a prerequisite to establishing mentoring programs.

African-American students enter college with connections to other African Americans (e.g., family, friends, former teachers), and the maintenance of these relationships helps with bonding and identity development. African-American students should connect with mentors who are best equipped to help them in their chosen career by sharing information they are unlikely to get elsewhere (Lee, 1997a). This early connection with faculty or staff mentors can help students clarify career aspirations and accurately assess the skills and educational expectations needed for that career. Moreover, these mentoring relationships can confirm students' initial career choices or provide support and direction to students who should make alternative choices.

Proactive services. There are two services that should be required for first-year African-American students: intrusive tutorials and student-specific advising. Tutorial services are typically offered to students who seek them, placing the responsibility on the student for seeking help. If the student does not seek help, then he or she is blamed for subsequent academic failure. However, intrusive tutorials are not only helpful for remediation, they are also useful forums for helping strong students accelerate learning. Structured, intrusive tutorials also provide an opportunity for African-American students to experience education as a socialization process rather than an isolation reality. These sessions, if properly implemented, can facilitate the transition from high school to college by demonstrating the importance of study groups, by minimizing feelings of isolation, and by orienting students to the availability of institutional resources.

The academic advising process should be student-specific, structuring course schedules based on African-American first-year students' present needs rather than future goals. The mass production approach that involves all students taking a prescribed combination of courses is not as effective as selecting courses based on students' fit to the institution's environment, their entering skill level, and their educational goals. It is important for advisors to use both quantitative assessments (e.g., the Learning Environment Preferences, the California Critical Thinking Disposition Inventory) and qualitative assessments (e.g., purposeful dialogue with the student) when making recommendations for course schedules.

Institutional Assessment

The institutional assessment phase of the process measures African-American students' progress and provides credible data for decisions regarding future iterations of effort (Lee, 1997b). The goal is to monitor students' academic achievement on traditional indicators to ensure educational equity and use these findings in strategic planning. The institutional assessment phase involves monitoring, classroom review, and dissemination of findings.

Monitoring. African-American students' academic achievement in the first year should be monitored on indicators such as persistence, progression, and grade point average. Persistence is important for academic success, but continuous enrollment can be a challenge for some students who are not financially prepared for college. Monitoring should determine whether they are consistently enrolled (i.e., complete all courses attempted) and that they are making normal or reasonable progress through the curriculum. Normal progress should not only involve assessing students' grade point average and the number of credits earned but should also include an assessment of the number of credits earned that apply toward degree-completion requirements.

Classroom review. African-American student experiences in the classroom should be continuously monitored to determine whether culturally valid assessments are used to measure academic achievement. Fair testing practices are not easily attained. However, at a minimum, the institutional assessment process should determine whether there are significant differences between African-American and other students' performance in courses and whether classroom content and tests are culturally offensive and demotivating to African-American students (Robinson, 1999). Culturally valid assessment should use a mixed methods approach (i.e., quantitative and qualitative measures) to determine mastery of course content, balance cognitive and affective measures of performance, and reflect on the impact of the language on the construct validity of classroom test items.

Dissemination of findings. Using assessment information is essential in any effort to bring about change (Patton, 1986). Attention should be given to the audience who will receive the assessment data generated. Data should be accurate and presented in an informative and balanced format, so that it will actually be used for improving the quality of the first-year experience for African-American students.

Conclusion

The first year of college is a memorable experience, and institutions bear the responsibility of making "quality" and "positive" accurate descriptors of that experience. While African-American students share many similarities as a group, there is also considerable diversity within this culture. Institutional personnel must avoid "'megagrouping,' that is, the tendency to identify as homogeneous the broad, diverse characteristics within a group" (Anderson, 1995, p. 71). Additionally, institutions should empower African-American students so that they are equipped to persist toward their educational goals. The best pathway to student empowerment is seeking the meaningful participation of students in the institutional planning process. This empowerment depends on the extent to which campuses can transform into culturally competent environments that recognize and honor African culture, without ignoring intra-group diversity among African-American students. Finally, institutions must understand that enhancing the first-year experience of African-American students is neither a one-size-fits all strategy nor is it a once-in-a-lifetime event, rather it is an iterative, continuous process that should be institutionalized into the values of the university.

References

Anderson, J. A. (1995). Toward a framework for matching teaching and learning styles for diverse populations. In R. R. Sims, & S. J. Sims (Eds.), *The importance of learning styles: Understanding the implications for learning, course design, and education*. Westport, CT: Greenwood Press.

Banks, J. A., & McGee Banks, C.A. (Eds.). (1997). *Multicultural education: Issues and perspectives* (3rd ed.). Boston: Allyn and Bacon.

Bolman, L. G., & Deal, T. E. (1991). *Reframing organizations: Artistry, choice, and leadership*. San Francisco: Jossey-Bass.

Boone, E. J. (1997). An introduction to the community-based programming process. In E. J. Boone & Associates, *Community leadership through community-based programming: The role of the community college* (pp. 1-20). Washington, DC: Community College Press.

Davis, J. E. (1998). Cultural capital and the role of historically black colleges and universities in educational reproduction. In K. Freeman (Ed.), *African American culture and heritage in higher education research and practice* (pp. 143-153). Westport, CT: Praeger.

Facione, P. A., Facione, N. C., & Sanchez, C. A. (1994). *Are college students disposed to think?* (ERIC Document Reproduction Service No. ED 368311)

Fleming, J. (1984). *Blacks in college*. San Francisco: Jossey-Bass.

Freeman, K. (1999). My soul is missing: African American students' perceptions of the curriculum and the influence on college choice. *Review of African American Education, 1*(1) 31-43.

Freeman, K. (1998). African Americans and college choice: cultural considerations and policy implications. In Freeman, K. (Ed.), *African American culture and heritage in higher education research and practice* (pp. 181-194). Westport, CT: Praeger.

Hamilton, D. M., & Jackson, M. H. (1998). Spiritual development: Paths and processes. *Journal of Instructional Psychology, 25*(4), 262-272.

Hernandez, M., & Isaacs, M. R. (1998). *Promoting cultural competence in children's mental health services*. Baltimore, MD: Paul H. Brooks Publishing Co.

Lee, W. Y. (1997a). University transition program baseline assessment. Raleigh, NC: North Carolina State University, Undergraduate Studies.

Lee, W. Y. (1997b). Evaluation and accountability in community-based programming. In E. J. Boone & Associates (Eds.), *Community leadership through community-based programming: The role of the community college* (pp.171-194). Washington. D.C.: Community College Press.

Lee, W. Y. (1992). *Fostering undergraduate minority student academic achievement*. Nashville, TN: Peabody College.

National Center for Education Statistics. (2000). *Digest of Education Statistics*. Washington, DC: U.S. Department of Education.

Nero, L. (2001, May). *How college freshmen value and express spirituality*. Paper presented at the Second Annual Conference on Diversity, Raleigh, NC.

Nettles, M. T., & Perna, L. W. (1997). *African American education data book:* (Vol. 1). Higher and Adult Education. Washington, DC: Frederick D. Patterson Research Institute of the College Fund/UNCF.

Nettles, M. T., Thoeny, A. R., Gosman, R. J., & Dandridge, B. A. (1985). *The causes and consequences of college students' performance: A focus on Black and White students' attrition rates, progression rates, and grade point averages*. Nashville, TN: Tennessee Higher Education Commission.

Nichol, B. (1997). Environmental scanning. In E. J. Boone & Associates (Eds.), *Community leadership through community-based programming: The role of the community college* (pp. 59-78). Washington, DC: Community College Press.

Patton, M. Q. (1986). *Utilization-focused evaluation.* (2nd ed.). Newbury Park, CA: Sage.

Robinson, S. (1999, June). *The meaning of 'fairness' in the context of testing.* Paper presented at AAHE's Annual Assessment Conference, Denver, CO.

Robinson, T. L. (2001). White mothers of non-white children. *Journal of Humanistic Counseling, Education and Development, 40,* 171-184.

Robinson, T. L. & Howard-Hamilton, M. F. (2000). *The convergence of race, ethnicity, and gender: Multiple identities in counseling.* Upper Saddle River, NJ: Merrill/Prentice Hall.

Ross, M. J. (1998). *Success factors of young African-American males at a historically black college.* Westport, CT: Bergin & Garvey.

Wells-Lawson, M. I. (1994, April). *The effects of race and type of institution on the college experiences of Black and White undergraduate students attending 30 predominately Black and predominantly White college and universities.* Paper presented at the Annual Meeting of the American Educational Research Association, New Orleans, LA.

Vaughan, G. (1997). The community college's mission and milieu: Institutionalizing community-based programming. In E. J. Boone & Associates (Eds.), *Community leadership through community-based programming: The role of the community college.* Washington, DC: Community College Press.

Resources

Assessment Tools

Facione, P. A., Facione, N. C., & Sanchez, C. A. (1994). The California critical thinking disposition inventory test manual. Millbrae, CA: California Academic Press.

Moore, W. S. (1990). The learning environment preferences: An instrument manual. Olympia, WA: Center for the Study of Intellectual Development.

Pace, C. R. (1994). Information for prospective users: College student experiences questionnaire. Bloomington, IN: Indiana University.

Books

Foster, L., Guyden, J. A., & Miller, A. L. (Eds.). (1999). *Affirmed action: Essays on the academic and social lives of White faculty members at historically Black colleges and universities.* Oxford, England: Rowman & Littlefield.

Freeman, K. (Ed.) (1998). *African American culture and heritage in higher education research and practice.* Westport, CT : Praeger.

Graham, L. O. (1999). *Inside America's Black upper class: Our kind of people.* New York, NY: Harper Collins.

hooks, b. (2000). *Where we stand: Class matters.* New York, NY: Routledge.

Kottak, C. P., & Kozaitis, K. A. (1999). *On being different: Diversity and multiculturalism in the North American mainstream.* Boston: McGraw-Hill.

Smitherman, G. (2000) *Black talk: Words and phrases from the hood to the amen corner* (revised edition). Boston: Houghton Mifflin.

Stanfield, J. H., II, & Dennis, R. M. (Eds.). (1993). *Race and ethnicity in research methods.* Newbury Park, CA: Sage.

West, C. (2001). *Race matters.* Boston: Beacon Press.

Periodicals

> *Journal of Negro Education*
> *African American Review*
> *Journal of Black Studies*
> *Journal of Blacks in Higher Education*
> *Black Issues in Higher Education*
> *Transition*

Videos/Films

> *African American Cultures*
> Insight Media
> 2162 Broadway, New York, NY 10024
> Toll Free: 1-800-233-9910
> Fax: 212-799-5309
> www.insight-media.com
>
> *Beyond Black and White: Affirmative Action in America*
> Films for the Humanities and Sciences
> P. O. Box 2053, Princeton, NJ 08543-2053
> Toll Free: 1-800-257-5126
> Fax 609-275-3767
> www.films.com
>
> *Facing Racism*
> Films for the Humanities and Sciences
> P. O. Box 2053, Princeton, NJ 08543-2053
> Toll Free: 1-800-257-5126
> Fax 609-275-3767
> www.films.com
>
> *Redefining Racism: Fresh Voices From Black America*
> Insight Media
> 2162 Broadway, New York, NY 10024.
> Toll Free: 1-800-233-9910
> Fax: 212-799-5309
> www.insight-media.com
>
> *The Price of Racism*
> Films for the Humanities and Sciences
> P. O. Box 2053, Princeton, NJ 08543-2053
> Toll Free: 1-800-257-5126
> Fax 609-275-3767
> www.films.com

The Two Nations of Black America
Insight Media
2162 Broadway, New York, NY 10024
Toll Free: 1-800-233-9910
Fax: 212-799-5309.
www.insight-media.com

Understanding Our Biases and Assumptions
Films for the Humanities and Sciences
P. O. Box 2053, Princeton, NJ 08543-2053
Toll Free: 1-800-257-5126
Fax 609-275-3767
www.films.com

When Is Race Black or White?
Insight Media
2162 Broadway, New York, NY 10024
Toll Free: 1-800-233-9910
Fax: 212-799-5309
www.insight-media.com

White, Black, or None of the Above?
Insight Media
2162 Broadway, New York, NY 10024
Toll Free: 1-800-233-9910
Fax: 212-799-5309
www.insight-media.com

Web Sites

Black America Political Action Committee
http://www.bampac.org/

Public Broadcasting Service (PBS)
http://www.pbs.org/wgbh/pages/frontline/shows/race/
http://www.pbs.org/aajourney/

Black Voices (Tribune Company)
http://new.blackvoices.com/

Innercity Software
http://www.blackfacts.com/about.asp

Chapter 8

Enhancing the Post-Secondary Experiences
of Latinos

Kenneth P. Gonzalez,
Louis Olivas,
and Mistalene Calleroz

Once social change begins, it cannot be reversed: you cannot un-educate the person who has learned to read; you cannot humili-ate the person who has pride; and you cannot oppress the people who are not afraid anymore.—Cesar Chavez as cited in Jenson & Hammerback, 2002, p. 28

Never before have major national newspapers and periodicals covered the growing Latino population with as much intensity as after the U.S. Census Bureau 2000 reports were released. Latinos, now numbering 35.3 million, represent 13% of the U.S. population. For the first time in U.S. history, the Latino population now surpasses the African-American population. Leading all population groups in percentage growth since 1990, Latinos grew by 57.9% from 1990 to 2000. Figure 1 compares population growth for all groups.

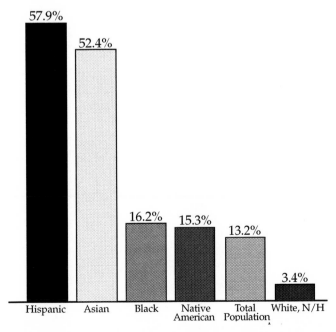

Figure 1. Percentage change by race/ethnicity from 1990 to 2000. Data from Census 2000 PHC-T-I, Table 4. (U.S. Census Bureau, 2000). Used with permission.

The U.S. Census Bureau (2001) also predicts that minority populations will continue to outpace non-minorities over the next 50 years. Over the past 10 years, Latinos have had the highest fertility and birthrates among all groups (averaging 83.3 births per 1,000 in comparison to 57.8 births of White, non-Hispanics), and predictions are that over the next 25 years, this birth trend will continue.

Not only is the Latino population growing at a faster rate than any other group, but it also is consistently the youngest population by a great margin. The median age is 27 compared to 38 for the White, non-Hispanic population. By 2020 that age disparity will increase: 29 for Latinos compared to 42 for White, non-Hispanics. Consequently, there are many enrollment implications for higher education.

The 1998 White House Initiative on Educational Excellence for Hispanic Americans tracked the demographic changes across two decades. From 1978 to 1998, Latino elementary school enrollment grew by 157%, eight times greater than African-American enrollment and 16 times greater than that of White, non-Hispanic. Latinos currently account for 15% of the elementary school enrollment. By 2025, it is estimated that Latinos will make up 25% of the elementary school-age population.

According to the 1998 White House Initiative report, the Latino enrollment for high school students, grades 9 to 12, have strikingly similar growth rates to K through 8. Today, Latinos account for 13% of the secondary school enrollment. Over the next 29 years, this population group will make up 23% of the secondary school-age population. The Western Interstate Commission for Higher Education report, *Knocking at the College Door* (1998) estimates that beginning with the high school graduating class of 2008, Latino high school graduates will surpass African Americans as the largest minority group for the first time. This will be the first in a continuing trend of large Latino graduating populations. Figure 2 describes the projected growth of Hispanic high school graduates as compared to other ethnic groups.

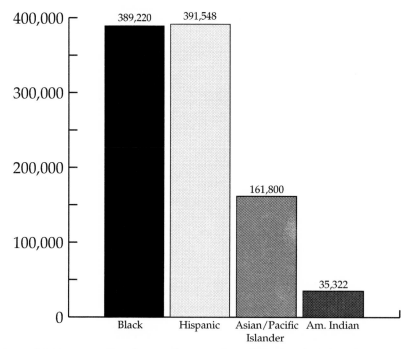

Figure 2. Projected Minority Graduates from U.S. Public High Schools, 2006-07. (Western Interstate Commission for Higher Education, 1998, p. 73). Reprinted with permission.

While the college age (18-24) participation rates for Latinos have grown over the past 10 years, the rates are still well below White, non-Hispanic rates. The *Minorities in Higher Education Annual Report, 1999-2000,* issued by the American Council on Education (ACE), identifies the trends for all racial and ethnic groups. Figure 3 illustrates the trend of college continuation rates of high school graduates for Latinos and White, non-Hispanic populations, from 1976-2000.

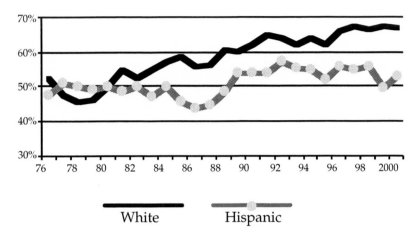

White　　　　Hispanic

Figure 3. College Continuation Rates for White and Hispanic High School Graduates, 1976 to 2000 (American Council on Education, 1999-2000, p. 47). Used with permission.

Finally, Latinos in undergraduate programs now represent 14.5% (3.6 million) of the U.S. undergraduate population. Within the next 20 years, it is estimated that the percentage will increase to 22% of the total undergraduate population. Over the next 14 years, the Latino undergraduate population will increase by over one million students.

Universities across the country will continue admitting students from diverse populations with larger net enrollments gained from the Latino population. The competition for these students among colleges and universities will increase as institutions attempt to capture a share of the growing Latino population to offset the leveling off or decrease of other student populations. In this new millennium, it is clear that successful institutions of higher education will be those that not only have acquired a deep understanding of the unique challenges and experiences of Latino college students but that also use that understanding in recruiting, retaining, and graduating these students. In an effort to aid in such understanding, the chapter outlines recent research concerning two major challenges to Latino college students' success and provides overviews of four model programs designed to aid these students in their transition to college.

Challenges for Latino/a Students

Negotiating the Institutional Culture

Although the numbers of Latino and other students of color entering colleges and universities are increasing, the culture or climate existing on many campuses endures as an obstacle in their path toward graduation (Hurtado, Carter, & Spuler, 1996; Skinner & Richardson, 1988). For instance, Latino students interpret the culture or climate of many colleges and universities as alienating, isolating, hostile, and unsupportive (Attinasi, 1989; Bennett & Okinaka, 1990; Hurtado, 1992, 1994; Hurtado, Carter, & Spuler, 1996; Olivas, 1986).

Hurtado et al.'s (1996) study of Latino student transition to college found that climate-related minority status stressors have a "depressing effect on Latino students' feelings of attachment to the institution" (p. 151). In an earlier study, Hurtado (1994) found that even high-achieving Latino students attending predominantly White universities viewed the climate of these institutions as hostile. In particular, Hurtado discovered that more than a quarter of these high-achieving Latino students felt like they did not fit in. Hurtado suggests that there are "elements of institutional culture, perhaps associated with its historical legacy of exclusion, that continue to resist a Latino presence on campus" (p. 35).

Smedley, Myers, and Harrell (1993) echo these sentiments, noting that the social climate for ethnic minority students attending predominantly White colleges and universities engenders an additional burden of stress in their academic adjustment to college. Moreover, Nora and Cabrera (1996) found that ethnic minority student perceptions of prejudice or discrimination on campus negatively affect their first-year experience in college and exert an indirect effect on their decisions to persist.

In short, ample corroborating evidence suggests that the culture or climate of many colleges and universities in the U.S. endures as an obstacle for Latino and other ethnic minority students. Unfortunately, few studies have produced an adequate understanding of the elements of campus culture that engender this adversarial relationship. One of the few studies that specifically sought to illuminate the various elements of the campus culture that either hindered or supported Latino students' transition to college was conducted by Gonzalez (2000). For more than two years, Gonzalez conducted interviews and observations of working-class, first-generation Latino students at a predominantly White university in the southwestern region of the United States. In this study, Gonzalez found that students were marginalized and alienated by three elements of the campus culture (See Figure 4). He referred to these elements as three asymmetrical systems of representation, labeling them (a) the *social world*, (b) the *physical world*, and (c) the *epistemological world*.

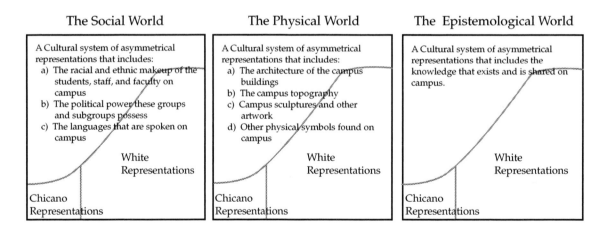

Figure 4. Elements of the campus culture that hinder the persistence of Latino students.

Gonzalez (2000) defines the social world as a system of cultural representations that includes the racial and ethnic makeup of individuals and groups on campus, the power relationships that exist among these groups, and the language spoken among them. He argues that within the social world, Latino students experience marginalization and alienation due to a lack of Latino representation among the students, staff, and faculty on campus; the lack of political power these groups possess; and the lack of the Spanish language spoken on campus.

The second asymmetrical system of representation existing on campus is the physical world. This world is viewed as a system of cultural representations that includes things such as the campus topography, the architecture of the campus buildings, campus sculptures, and other physical symbols found on campus such as posters and flyers. Within the physical world, marginalization and alienation are often experienced due to a lack of Latino representation among these elements.

The final asymmetrical system of representation Gonzalez (2000) identifies is the epistemological world. This system of cultural representations includes the knowledge existing and being shared within various social spaces on campus. Within the epistemological world, Latino students were found to have experienced marginalization and alienation due to a lack of Latino knowledge existing and being exchanged within and outside of the classroom environment.

Viewed in total, Gonzalez (2000) makes the salient point that Latino students must often survive in a college or university environment of asymmetrical systems of representation. He goes on to suggest that it is within these systems that the dominant, White cultural representations not only function as key mechanisms toward the reproduction of the existing campus culture (Althusser, 1971) but also simultaneously marginalize and alienate the few Latino representations and, therefore, Latino students themselves.

In addition to identifying elements of the campus culture that hinder the persistence of Latino students, Gonzalez's (2000) research highlights the critical sources of support Latino students draw from in order to persist at the university. He conceptualizes these support systems as sources of cultural nourishment. Latino students are viewed as carrying the burden of experiencing cultural starvation on predominantly White campuses; thus support systems primarily exist for cultural replenishment.

Gonzalez (2000) proposes that sources of cultural nourishment exist in social, physical, and epistemological forms. Within the social world, students' families, friends, music, and language are identified as notable sources of cultural nourishment and support. Sources of support within the physical world emerge as pictures, paintings, posters, and other material artifacts. Within the epistemological world, Gonzalez suggests that cultural nourishment exists in the form of knowledge constructed and shared from such sources as family members, Chicano literature, Chicano faculty, and courses in Chicano studies.

This research provides additional support for reform efforts focusing on the transformation of campus culture. Gonzalez's (2000) findings point to the very elements of the campus culture that must be changed to ensure the successful transition to college for Latinos, namely the social, physical, and epistemological worlds of the campus environment. Notable changes would involve transforming these three worlds so that a more adequate representation of the Latino culture exists.

Transforming the social world of a college campus to support Latino students would involve increasing (a) the number of Latino students, staff, and faculty on campus; (b) the political power these groups possess; and (c) the use of the Spanish language on campus. Transforming the physical world of a college campus would involve increasing (a) Latino cultural representations within the architecture of the campus buildings, (b) the number of Latino sculptures and other artwork, and (c) other physical images on campus that represent the Latino culture. Finally, transforming the epistemological world of a college campus would involve increasing the amount of Latino knowledge created and shared on campus. This could take the form of increasing the number of Latino studies courses offered on campus, as well as transforming existing curricula so that it includes a greater emphasis on Latino worldviews or contributions to the disciplines. These transformations would simultaneously increase the sources of cultural nourishment for Latino students.

Challenges Unique to Latinas

In concert with the attention paid to the demographic changes within the Latino population, recent reports (e.g., Ginorio & Huston, 2001) have highlighted the troubling educational status of Latino females. For example, on March 25, 2001, the caption on the front page of the Sunday edition of the *New York Times* read: "Troubling Label for Hispanics: Girls Most Likely to Dropout" (Stanz). The article bluntly described the poor educational achievement of Latinas. Citing recent U.S. Census data, the author indicated that Latinas are dropping out of high school at a far greater rate than other groups of young women in the United States. The article showed that the dropout rate for Latina female high school students has reached 26% compared with 13% and 6.9% for African Americans and Whites, respectively. The implications of such high dropout rates for Latina high school students are clear for school officials concerned with improving the rates of postsecondary attendance for these young women. The first step is to ensure that Latinas graduate from high school.

In addition to lowering the dropout rate for Latina high school students, other issues must be addressed. There are numerous hurdles to overcome to gain access to a college or university. However, in the Latino community, females are confronted with barriers that their male counterparts are not. In the traditional Latino family, Latinas are not often encouraged to move away from home to attend college (Ceja, 2000; Vasquez, 1982). Consequently, of the small minority of Latinas who do decide to enroll in college, many attend community colleges close to home. Institutional data suggest that Latinos are much more likely to move away from home to attend college than Latinas (Nieves-Sequires, 1991). Moreover, the transfer rates from community colleges to four-year colleges and universities are lower for Latinas than Latinos. In short, for a variety of reasons, Latina participation in four-year colleges and universities has been thwarted.

Although research on Latinas in college is far from extensive, consensus exists that their presence in college is constrained as a result of parental pressure to remain close to home (Ceja, 2000; Vasquez, 1982). To understand the unique tension of Latinas leaving home for college, Gonzalez and Stoner (2001) conducted a study of Latinas who left home after high school to attend a prestigious university. They designed their study with Vasquez's (1982) and Ceja's (2000) findings in mind, and asked how the decision-making process of Latinas who chose to leave home after high school to attend an elite university might be explained. Gonzalez and Stoner employed qualitative research methods to answer the following research questions: (a) What was the experience of Latinas who chose to leave home after high school to attend a prestigious university, and (b) Do Latinas, in fact, experience pressure from their parents to remain close to home while attending college? If so, what might explain their parents' needs to have their daughters remain close to home?

Interviews with 14 Latinas who left home after high school to attend an elite university were conducted. Ten research participants were from the Los Angeles metropolitan area, and four were from rural communities in central California. Eight of the students attended Stanford University and six attended the University of California at Berkeley. Both institutions are more than 350 miles away from their hometowns. All participants were raised in monolingual Spanish or bilingual home environments. All but one of the students attended public schools that were predominantly Latino; one student transferred from a predominantly Latino public elementary school to a private, largely White, middle and high school. All participants were from working-class families and were first-generation U.S. citizens.

Gonzalez and Stoner (2001) found that their participants' decisions to leave home to attend college began with their desire for independence. Many students commented that although they "felt bad" about leaving home, they knew they needed to leave in order to become independent. For example, one of the students stated:

> *I knew from the beginning that I wanted to leave Southern California and my family. It was because I needed to get away from my family. I was too dependent on them. I was the youngest and all my problems were always taken care of for me. I had six people ahead of me to turn to, plus sisters-in-law and brothers-in-law. So I remember I felt weak as a person being so dependent; and I wanted to leave. I love my family, but I just needed to go away so I could be independent.*

Not all of the students in the study were the youngest in their families, but they all shared the desire to become independent. Each of them voiced a concern about remaining dependent on their family and others if they remained close to home. In addition to a desire for independence, the students chose to leave home because of the unique opportunity to attend one of the top institutions in the country. They shared stories about the experience of opening their acceptance letters and being pleasantly surprised about the opportunity to attend a prestigious university; the opportunity was not something they could easily ignore.

Despite the students' acceptance into two prestigious universities, Gonzalez and Stoner (2001) discovered that tensions with their parents were prominent in the decision to leave home. In fact, only one student did not experience any tension or conflict about her decision to leave home to attend college. One student described her mother's subdued reaction in the following way:

> *My mom was sad. I remember when I found out, she was in the kitchen. I said "Mom! I got in!" And she said, "Oh, now you are leaving." And then she stayed quiet. I felt like I had to apologize even though I was happy.*

Another student described her father's reaction below:

> *My dad was actually mad back then. He was really mad that I did not go to UCLA. He really wanted me to go to UCLA. He was really mad that I did not even apply there. He wanted me to stay in Southern California. He wanted me to go to college, but he also wanted me to stay nearby.*

This quote alludes to Gonzalez and Stoner's finding that at the other extreme of the students' desire for independence and acceptance of a unique college opportunity was their parents' need for them to remain close to home. The students and their parents were caught in an uncommon web of opportunity woven with threads of conflict.

One of the more insightful findings of Gonzalez and Stoner's study involved uncovering the underlying rationale of the parents' need for their daughters to be close to home. A student commented:

> *My mom was like, "Why do you have to move? Why can't you stay here?" She was really afraid for me more than anything else. I think she was worried about what was going to happen to me, who was going to take care of me, things like that. I think those were the greatest concerns of people.*

A second student highlighted how her parents' concern about who would take care of her was gender specific:

Oh yeah, the boys could do whatever they wanted. They could leave when they wanted. They did not have to go to school to leave the house. One of my brothers left the house without even being married. It was not a big deal. But for us, the only way you can leave the house is to go to school or get married. Even now, my mom feels like she is still taking care of me because I am not married. It's like, the girls have to be taken care of until there is a man to do it. It's different for the boys, they can leave the house without being married or going to school. It's because everyone thinks they can take care of themselves, but not us.

For more than 20 years, scholars have consistently found that one of the major barriers to college attendance opportunities for Latinas is parental pressure to remain at home. Unfortunately, these scholars often have neglected to adequately describe the roots of such pressure. From the interviews Gonzalez and Stoner (2001) conducted, they learned that parental pressure to have their daughters remain close to home was rooted in the question, "Who will take care of her?" They also discovered that this question was gender specific. Gonzalez and Stoner uncovered a particular belief system that most of these women confronted in their decision to leave home for college. This belief system maintains that women (a) are unable to take care of themselves and (b) can only be "taken care of" by the parents and family or a spouse. Leaving home without being married was only possible by going to college. But even this scenario did not provide an answer to the question of "Who would take care of her?" It was difficult for the parents to believe, understand, or even consider that these women could take care of themselves.

The findings of Gonzalez and Stoner (2001) have potentially important implications for researchers and practitioners. For researchers, these findings suggest the importance of continuing to examine the role of gender in the college choice process. In the case of Latinas, gender roles and expectations were found to be salient in choosing to attend a university away from home. Institutions of higher education would benefit by putting this knowledge to work when creating support systems for this growing Latina population. For practitioners, the findings of this study offer a more comprehensive understanding of the tensions underlying Latinas' decisions to attend a college away from home. Such understanding may be especially helpful for high school counselors or other school personnel who may want to help ameliorate the tension between the desires of Latinas to attend a college away from home and their parents' concerns about who will take care of them.

Although some of the challenges Latinos experience in their pursuit of a college degree are not uncommon to other ethnic minority groups, unique differences exist. Moreover, some challenges are gender specific. In our review of the literature, we focused on two major challenges that Latinos experience in making the transition to college: (a) negotiating the institutional culture and (b) the tensions of Latinas leaving home for college. Although much needs to be done, a number of programs have made significant progress in easing the first-year transitions of Latino college students. The remaining section describes exemplary programs that have responded to the unique challenges of Latino students.

Latino/a Support Programs

The Doran Community Scholars Program

In 1997, Arizona State University (ASU) initiated the Doran Community Scholars Program, a scholarship effort recruiting from the largest inner-city high school district in Arizona. Although open to all students, most Doran scholars are Latino because of the targeted geographic area. The purpose of this scholarship program is threefold: (a) to prepare the next generation of leaders who are committed to improving the social conditions of their community; (b) to facilitate the academic success and leadership development of student participants; and (c) to offer financial scholarships of up to $3,000, renewable for four years.

The Doran program differs from most scholarship efforts in that a high grade point average is not necessarily a guarantee that a student will be awarded. Rather, the criteria focuses on the student who may not have performed to his/her potential in high school but who shows the potential to succeed at ASU with the help of financial support, encouragement, and mentoring. Doran scholars are required to attend the ASU Summer Transition Academy (ASTA). This free, week-long orientation offers students the opportunity to learn more about the university and to connect with other Doran applicants who will be attending ASU.

Other components of the program include peer mentoring with continuing Doran scholars, tutoring, academic and personal development workshops, and direct interaction with staff. The coupling of the services and the close, supportive network of staff and upper-division students contribute to the success of the program. A final key to the success of the program is its central location on campus. Students spend time in the office; use the computer lab, printer, or copier; and simply congregate and connect with other students.

To renew their scholarship, students must maintain a 2.7 cumulative GPA, register for the "Doran Community Scholars" Pro-Seminar course, complete 45 volunteers hours, attend monthly group meetings, and actively serve on a Doran Scholars committee.

The goals of the program are achieved, in part, by the Pro-Seminars, year-long, cohort-based academic courses that focus on social problems, community service, and leadership in the Phoenix metropolitan area. Each class level has a different focus, and an internship is incorporated within the classroom structure. First-year students focus on leadership and service-learning related to the social conditions in the surrounding area; sophomores focus on understanding the impact of the local government on the community; juniors focus on career development (e.g., resume writing, interviewing skills) and personal exploration; and seniors focus on leadership and special event coordination. This senior cohort organizes a large event that provides volunteer services to the local community. The final event for the senior cohort of 2001 was a trip to Washington, D.C. that included a visit to the office of Arizona's state representative and historical landmarks. The seniors solicited donations to fund the trip, developed a budget and a timeline, and connected with potential donors.

In May 2001, the Doran Community Scholars program completed its fourth year and graduated its first cohort. Of the 12 charter students, eight students graduated for a completion rate of 67%.

The Puente Project

The Puente Project, initiated in 1981, reaches out to both the Latino high school and community college population, serving roughly 63,000 students in 38 community colleges and 32 high schools throughout California. Seeking to increase the number of "educationally underserved students who enroll in four-year colleges and universities; earn college degrees; and return to the community as mentors and leaders to future generations" (http://www.puente.net), Puente focuses on mentoring, teaching, and counseling students. In addition, the program offers training to high school and college staff members to conduct the Puente program at their respective institutions.

At the community-college level, the specific goal is to increase the number of students who transfer to four-year colleges and universities and ensure that they complete their degrees. Puente students are mentored by a community member who has achieved success in the academic and professional world. This relationship partners students with business leaders, educators, and others who can provide an important role model. Teaching is also a crucial component of the Puente program; students enroll in two accelerated English courses that focus on Latino literature and experience. A former Puente student who returned to work with the program after he graduated recalled that the Latino focus in the classroom was encouraging and, in many ways, legitimized his own experiences outside the classroom (Laden, 1999). Finally, students visit college campuses and have regular meetings with a Puente counselor who facilitates the transfer application process and ensures the students are taking the appropriate college-prep classes.

Puente has seen the fruits of its labor over the course of 20 years. The four-year college or university enrollment of Puente high school students in 1998 was 43%; for non-Puente students, the percentage was 24% (Gandara, 1998). The term-to-term retention of students in California community colleges varied dramatically between Puente students and all students: 92% (Puente) versus 60% (student statewide) (http://www.puente.net/results_pg.html).

Hispanic Mother Daughter Program

For the past 17 years, the Hispanic Mother Daughter Program (HMDP) at ASU has worked with students and their mothers from 41 feeder schools in two local school districts. The mission of the HMDP is to increase the number of Hispanic women who complete a four-year college degree. The emphasis is keeping the student on track academically and ensuring that she fulfills the university requirements for entrance. Although the program encourages attendance at any college, ASU is the primary choice as students are offered a tuition waiver and an established support network. The program helps participants (eighth grade through college) recognize the benefits of higher education through a support network of school counselors, community leaders, and role models; it uses a team approach, involving the mother directly in the educational process of her daughter.

A unique characteristic of the HMDP is the outreach that begins five years prior to enrolling in college. Fifty mother-and-daughter teams are selected from approximately 200 applicants each year. In addition to a written application, two letters of recommendation are required from the student's math and English teachers, and an interview is conducted with mother and daughter together. Awardees receive a tuition waiver, renewable for up to four years. Students must maintain a 2.75 GPA in the core coursework of math, science, and English; be the first in their families to attend college; and be proficient in English. Once selected, mothers and daughters attend monthly workshops designed to increase understanding of and comfort with the university environment. Separate monthly workshops take place for the high-school cohort as well as the college cohort. In addition to workshops, one-on-one advising with HMDP advisors offer students the opportunity to receive individual academic guidance and monitoring and social and personal development. Tutoring in the Math and Science Program at ASU and the high schools completes the programmatic components of the HMDP.

The inclusive approach of bringing both mothers and daughters to campus appears to have influenced mothers' support for their daughters to attend higher education institutions. The program encourages mothers who speak only Spanish to learn English so that they will understand the different education expectations that their daughters must fulfill for college entry. Thus, the mothers are better equipped to champion their daughters through the high school system and on to college graduation. A byproduct of this high level of parental involvement is that mothers often are energized to continue their own education. Through the HMDP, mothers have received high school, associate's, bachelor's, and master's degrees.

The program boasts strong results. The average time to degree completion is five to five-and-a-half years. Of those who participated in the program beginning in their eighth grade year, 84% of them graduated from college in 1998 and 1999, and 100% for academic years 2000 and 2001. An equally impressive statistic is that the average GPA for high-school participants in 1999-2000 was 3.22. Over seven years, a total of 90 college graduates, averaging 13 per year, successfully completed this program. Included in this number is an undergraduate degree completed by a mother in the Program, two master's degrees (one a daughter, one a mother), and two juris doctorate degrees.

Institutionalization of the HMDP at ASU has contributed to its success. The initial grant from the Ford Foundation concentrated on persistence through high school. When the grant ended, ASU incorporated the program within the university. The formal adoption of this program by the institution sent a message of support to the community and facilitated the slight shift in focus from high school graduation to include completion of a four-year degree.

Hispanic Business Student Association

The Hispanic Business Students Association (HBSA) was established at ASU in 1974. Its mission is to meet the challenges of the 21st century by providing leadership skills for students and preparing them to be future leaders who serve Hispanic communities, promote diversity, and bring about positive change. Members of HBSA come from different colleges and represent a variety of academic disciplines beyond business: communications, social and applied sciences, and liberal arts. HBSA has a long history of collaboration with other groups within and outside the university, including other student organizations, community organizations, and business and industry. The leaders of HBSA are committed to enhancing the cultural and social awareness of members by sponsoring various events throughout the year.

HBSA officers are elected each semester, providing ample opportunity for all members to hold leadership positions of increasing responsibility. A close working relationship with the organization's advisor of 23 years, strong ties to the university and local community, and an active network of HBSA alumni in the local community facilitate the tradition of professionalism of HBSA. This campus organization maintains a close relationship with community groups precisely because so many HBSA alumni work in Arizona businesses and continue to foster collaborations with their alma mater. These close relationships offer wonderful opportunities to HBSA members: Students are able to network with potential employers, and employers are provided a chance to recruit students with strong leadership skills. Alumni have risen to positions of influence and are able to direct money and efforts back to HBSA, thus creating a cyclical pattern of recruitment and support. Many opportunities are offered specifically through the Spring Recruitment workshop, an HBSA career fair that has occurred annually for the past 18 years.

HBSA's focus is the overall success of its members, and the students' commitment to excellence on the university campus extends to the surrounding community. Each year, the organization identifies one major community service project, and students work throughout the year in support of this project. In addition to community service, there are a number of events sponsored by HBSA that promote and celebrate college success in and out of the classroom. These include career fairs, workshops with local leaders, social events, leadership conferences, award ceremonies, and Target 4.0 luncheons, where students who received 4.0 on a test, paper, or as an overall GPA are recognized. The majority of HBSA members are female, and while the membership is open to all students, almost all members are Hispanic. Approximately 2,700 students have participated in HBSA over the past 27 years, and roughly 92% of HBSA members have completed their undergraduate degrees.

Leadership opportunities are identified as the key ingredient to success offered to HBSA members. Students learn to plan, communicate with students, faculty, and other individuals, and most important, learn to deal with unexpected difficulties and obstacles. These skills are invaluable during the college experience, in particular for ethnic minority students, enabling them to navigate the university system successfully.

Summary

Four themes run consistently through these programs designed to support the college transitions of Latinos: (a) creation of community, (b) collaboration with other groups, (c) community service, and (d) validation of students. The creation of community is essential to make a successful transition in college. Academic learning communities are facilitated by tutoring, workshops that focus on academic skills, and in the case of the HBSA, identifying students who have the same major. The importance of a social connection with other students and with faculty and staff is not overlooked; in fact, the academic and social communities are often intertwined. For example, students attend social gatherings immediately after most HBSA meetings. Vital in the establishment of a community is a physical space where students can gather. The Doran program views its central location on campus as one factor that contributes to the success of the program; students are able to spend time in the office between classes, connecting with others in the program. The emphasis on belonging to a community is cited by all four programs as a key factor of success.

Collaboration with other university departments as well as outside organizations round out each of these programs. The programs acknowledge that they cannot provide a comprehensive program for students without assistance from other areas. Puente works in collaboration with not only high school counselors and teachers but also with college professors and community leaders. When such programs partner with university academic departments, tutoring services, or admissions counselors, they are better equipped to educate the students and introduce them to various aspects and services of the campus.

Community service is a formalized component in three of the programs. Student engagement in community service not only enhances the resources available to the local community but also facilitates a sense of responsibility and accomplishment within students themselves. In addition, engagement with the local community enables students to develop organizational and leadership skills.

Finally, validation of students plays a premier role in the success of the programs. Validation theory, as introduced by Rendón (1994), highlights the importance of institutional support and acknowledgement, particularly for Latino/a students. These programs hold recognition ceremonies, ranging from monthly luncheons to annual award receptions. Beyond the formal recognition programs; however, there is a need to validate students in informal ways as well. Connecting students with peer mentors is a practice each of the programs employs. In addition to pairing students with one another, a connection with faculty and/or staff is viewed as important. The HMDP's monthly one-on-one meetings have offered HMDP staff the opportunity to know students on an individual basis, as well as provide the student a chance to strengthen the connection with the program, the staff, and the university.

The themes discussed above support Gonzalez's (2000) assertion that when institutions of higher education address the social, physical, and epistemological worlds of Latino college students, increases in persistence and graduation rates may be achieved. The K-16 Latino/a student population in the United States will continue to grow at a faster rate than any other ethnic group. As this group reaches college age, institutions of higher education must focus on new recruitment and retention strategies. Successful strategies and programs currently exist in a multitude of designs and fashions and, when institutionalized, can provide a venue for wide-scale efforts to assist postsecondary institutions in the persistence of Latino students. At a minimum, existing programs can also serve as a guide to develop, fund, and generate programs that best fit the institution and the Latino population it purports to serve.

Authors' Note

The terms Hispanic and Latino/a are used interchangeably throughout this chapter. There is no "universal" term which best describes the largest ethnic minority group in the United States. Hispanic and Latino/a are the two most common terms used among this group and also widely used in research and various other publications. Moreover, Hispanic and Latino comprise two "umbrella" terms that attempt to represent a diversity of the ethnic populations including, but not limited to Mexican Americans or Chicanos, Puerto Ricans, Cubans, Dominicans, South Americans, and Central Americans. Moore and Pachon (1985) state that a number of factors bring Latinos or Hispanics together as a group: "urban residency, disproportional poverty, the experience of prejudice and discrimination, ...and the large increase in their total number" (p. 37).

References

Althusser, L. (1971). Ideology and idealogical state apparatuses. In *Lenin and philosophy, and other essays* (B. Brewster, Trans.). New York: Monthly Review Press.

American Council on Education (1999-2000). *Minorities in higher education 1999-2000: Eighteenth annual status report*. Washington, DC: Author.

Attinasi, L. C. (1989). Getting in: Mexican American's perceptions of university attendance and the implications for freshman year experience. *Journal of Higher Education, 60*, 247-277.

Bennett, C., & Okinaka, A. M. (1990). Factors related to persistence among Asian, Black, Hispanic, and White undergraduates at a predominately White university: Comparisons between first- and fourth-year cohorts. *Urban Review, 22*, 33-60.

Ceja, M. (2000). *An exploratory study of first-generation Chicana college choice.* Paper presented at the annual meeting of the American Educational Research Association, New Orleans, LA.

Gandara, P., (1998). Capturing Latino students in the academic pipeline. *Chicano/Latino Policy Project Report*. Berkeley, CA: Institute for SocialChange.

Ginorio, A., & Huston, M. (2001). *Yes we can: Latinas in school*. Washington, DC: American Association of University Women Educational Foundation.

Gonzalez, K. P. (2000). Toward a theory of minority student participation in predominately White colleges and universities. *Journal of College Student Retention, 2*, 69-91.

Gonzalez, K. P., & Stoner, C. (2001). *"But who will take care of her?" The tensions of Latinas leaving home for elite universities.* Paper presented at the annual meeting of the Association for the Study of Higher Education, Richmond, VA.

Hurtado, S. (1992). Campus racial climate: Contexts of conflict. *Journal of Higher Education, 102,* 330-351.

Hurtado, S. (1994). The institutional climate for talented Latino students. *Research in Higher Education, 35,* 21-39.

Hurtado, S., Carter, D. F., & Spuler, A. (1996). Latino student transition to college: Assessing difficulties and factors in successful college adjustment. *Research in Higher Education, 37,* 135-157.

Jenson, R. J., & Hammerback, J. C. (2002). *The words of Cesar Chavez.* College Station, TX: University of Texas A&M Press.

Laden, B. V. (1999). Socializing and mentoring college students of color: The Puente Project as an exemplary celebratory socialization model. *Peabody Journal of Education, 74,* 55-74.

Moore, H., & Pachon, J. (1985). *Hispanics in the United States.* Englewood Cliffs, NJ: Prentice-Hall.

Nieves-Sequires, S. (1992). Hispanic women in the U.S. academic context. In L. Welch (Ed.), *Perspectives on minority women in higher education,* (pp. 75-76). Westport, CT: Praeger.

Nora, A., & Cabrera, A. F. (1996). The role of perceptions of prejudice and discrimination on the adjustment of minority students to college. *Journal of Higher Education, 67,* 119-148.

Olivas, M. A. (1986). *Latino college students.* New York: Teachers College Press.

Rendón, L. (1994). Validating culturally diverse students: Toward a new model of learning and student development. *Innovative Higher Education, 19,* 33-51.

Skinner, E., & Richardson, R. (1988). Making it in a majority university. *Change, 20,* 34-42.

Smedley, B. D., Myers, H. F., & Harrell, S. P. (1993). Minority-status stresses and the college adjustment of ethnic minority freshmen. *Journal of Higher Education, 64,* 434-451.

Stanz, M. (2001, March 25). Troubling label for Hispanics: Girls most likely to dropout. *New York Times.*

U.S. Census Bureau. (2001, April 2). *Difference in population by race and Hispanic or Latino origin, for the United States: 1990 to 2000.* Retrieved on April 1, 2003, from http://www.census.gov/population/cen2000/phc-t1/tab04.txt

Vasquez, M. J. T. (1982). Confronting barriers to the participation of Mexican American women in higher education. *Hispanic Journal of Behavioral Sciences, 4,* 147-166.

Western Interstate Commission for Higher Education, & The College Board. (1998). *Knocking at the college door: Projections of high school graduates by state and race/ethnicity 1996-2012.* Boulder, CO: Authors.

White House Initiative on Educational Excellence for Hispanic Americans. (1998). *Latinos in Education.* Retrieved from http://www.ed.gov/offices/OIIA/Hispanic/new/fact.pdf

Web Resources

Hispanic Mother Daughter Program:
http://www.asu.edu/studentlife/msc/hmdp.html
Puente Project:
http://www.puente.net/
Hispanic Business Student Association:
http://www.hbsa.org/

Chapter 9

Enhancing the First-Year Experience for Asian/Pacific Americans

Xiaoyun Yang and Xiaomei Feng

An Asian/Pacific American Student's Story

Min, a tall, shy, 20-year-old sophomore at a four-year public university in the southeastern United States, describes his college experience:

I was born in Korea and finished high school in the U.S. My dad has a Ph.D., and my mom has a bachelor's degree. They expect me to at least go to a graduate school and get a doctoral degree. My high school GPA was 5.6 [on a 6- point scale], and I was an honor student. In my freshman year [at college], I spent about 14 to 16 hours a week studying and spent more time if there were exams. I thought it would be easy to make straight A's at college, but it's not. English was the most difficult course. I have been through ESL courses. My English is okay, but [I] still have hard time to express my ideas [in class] and make them sound good. My peers think that I am a[n] "FOB" (fresh off the boat) because I am from Asia and not familiar with American culture. I live at home. My parents and family definitely provided the most support for me during my freshman year. After the first semester when I made my good friends, they [my new friends] also provided me with the kind of support my family couldn't. I liked the fact that we had a lot of different type[s] of people [on campus], including more Asians. I also liked different various types of clubs we could join, such as Kamikazi Dance Team and Asian Students Association.[1]

When asked whether the university had made an adequate effort to make him feel comfortable, he answered "yes" and "no." He explained,

I can definitely see that university is trying to reach out to all of the students to get them involve[d], especially the incoming students. For example, all of the different types of activities going on in freshmen dorms [such as] Freshmen Camp, etc. Since the university is so large, it is difficult to reach out to every student to get [everyone] involve[d]. I can see that the university is putting in effort, but sometimes I don't think they are trying hard enough. As an Asian-American student, I always think it would be great to have more programs and activities for us to get involve[d in] and feel comfortable.

If given another chance to start college, Min said,

> *I would have definitely lived on campus, because you meet a lot of people there....Being an Asian, I felt the pressure to study hard and get really good grades. Sometimes I wish I partied more and met more interesting people during my freshmen year, instead of staying at the library most of the time.*

Is Min's experience unique? What is the first-year college experience like for Asian/ Pacific Americans? How can their first-year experience be enhanced? To address these questions and gain understanding about Asian/Pacific Americans, this chapter discusses their diversity as well as their cultural, academic, and social adjustment during the first year of college. The discussion is framed by the use of national and institutional data as well as focus group interviews, so that both a macro- and micro-level view can emerge. Recommendations for serving this population are provided.

Diversity of Asian/Pacific American Students

College transition is stressful and difficult for all students. However, many Asian/ Pacific American (APA) students encounter additional problems that are unique to their transition to college, including language and cultural differences. Treating APA college students as a homogenous group and failing to take their extreme diversity into account exacerbate their difficulties. Additionally, the notion that all Asian Americans fit the "model minority" stereotype assumes that the group, as a whole, has no problems succeeding in college. This presumption masks individual and cultural differences (Goyette, 1999), which must be understood in all their richness and complexity if educators are to provide these students with much needed support.

Geography, Culture, and Religion

To begin to understand the APA population, it is necessary to recognize their diversity in terms of their immigration origin, history, culture, values, and religion. Geographically, they can be divided into four major groups:[2] East Asian, Pacific Islander, Southeast Asian, and South Asian. East Asian countries include China, Japan, Korea, and the Philippines; Pacific Island countries/areas include Fiji, Hawaii, and Samoa; Southeast Asian countries include Vietnam, Cambodia, Laos, Burma, Thailand, and Indonesia; and South Asia countries include India, Nepal, Bangladesh, and Sri Lanka (Trueba, Cheng, & Ima, 1993; see Figure 1). These groups share some commonalties, but differ in ethnicity, language, history, religion, culture, and values. For example, English is the official language for Indians and Filipinos. However, Chinese, Japanese, and Koreans have their own unique languages. Not surprisingly, the language barriers that many non-English speaking Asians face after immigrating to the United States can lead to academic challenges.

Diversity also exists among these groups in terms of their culture, values, and religion. For example, APAs have very diverse religious beliefs that range from Taoism (or Daoism), Buddhism, and Hinduism to Catholicism, Protestantism, and Islam. Buddhism and Taoism are the major religions in China and Vietnam. Buddhism is also a major religion in Japan, Korea, and many Southeast Asian countries, such as Cambodia, Laos, Thailand, and Burma. The dominant religions in the Phillipines are Catholicism and Protestantism. Indians are typically Hindu or Muslim; and Islam, Buddhism, and Christianity are the primary religions in Malaysia.

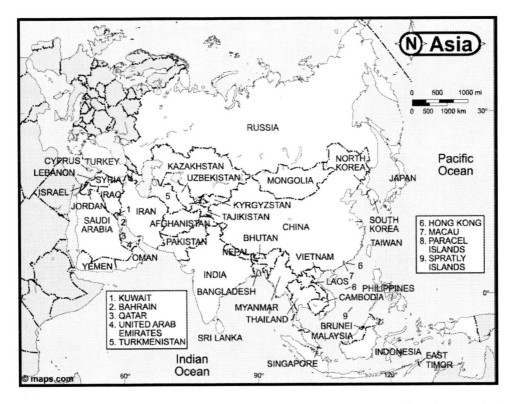

Figure 1. Map of Continental Asia. Copyright 1999 maps.com. Used with permission.

Different religions and unique cultures affect the value systems of APA students, which, in turn, impact their first-year adjustment to college life. For instance, the Confucian philosophy is very much alive in the daily behaviors, attitudes, and practices of Chinese, Koreans, Japanese, and Vietnamese (Trueba et al., 1993). This philosophy emphasizes the importance of education and hard work, which has played an important role in many Asian immigrants' success. Yet, it also demands self-reflection, moderation, and obedience to authorities or superiors. These values often conflict with those stressed "in modern, competitive industrial and technological societies" like the U.S. (Trueba et al., p. 29). Thus, it may be harder for Asian-American first-year students who follow these tenets to adjust to college.

Place of Birth

Differences between American-born Asian Americans and first-generation Asian-American immigrants may also impact their transition and adjustment to college. For example, American-born Asians experience a lifetime exposure to English and U.S. culture, which minimizes their college transition difficulties. In contrast, new immigrants face many more language and cultural barriers, because they are relatively new to the United States. According to Jamieson, Curry, and Martinez (2001), almost all APA college students have at least one foreign-born parent (91%). Among these students, 60.6% were foreign-born. Many of these foreign-born students have language problems in the classroom, and some reports suggest they score lower on the verbal portion of the SAT than White students (*The Chronicle of Higher Education*, 1999). This finding has negative implications for their college admission and classroom success if and when they get to college.

Academic Achievement

Differences also exist among Asian groups in their academic motivations and achievements. Although many Asian Americans are highly motivated to succeed academically, Cambodian and Laotian immigrants are often seen as lacking motivation. One reason for this is that their communities fail to see learning as necessary or desirable (Trueba et al., 1993). Thus, college-age students from these groups have enormous obstacles to overcome. Not only do they lack familial and community support for going to college, they must also overcome barriers other first-generation college students face because very few of their families have any college experience. Limited experience with higher education causes many first-generation students to see college as a "significant and intimidating cultural transition" (Terenzini et al., 1994). Thus, this segment of the APA population confronts both cultural and situational issues that other students do not face.

As stated previously, many APAs encounter language barriers. In order to accommodate their language deficiencies, they tend, or are advised, to choose quantitative-related careers or majors, such as engineering, health professions, and pre-professional programs, rather than social sciences or humanities (Hune & Chan, 2000; Suzuki, 1994; Tan, 1994). Because of their own academic insecurities and an inaccurate assumption of their strengths, entire fields and professions are foreclosed to them.

Socioeconomic Status

APA students' problems are not limited to language alone. Although they are thought to be better off economically than other ethnic groups, the truth is that some Asian groups are struggling to make ends meet. Foreign-born APAs tend to have lower socioeconomic status than their American-born counterparts (Kitano & Daniels, 2001; Osajima, 1995; Trueba et al., 1993). Statistically, poverty rates for Asian Americans are slightly higher than the national average (14%, compared to 13%), and "foreign-born Asian Americans [have] a higher rate of poverty, 16 percent, than native-born, 10 percent" (Kitano & Daniels, p.183). The socioeconomic status of many south Pacific and Southeast Asians is far lower than that of White Americans and other Asian-American groups (Goyette, 1999). Indeed, "Southeast Asian refugees had the highest rates of poverty: 26 percent of Vietnamese Americans, 35 percent of Laotian Americans, 43 percent of Cambodian, and 64 percent of Hmong were in poverty status" (Kitano & Daniels, p.183).

With lower economic capital, these students may also be less familiar with and have less access to the educational system than their American-born peers. Research confirms that students from lower socioeconomic status families feel academic and aspirational limits, as well (Walpole, 1998). Thus, these students tend to confront more college transition challenges for a number of reasons.

Therefore, diversity in terms of culture, religion, values, socioeconomic background, and academic achievement exists among this population. Language deficiencies, financial issues, and first-generation status are just a few of the challenges that some APA students face. Thus, it is misleading to put APA students under one umbrella and assume they will have no or very few problems in their first year in college.

Overview of Research

To identify the unique circumstances first-year APA students face, we studied national, institutional, and individual data. At the national level, we used the National Education Longitudinal Study (NELS) data (National Center for Education Statistics, 2000), which provides aggregate, national demographic information about first-year APA college students. At the institutional level, we used data from a U.S. west coast two-year institution, which represents an educational sector seeing a rapid increase in the enrollment of APAs. Finally, qualitative data were collected in a southeastern university, where 16 APA students were interviewed. These interviews allowed us to get a more in-depth understanding of the first-year college experience of these Asian Americans.

The national data. The National Education Longitudinal Study (NELS) was first administered in 1988 to an eighth-grade cohort. Follow-ups took place in 1990, 1992, and 1994 when the students in the baseline sample were high school sophomores, seniors, and first-year college students or in the labor market. The NELS data were used to obtain some demographic information about first-year APA college students nationwide. It provided comparison information among APAs, Whites, and Blacks and made comparisons within APA groups, as well. For this study, 950 White (non-Hispanic) and 737 other ethnic minorities including Hispanic, Black (non-Hispanic), and American Indian were randomly selected to compare with 950 APA students in the sample, which included Chinese (24%), Filipinos (20%), Japanese (7%), Koreans (15%), Southeast Asian (19%), South Asian (9%), and Pacific Islanders (6%).[3]

Institutional data. A study was conducted at a community college on the west coast of the U.S. exploring the needs and characteristics of the first-year APAs at this institution. The ethnic distribution at the college was 31.6% White, 29.7% Hispanic, 22.0% APA, 12.4% Black, 3.3% Other Non-White, and 1.0% Native American. The target population in this study was first-time admitted students who had indicated that their educational goal was to transfer to a four-year university or to earn an associate degree. These students had no previous college experience. In order to increase the sample size of certain small sub-groups within the APA student sample, six semesters' worth of data, from Fall 1997 to Spring 2000 (excluding summer sessions), were pooled and included in the study. A total of 1,070 APA students were in the sample: 42.2% were Cambodian, 20.7% Filipinos, 3.6% Chinese, 2.0% Japanese, 2.0% Koreans, 7.3% Pacific Islanders, 5.4% Vietnamese, and 16.8% other Asian groups.[4]

Individual data. A qualitative study provided a closer examination of APAs' adjustment to college life at a predominantly White southeastern, four-year public university. A "snowball" sampling method was used, beginning with a first-year Korean-American student who was recommended by a student worker in our office. In turn, this Korean-American student recommended three other Asian-American students. These students participated in the first focus group interview that lasted three hours. Through them, more Asian-American first-year students and sophomores were identified and more group interviews were conducted. Sixteen APA students participated in the study: five were males and 11 were females. Four Chinese Americans, four Korean Americans, two Japanese Americans, two Indian Americans, one Thai American, one Laotian American, one Vietnamese American, and one Hmong American were among the participants. Twelve of the students participating were in their first-college year; four were sophomores. Their majors included business, biology, chemistry, engineering, and pharmacy. Two were majoring in arts and science, and one was undecided.

Issues and Challenges: Findings from the Research

Student Background

The national profile provided by the NELS data confirms a wide diversity among APA students. For more than half of the APA families, English was not the only or dominant language in their households. In addition, when comparisons were made within APA groups, South Asian and Japanese students were more likely to come from higher socioeconomic backgrounds, while Southeast Asian and Pacific Islanders were less likely to come from such backgrounds. South Asian, Chinese, Korean, and Japanese students had higher scores on standardized tests than other Asian groups. Not surprisingly, they also had higher educational expectations, as more than four fifths of them planned to pursue advanced degrees after college education.

Cultural Adjustment

NELS data suggest that the majority of first-year APA college students are immigrants. As previously stated, they often have language deficiencies and experience cultural conflicts at school. Some of these conflicts are the result of the students' Confucian values, and the students may feel challenged by the educational environment and teaching and learning styles advocated in the United States. Immigrant students tend to be passive learners and lack critical thinking skills because of their backgrounds, thus they have to adjust to the active learning style that dominates many U.S. classrooms. Unfamiliar with the concept that they play a crucial role in the educational process, these students tend to withhold their questions during the learning process and avoid confrontations with faculty when problems occur.

This perspective was confirmed in the focus group interviews we conducted. During the interview, when asked "How involved in class were you in your freshmen year?", most of the students answered that they "keep quiet most of the time" in class. One student said, "I think it's the culture and a courtesy. It's a matter of consideration. I would feel selfish to ask questions in class that others may not be interested [in]. I don't think I have the right to waste other people's time."

As noted, the culture and language barriers may be less problematic for American-born Asians. Two of the three students who said that they "actively engage in class discussions" and "ask questions in class" were American-born and the other one finished high school in the U.S. Thus, inherent cultural differences may be more profound in immigrant populations, resulting in negative educational experiences.

Academic Adjustment

Expectations. Asian parents generally have high expectations for their children's education. The NELS data showed that 42% of Asian parents compared to 18% of White and 19% of other ethnic minority parents expected their children to receive a post-graduate education. These educational expectations may be internalized, as more than half of the APA students wanted to pursue advanced degrees after college.

Academic preparedness. Academic preparedness is a key factor to a successful college transition. The NELS data showed that Asian and White student achievement was similar in reading and on standardized tests of science. Asian students performed better in math than their White peers. Among the APA groups, South Asian students achieved the highest scores in reading and science. Chinese and Korean students performed as well as the South Asian students in math. However, academic achievement is not a given among APA students: Pacific Islanders ranked the lowest of all ethnic groups on the three standardized tests.

The data from the community college on the west coast provide a possible explanation for the differences in academic preparation. At this institution, first-year APA students had the lowest skill levels in English and reading of all ethnic groups including Whites, Blacks, and Hispanics. The data also showed that these APA students were less likely to use English as their primary language than other groups. The findings suggest that first-year APA college students whose dominant language is not English face serious language challenges, which may affect their performance in English, reading, and other subjects and in other aspects of college life.

Discrimination

In terms of school environment, some first-year APA students experienced racial and ethnic discrimination on campus. The focus group interviews help us gain a deeper understanding of the students' experiences. Among the 16 Asian-American students interviewed, eight felt that the university had made an adequate effort to make them feel comfortable. They had not experienced or paid attention to racial harassment or discrimination during their first year. However, six students stated that they had personally experienced, witnessed, or heard about incidents of racial harassment or discrimination during their first year at the university. These students did not think that the university's efforts were adequate in dealing with problems of racism on campus, especially racism directed against Asians. One student stated,

> *I think that racism regarding black and white, yes there is lots of awareness and publicity surrounding that issue, sometimes too much, because people are reminded of the division every day through the editorials or hearing others speak and not necessarily their own experience. As for Asian Americans, there are not enough of us [on this campus] that are political enough to confront the issue and there is not much awareness at all.*

Another student said, "I don't think the university does anything to alleviate this. In fact, the administration is rather lax on this issue, and I think it neglects the topic and leaves most of this responsibility to the students and student-run organizations." Therefore, this institution could do more to create a healthier and more comfortable environment for these students. Offering various support services and programs on campus is essential, but students must also feel empowered to develop their own support systems.

Support Systems

Student support systems. It is critical for the first-year APA students to have their own support system in the transition to college—one that helps them make good academic decisions and develop a sense of belonging. Those who were interviewed felt that the most difficult obstacles in their first year included: "choosing a major," "having a sense of belonging," achieving "English proficiency," dealing with "homesickness," and "staying focused on my studies." When asked who helped them most during their first year in college, they listed friends, family members/relatives, roommates, and upper-class peers. Some students noted that "finding friends of their own culture" helped them establish their own identity and a sense of belonging on campus.

School support services and programs. The institutional data provides a revelatory snapshot of the diverse interests in services that these community college APA students want or need (see Figure 2). The support services and programs provided by the college fall into four categories: (a) financial aid; (b) employment-related services—career planning, job placement, and work experience; (c) academic counseling—orientation, major selection, counseling, Extended Opportunity Program and Services (EOPS)[5], and transfer; and (d) tutoring in a wide range of subjects. The value from 1 to 8 reflects the degree of importance (from least to most important) of a program to a particular group.

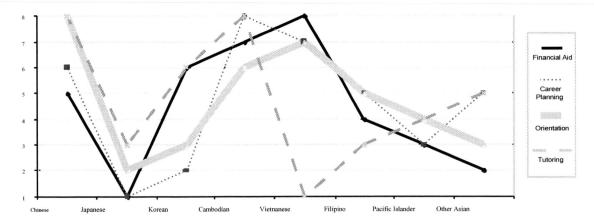

Figure 2. Comparison of First-Year Asian/Pacific Americans' Interests in School-Provided Support Programs and Services. Importance of programs measured on a scale of 1 to 8, with 8 being the most important.

The results show that different types of students desire different types of services. The variance reflects the great diversity in the APA student population. For example, Chinese students were most interested in academic counseling services and tutoring programs and fairly interested in employment-related services, whereas Korean students showed interest in financial aid and tutoring programs. Cambodian students were interested in all the programs and services, but Japanese students did not show high interest in any of the support programs and services. Thus, each group had very different needs.

Suggestions and Recommendations

In order to enhance the experience of this widely diverse group, the following suggestions and recommendations are provided.

Understand the diversity among this population. First-year APA students come from various backgrounds with different needs. Each group has its own unique culture, religion, and history. Treating APA students as a homogeneous group neglects the unique problems some sub-groups face. Workshops on this group's diversity and wide-ranging needs will help administrators, faculty, counselors, and student services staff promote cultural awareness and sensitivity. Regularly held workshops better prepare administrators, faculty, counselors, and student services staff to help these first-year college students.

The entire college/university community must work together to create an accepting, understanding, and comfortable climate on campus where biases are challenged and differences are understood and appreciated. This, in turn, leads to an environment that facilitates personal and professional growth for not only first-year APAs, but for all students.

Make continuous collaborative efforts on campus. As implied above, collaborative efforts from decision-makers, administrators, counselors, faculty, staff, and students themselves are required for first-year APA students to have a smooth college transition. Collaboration between all administrative units and faculty is crucial to develop effective and inclusive first-year experience, outreach, academic assistance, and mentoring programs so that these students can receive the academic and social support they need.

Setting up an APA leadership program, like the one at the University of California at Davis, is a good way to involve a wide range of constituencies. Students provided the impetus for the Asian Pacific Islander Leadership Program (APILP) at UC Davis, but they had support from faculty and staff. In addition to other activities, the students hold Asian Pacific Islander Leadership retreats twice a year. The retreats include keynote speaker(s), workshops, social and team-building activities, and "family group" meetings. The workshops are led by students, alumni, graduate students, Counseling Center staff, Cross Cultural Center staff, and Student Programs and Activities Center staff, as well as Asian-American Studies faculty and staff. Students who have established themselves in the campus community are asked to be facilitators for the "family groups," small groups designed to encourage reflection and personal dialogue. To involve administrators directly in the program, retreat planners invite upper-level administrators, such as the vice chancellor for student affairs, to serve as the keynote speaker.

The retreat is a very effective way for the first-year APA college students to network with older, more established students, and with new students like themselves. These students also get to meet and work with staff, faculty, and administrators outside the traditional classroom or office setting. These opportunities enable the first-year students to feel more connected to campus.

Establish mentoring programs and support groups on campus. "Living on campus" and "experiencing college life with their fellow students" are viewed as very important by the first-year APA students. As Min, a sophomore student, recommended, "make friends, they'll help you through college." Like many first-year students, these students especially enjoy the opportunity to learn from their upper-class peers.

One way universities and colleges can foster these connections and assist first-year students in their college transition is through special mentoring programs that pair upper-class students and first-year APA students. Ideally, students should be paired with students who are from the same cultural backgrounds whenever possible. Connecting new students with an older, already successful student with whom they share a cultural history facilitates the mentoring relationship, making its impact on the transition experience more profound. Such mentoring relationships help first-year college students choose a major and improve their time management skills, in addition to acclimating them to the social aspects of campus life. An added benefit is accrued by the upper-class student, who gains a sense of pride and community spirit in guiding younger peers.

In addition to these peer relationships, it is important to pair first-year APA students with faculty from similar cultural backgrounds or faculty who are willing to mentor APA students. These faculty-student connections allow students the opportunity to have informal, one-on-one contact with faculty members outside the classroom, which is viewed as one of the most important factors in retaining APA students in college (Hodne, 1997).

Recruit more APA faculty and staff. Students of color feel that mentoring relationships with individuals from similar cultural backgrounds provide critical support (Ancis, Sedlacek, & Mohr, 2000). APA students are no different. They feel comfortable seeking help from faculty, staff, or counselors who share similar cultural backgrounds (Yeh & Wang, 2000). Thus, it is important for universities to recruit APA faculty and staff. However, there is a gap between the proportion of APA faculty and students on campus (Hune & Chan, 2000). In 1999, 6.4% of students in degree-granting institutions were APA, but only 5.7% full-time faculty members were APA (NCES, 2001). The picture among administrators is even less encouraging, because Asian Americans "represent less than 2 percent of all college and university administrators" (Harvey, 2001, p. 45). In order to close the gap and better serve first-year APA college students, institutions must hire more APA faculty, administrators, counselors, and staff, so that they can be advisors, mentors, and role models and serve as a bridge between campus decision-makers and students.

Assist in the improvement of English language skills. First-year APA college students whose dominant language is not English have more difficulty making the transition to college. These students need additional support to enhance their understanding of, participation in, and integration into mainstream America. It is critical for these students to develop their verbal ability and writing skills during the first-year in college because their English proficiency affects academic progress, first-year college transition, college life, careers, and future social mobility.

To help APA students improve their English verbal and written skills, English language courses at all levels should be available. Additionally, faculty can use different pedagogical strategies, such as small-group discussions, group projects, and class presentations, to encourage any reticent students to speak up, be more involved in class, and interact more with their peers after class. In addition, faculty should be more patient and encouraging when these students have difficulties expressing their ideas in class. Faculty can also help APA students realize that asking questions and participating in discussions will benefit other students.

Organize diversified cultural events and club activities on campus. Offering a variety of extracurricular activities will help first-year APA students persist in college. Two students who were interviewed said that they wished they had participated in more activities outside the classroom. Another one wished that she had taken on some leadership roles the first year in college. Institutions can and should support specialized, student-run organizations on campus, such as Asian Students Organization, Asian Culture Club, and Asian/Pacific American Leadership Program. These organizations provide tremendous opportunities for the first-year Asian/Pacific Americans to learn and grow, as UC Davis has done with their Asian Pacific Islander Leadership Program. Campuses can also host cultural and academic events (e.g., Asian culture week) to promote awareness and understanding. In addition, providing multiple social opportunities for all first-year students and for more advanced students promotes cultural understanding and tolerance, helping these students have a more inclusive sense of community.

Help students overcome cultural barriers. Promoting both western and eastern culture awareness is essential. Some first-year APA college students, especially those who are foreign-born and influenced by Confucian philosophy, experience cultural conflicts and constantly try to balance two competing value systems. When they have problems, they traditionally keep the problems to themselves or blame themselves for not having tried harder. As one Korean-American student put it, "my parents have taught me that if I have a problem, it's because I have not tried hard enough." Helping students find the common ground where the east and west cultures and values overlap is essential if they are to maintain their own cultural identities and participate successfully in western culture. Such an effort requires collaboration from faculty, administrators, staff, counselors, and students themselves. For example, by providing support programs and cultural awareness workshops open to everyone on campus, institutions can help students overcome cultural barriers and realize that they do not have to struggle alone. Faculty and staff can encourage all students to take advantage of the programs and services on campus and seek professional help when they face obstacles or challenges. Students also need help negotiating experiences of prejudice and racism so that they do not internalize negative beliefs about themselves. Because high achievements are valued by many Asian Americans, APA students need to learn to reward themselves and give themselves credit for their hard work and accomplishments. By doing so, they will learn to evaluate and position themselves appropriately so they can adopt positive strategies that help them overcome obstacles. A successful first-year experience will help these students achieve a satisfying college experience, which will lay the foundation for their integration into mainstream America and subsequently, a successful career and happy life.

Summary

Colleges and universities provide students with tremendous opportunities. APA first-year college students view study as the most important aspect of college. They are also willing to and interested in participating in other activities on campus. However, some students, because of their background, culture, and the pressure to be a "model minority," feel compelled to be exemplary students. While their dedication to academic excellence should be encouraged, colleges also need to help these APA students realize that learning has a broader meaning, which includes academic success, personal growth, political maturity, and future preparedness. The role of the college is to help students grow in each of these aspects.

Colleges and universities are places where first-year APA students overcome their cultural barriers, master English for their survival needs, seek knowledge and skills, and combine the strengths of both western and eastern cultures and values for their academic success and personal growth. Some enter college unsure of themselves and their futures. Only with combined efforts from the whole campus community can they have a successful first-year college transition and become actively engaged in a wide range of extracurricular activities, such as sports, social events, student government, and political activism. Colleges can help first-year APA students realize that both a focus on academics and an openness to a wide range of interests are essential in reaching their full potential.

First-year APA students can achieve a sense of belonging by interacting with students from similar cultural backgrounds. However, universities must also provide opportunities for students, faculty, and administrators from different backgrounds to learn and gain strengths from other cultures and values. A truly diverse and welcoming environment will foster learning, understanding, acceptance, and tolerance. These environments can only be created and maintained through continuous efforts from the whole campus community. Only in positive, culturally diverse environments, can the first-year APA students and all other first-year students truly learn, succeed, and become prepared for the ever changing and diverse world.

Notes

[1]Quotes from Min and other students in this chapter are taken from focus group interviews conducted by Xiaoyun Yang.

[2]The Middle East Asian Americans are not included in this study.

[3]Xiaomei Feng conducted the analysis of NELS data reported on in this chapter.

[4]Laura Tang at Long Beach City College conducted the study on the experiences of APA college students in the community-college setting. The authors would like to thank her for her contribution to the chapter.

[5]Extended Opportunity Program and Services (EOPS) program's primary goal is to encourage the enrollment, retention, and transfer of students disadvantaged by language, social, economic, and educational barriers and to facilitate the successful completion of

their goals and objectives in college. EOPS offers academic support, counseling, financial aid, and other support services.

References

Ancis, J. R., Sedlacek, W. E., & Mohr, J. J. (2000). Student perceptions of campus cultural climate by race. *Journal of Counseling & Development, 78,* 180-185.

Chronicle of Higher Education. (1997, August 27). Almanac Issue 1999. Washington, DC: The Chronicle of Higher Education.

Goyette, K. (1999). *Application to college: A comparison of Asian American and White high school students.* Paper presented at the Annual Meeting of the American Educational Research Association. Montreal, Canada. (ERIC Document Reproduction No. ED 432 623)

Harvey, W. B. (2001). *Minorities in higher education. 2000-2001: Eighteenth annual status report.* Washington, DC: American Council on Education.

Hodne, B. D. (1997). Please speak up: Asian immigrant students in American college classrooms. *New Directions for Teaching and Learning, 70,* 85-92.

Hune, S., & Chan, K. S. (2000). Educating Asian Pacific Americans: struggles and progress. In T. P. Fong & L. H. Shinagawa (Eds.), *Asian Americans: Experiences and perspectives.* Upper Saddle River, NJ: Prentice Hall.

Jamieson, A., Curry, A., & Martinez, G. (2001). *School enrollment in the United States—social and economic characteristics of students, October 1999, current population reports.* Washington, DC: U.S. Department of Commerce, U.S. Census Bureau.

Kitano, H. H. L., & Daniels, R. (2001). *Asian Americans: Emerging minorities.* Upper Saddle River, NJ: Prentice Hall.

National Center for Education Statistics. (2000). National education longitudinal study of 1988. [Data set]. Retrieved March 25, 2004, from http:/www.nces.edugov/surveys/nels88/index.asp

National Center for Education Statistics. (2001). Fall enrollment survey, 1999. Washington, DC: U.S. Department of Education, Integrated Postsecondary Education Data System.

Osajima, K. (1995). Racial politics and the invisibility of Asian Americans in higher education. *Educational Foundations, 9,* 35-53.

Suzuki, B. H. (1994). Higher education issues in the Asian American community. In M. J. Justiz, R. Wilson, & L. G. Bjork (Eds.), *Minorities in higher education.* Washington, DC: American Council on Education, Oryx Press.

Tan, D. L. (1994). Uniqueness of the Asian-American experience in higher education *College Student Journal, 28*(4), 412-421.

Terenzini, P. T., Rendon, L. I, Upcraft, M. L., Millar, S. B., Allison, K. W., Gregg, P. L., & Jalomo, R. (1994). The transition to college: Diverse students, diverse stories. *Research in Higher Education, 35*(19), 57-73.

Trueba, H. T., Cheng, L., & Ima, K. (1993). *Myth or reality: Adaptive strategies of Asian Americans in California.* Washington, DC: The Falmer Press.

Walpole, M. (1998). *Class matters: How social class shapes college experiences and outcomes.* Unpublished doctoral dissertation. University of California, Los Angeles.

Yeh, C., & Wang, Y. W. (2000). Asian American coping attitudes, sources, and practices: Implications for indigenous counseling strategies. *Journal of College Student Development, 41*(1), 94-103.

Recommended Books and Articles

Books

Fong, T. P., & Shinagawa, L. H. (2000). *Asian Americans: Experiences and perspectives.* Upper Saddle River, NJ: Prentice Hall.

Lee, S. J. (1996). *Unraveling the "model minority" stereotype.* New York: Teachers College, Columbia University.

Liu, E. (1998). *The accidental Asian: Notes of a native speaker.* New York: Random House.

Nakanishi, D. T., & Nishida, T. Y. (1995). *The Asian American educational experience: A source book for teachers and students.* New York: Routledge.

Pang, V. O., & Cheng, L. R. L. (1998). *Struggling to be heard: The unmet needs of Asian Pacific American children.* New York: State University of New York Press.

Weinberg, M. (1997). *Asian-American education: Historical background and current realities.* Mahwah, NJ: Lawrence Erlbaum Associates.

Wu, F. H. (2001). *Yellow: Race in American beyond black and white.* New York: Basic Books.

Articles

Gregory, S. T. (2000). Strategies for improving the racial climate for students of color in predominately White institutions. *Equity & Excellence in Education, 33*(3), 39-47.

Hune, S. (1998). *Asian Pacific American women in higher education: Claiming visibility and voice.* Washington, DC: Association of American Colleges and Universities.

Liu, W. M., & Sedlacek, W. E. (1999). Differences in leadership and co-curricular perception among entering male and female Asian-Pacific-American college students. *Journal of The First-Year Experience, 11*(2), 93-114.

Solberg, V. S., Choi, K. H., Ritsma, S., & Jolly, A. (1994). Asian-American college students: It is time to reach out. *Journal of College Student Development, 35,* 296-301.

Ting, S. R. (2000). Predicting Asian Americans' academic performance in the first year of college: An approach combining SAT scores and noncognitive variables. *Journal of College Student Development, 41*(4), 442-449.

Yee, J. A., & Kuo, E. W. (2000). Bibliographic review essay: The experiences of Asian Pacific Americans in higher education. *Journal of Asian American Studies, 3*(1), 101-110.

Chapter 10

Enhancing the First-Year Experience for American Indians/Alaska Natives

Charles R. Colbert,
Joseph J. Saggio,
and Dawn Tato

Sophie became very animated and intense as she described her experience attending a small Bible college for American Indians and Alaska Natives (AI/ANs) in the southwest, several hours from her home in the White Mountains of northern Arizona. Her description was, in part, a response to a focus group question about difficulties she initially encountered as a first-year AI/AN college student:

> *[Anglos are] always moving and roaming these places, and Native Americans have that tie back home and I think that's what it is sometimes with students that go off the reservation . . . to this college . . . People don't care what you are doing or who you are—you're just another face in the crowd. And at home, you're somebody [because] they know your name. They know who mom and dad is, they know your clan, they know what community you came from. (Saggio, 2000a).*

Sadly, Sophie's case is not a unique one. Many AI/ANs feel lonely, disconnected, and disengaged from higher education. Ironically, the very vehicle (i.e., a college education) that is supposed to provide them with opportunities to improve the quality of their lives becomes for many an extremely disappointing experience. Although Sophie went on to graduate and pursue a career in teaching, many AI/AN students have been less fortunate.

Historically, AI/ANs have not fared well in gaining access and finding academic success in higher education (Colbert, 1999; Pavel, 1999). Many AI/ANs have consistently resisted federal policies of assimilation and have chosen to perpetuate their traditional ways of life. These roots of cultural persistence and the legacies of colonialism continue to result in their rejection of the higher education enterprise (Colbert; Wright, 1985). Pre-college data still suggest an inability of American Indians to perform well on standardized tests and meet important admission criteria (Pavel). The cultural-deficit model that attempts to correct the problem of AI/ANs' poor performance in higher education by suggesting that AI/AN cultures are "inferior" and need to be changed to be more like "White" culture is highly ethnocentric and fails to adequately address the overall complexity of issues that conspire to undermine attempts by American Indians to gain access to postsecondary institutions (Colbert; Pavel).

The Legacy of Colonialism

American Indians and Alaska Natives have a long history with higher education in the United States, and much of that experience has been unsuccessful by any standard. Much of mainstream America's knowledge of AI/ANs lies in the Indian-White relations over the past 500 years. As a consequence of forced colonial policies and systematic genocide during those years, AI/ANs have been reduced to 2 million members of 557 federally recognized tribes (220 of which are found in Alaska) living on 311 reservations (Russell, 1997).

According to current census figures, individuals identifying AI/AN as their only race, account for 0.9% of the total U.S. population (U.S. Census Bureau, 2001). Though small in total numbers, AI/ANs are proportionately represented within higher education as indicated by the National Center for Education Statistics (NCES). The Center (2002) reports that since 1996, AI/ANs comprised 1.0% of the higher education enrollment in degree-granting institutions. However, NCES data reveal that only 6.7% of AI/AN high school sophomores in 1980 earned a bachelor's degree by 1992, whereas 20% of the total number of high school sophomores completed a bachelor's degree during the same period.

Some effects of colonialism have been poor education systems, oppressed intellect (i.e., inability or inappropriate forums to use indigenous knowledge), and a negative impact on self-esteem and other self-development factors that are critical for success in the academic arena. Thus, the colonial legacy of AI/ANs continues to result in high drop-out rates from both high school and college, as well as enormous poverty for this population.

Further, much of the research on AI/ANs continues to be from a homogenous standpoint, viewing the AI/AN as a single ethnic group, though each individual and tribal group has different political and conceptual identities. Thus, this chapter addresses issues for first-year AI/AN college students in aggregate, while recognizing the wide diversity of this group.

Cultural Conflict

In their book *Native American Postcolonial Psychology*, Duran and Duran (1995) present "alternate" psychological approaches to the treatment of native peoples by incorporating indigenous worldviews. They challenge the mainstream theories of psychology and its practice, incorporating native approaches to healing, stating that "Without proper understanding of history, those who practice in the disciplines of applied social sciences operate in a vacuum, thereby merely perpetuating this ongoing neocolonialism" (p.1). This premise can be applied to education as well.

Many AI/AN students struggle to learn in the culture of mainstream institutions of higher education. Reports of high attrition rates from high school through postsecondary education have prompted traditional AI/ANs to encourage the next generation to learn the ways of both worlds so that they will not feel lost in either (Winik, 1999).

The cultural correlates of AI/AN college student success have been the target of some research studies. Such research has indicated that the extent to which Native American college students identify as being traditional (versus being acculturated, assimilated, or modern) contributes to their success. One study found that of five groups of Navajo students, those who described themselves as being of traditional Navajo background were more academically successful than those Navajos who were described as more acculturated (Deyhle & Swisher, 1997). Similarly, Lin (1990) looked at family value orientation of Native-American college students in Montana. Those students from families that were more modern reported skipping classes more often and having lower GPAs than those students whose families were more culturally traditional.

Another study by Lin, LaCounte, and Eder (1988) looked at 1986 institutional data to determine the effect of school environment on academic performance. They surmised that poor academic performance of AI/AN students is "...rooted in the 'concrete' difficulty experienced within the contextual situation of a college campus." (p.14). Specifically, environmental factors such as hostile attitudes of professors and feelings of isolation felt by AI/AN students on a mainstream campus contribute to lower GPAs for these students across disciplines and courses.

Kirkness and Barnhardt (1991) and Tierney (1992) have addressed the importance of cultural relevance for AI/AN students. They have discussed at length the importance of institutions recognizing and respecting the ethnic cultural needs of indigenous peoples. Both have stated that culturally responsive higher education institutions should provide programs and services that are more relevant for these students.

Other articles have emphasized the importance of a culturally sensitive faculty, which can greatly increase retention of AI/AN college students (Wright, 1985). Hornett (1989) recommends ways in which faculty may work more effectively with these college students, suggesting that faculty should remember that students respond differently in various situations. Therefore, instructors need to find effective ways of interacting with each student. Hornett offers some cultural considerations that faculty should take into account when interacting with Native students, for example, recognizing and dealing with subtle racial statements made in the classroom as well as recognizing and respecting Native leadership skills (i.e., collaborative versus authoritarian, multiple leaders versus single leader).

A study of First Nations students used Freire's dialogical inquiry method to examine oppression and levels of consciousness (Melchoir-Walsh, 1994). The study revealed a sense of sociocultural alienation among the First Nations students attending a Canadian higher education institution. These students expressed a sense of isolation on their campus even though this population represented 10% of the overall student body.

Similarly, Tierney (1991) points out that institutional integration often translates into assimilation for Native students. He claims that mainstream higher education expects all of its students to adapt to the institution rather than the institution adapting to the students. Likewise, Kirkness and Barnhardt (1991) criticize the assumptions of mainstream integration models and suggest that alternate institutional practices such as culturally relevant student services may increase participation and retention of AI/AN students.

Institutional responsibility and cultural relevance are evident in tribal colleges. More than a quarter of tribal college graduates are employed in critical fields on reservations (Wright, 2000). In addition, some research suggests that students who attend tribal colleges before attending mainstream institutions are more successful than those who do not first attend a tribal college (Yates, 2001). Mainstream institutions learning from and working with tribal colleges have the potential to strengthen the higher education pipeline for AI/AN students.

As the number of AI/AN students pursuing higher education increases, mainstream college and university administrators face mounting pressures from tribal communities to be accountable for serving the needs of Native students. The increased awareness of Native American higher education issues through research and practice will pave the way for a better learning environment for students of all nations.

Experiences that Enhance or Preclude First-Year Retention

Current research has identified a number of areas with which AI/AN first-year students struggle in their quest to persist in college. These relevant areas include cultural discontinuity (Colbert, 1999; Demmert, 1994; Saggio, 2000b, 2001; Saggio & Dempsey, 2003), low academic attainment (Benjamin, Chambers, & Reiterman, 1993; Gilbert, 1996; Pavel, 1999; Rendón, Nora, Gans, & Calleroz, 1997; Swisher & Hoisch, 1992; Wells, 1997), deficiencies in college preparation (Gilbert, 1996; Hill 1991; Lee, 1997; Pavel), the need for summer bridge programs (Kleinfeld, Cooper, & Kyle, 1987; Robert & Thomson, 1994), high school and college teachers who lack adequate cultural training (Almeida, 1996; Bowker, 1992; Demmert, 1996; Ledlow, 1992; Pavel; Pavel & Colby, 1992; Rehyner, 1991; Wells), and the lack of AI/AN role-models on college campuses in faculty and staff roles (Bowker; Falk & Aitken, 1984; Hill; Wells; Wright, 1991).

There are additional areas of concern outside of academe. Alcohol and drug problems are well documented in AI/AN communities and often begin long before college matriculation (Curley, 1984; Dehyle, 1992; Hodgkinson, 1992; Rehyner, 1991; Swisher & Hoisch, 1992). Educational opportunities for many AI/ANs are extremely limited because of the lack of a strong economic base and adequate financial aid. Many AI/ANs are either excluded from the academy or relegated to community colleges (Boyer, 1989; Brown, 1996; Rendón & Garza, 1996; Wright, 1991). The role of family support is paramount in helping students negotiate the cultural dynamics inherent in making the transition into higher education (Bowker, 1992; Pavel, 1991; Pavel & Padilla, 1993; Saggio, 2000b; Tinto, 1975, 1987, 1993; Wright, 1991). Students with strong family support are at a decided advantage over those who do not have it. AI/AN students transitioning into their first year will look to various family members for emotional and psychological support (Bowker; Saggio, 2000b).

AI/AN First-Year Retention Rates

Higher education researchers have clearly identified the first year of college as a crucial time in the academic and social formation of college and university students (Astin, 1991; Daughtry, 1992; Gardner, 1980, 1990; Tinto, 1987, 1993; Upcraft, 1991; Upcraft, Gardner, & Associates, 1989). For students, the first year is a critical time that determines the likelihood of continued persistence towards a bachelor's degree. Tinto (1993) determined that attrition for all full-time, first-time degree-seeking students is 53.3% in four-year colleges and 67.7% in two-year colleges.

If the problem of academic persistence is difficult for students in general, it is even more difficult for minorities, and especially for AI/AN students. Wells (1989) determined that more than half of AI/AN students who leave college before their graduation do so as first-year students. Pavel's (1999) data on AI/AN first-year persistence rates at Division II and Division III institutions (both public and private) show that AI/AN students persisted to their sophomore year at a rate of 14% lower than that of mainstream students in public Division II institutions and 17% lower in private Division II institutions. They fared slightly better in Division III institutions, with a persistence rate of 12% lower in both public and private institutions. Nonetheless, in all categories they persisted at a lower rate than the combined cohort of other students.

Even though persistence is an issue for AI/AN students, very few studies are available that specifically document first-year retention rates for AI/AN students (see Swisher & Hoisch, 1992; Wells, 1997). Retention models such as Tinto's (1975, 1987, 1993) and Astin's (1984, 1985a, 1985b) are undergirded primarily by data from mainstream majority college and university students and thus have their limitations when dealing with AI/AN students. Indeed, Rendón, Jalomo, and Nora (2000) have expressed criticism of mainstream models that do not take into account the unique dynamics of many minority students. Likewise, Tierney (1992) has expressed concern with the limitations of Tinto's research vis-à-vis AI/ANs.

Saggio (2000b) conducted one notable study on this issue. His research investigated persistence at a Bible college with a 78% AI/AN student population and an 86% first-year retention rate to gain a better understanding of why this institution succeeded in retaining its students. For this study, 29 students from 18 different tribes were interviewed, and their comments revealed four grounded concepts (i.e., family, spirituality, life experiences, and institutional culture) that impacted their persistence beyond the first year. Though no generalizations can be made from this study, it does give some insight into what helped AI/AN students persist beyond the first year at one institution.

For example, a strong supportive family background, where family members validated the students' institutional choice and ability to persist in their academic programs, was helpful. Strong religious faith, as expressed through spirituality, was also a determinant of successful persistence. The study also found that the students' life experiences, including positive and negative pre-collegiate experiences, as well as the development of time management and personal organizational skills helped students as they navigated their first year. Finally, the institutional culture, including the presence of culturally sensitive faculty and staff who validated students by encouraging their enrollment and persistence, made a positive impact in the lives of these AI/AN students.

Finally, according to "Creating Role Models for Change: A Survey of Tribal College Graduates" (2000), tribal colleges have a remarkable track record working with non-traditional students who are often female, single mothers, over 30 years of age, and first-generation college students (see also Boyer, 1989). Tribal colleges and universities have been successful at retention because they make it easier for non-traditional students to remain in school. For example, offering day care allows single mothers to pursue their education while providing a safe, nurturing environment for their children. These colleges also offer a curriculum that is tribally relevant and includes language studies. Further, they offer remedial instruction to those needing it and are close to home for most of the students, eliminating the necessity of lengthy travel to unfamiliar places where the student may not be comfortable (Boyer, 1989; Pavel, 1999; Stein, 1999). Finally, the majority of tribal colleges are two-year colleges that are able to focus on the specialized needs of lower-division students, including first-year students.

Strategies

This section includes strategies to help practitioners facilitate an increased likelihood of retention for AI/AN students past their first year. It seems important to recognize that just as Tierney (1995) has decried the "one size fits all" model used by American institutions, colleges and universities wishing to enroll and retain AI/AN students must make institutional adaptations so that AI/AN students who have different cultural needs from mainstream students can find their place within the academy. Based on Saggio's (2000b) findings, this section offers strategies from four perspectives or influences: (a) family, (b) spirituality, (c) life experiences, and (d) institutional culture.

Family

Institutions serving significant numbers of AI/AN students should keep the importance of the family's influence in mind when working with these students. Student affairs professionals must be aware that when they recruit AI/AN students they must attempt to involve various members of the student's family in the recruitment process. The nature of the familial influence may vary somewhat from tribe to tribe. For example, Bowker (1992) found that for Navajo females, the maternal influence was particularly strong. Because this may not be true for all tribal groups, the recruitment strategy must be tribally sensitive, and recruitment personnel must be appropriately trained to deal with the diversity of the tribes represented at their respective institutions. Recruitment practices should be reviewed periodically as new tribal groups are added to the pool of applicants. Tierney (1995) recommends to Native families that serious discussion about college choices should take place no later than ninth grade. The discussions should involve parents, grandparents, aunts, uncles, cousins, and siblings since Native American families typically operate as an "extended family" unlike many other segments of society (Martin & Farris, 1994). Recognizing the importance of extended family in college decisions of AI/AN students is essential for admissions counselors and for faculty and staff who encounter students after enrollment.

Classroom instructors need to be aware that AI/AN students may be called on to intervene in family emergencies such as illnesses, incarceration, and funerals. Cultural training should be provided to those educators working with significant numbers of AI/AN students so that they can be sensitive to these students and accommodate the students' needs, thus helping them to remain in the educational pipeline.

Spirituality

Institutions serving a large AI/AN population need to be cognizant of the influence of spirituality on these students. Tierney (1991, 1992) and Wright and Tierney (1991) have noted the importance of spirituality in their writings, although they emphasize traditional Native religions rather than Christianity. Saggio (2000b, 2001), on the other hand, notes the role of Christianity as a spiritual force among AI/AN students at a Bible college.

Certainly the impact of spirituality in AI/AN retention cannot be underestimated (Boyer, 1989; Colbert, 1999; Demmert, 1996; Saggio, 2000b, 2001; Tierney, 1991, 1992; Wright & Tierney, 1991). Historically, many educators have sought to "Christianize" Indians through forced indoctrination (Colbert, 1999; Demmert, 1996; Wright, 1991; Wright & Tierney, 1991). There have been sharp repercussions to this attempted "cultural genocide" (Colbert, 1999). As a result of the forced assimilation attempts by some missionaries in the past, today many AI/AN people wish to have nothing to do with the "White man's religion" and have rejected Christianity in favor of traditional Native beliefs. Boyer (1989) indicates that tribal colleges have been positively impacted by giving preeminence to tribal religious practices as well as allowing shamans, medicine men, and tribal elders to promote the practice of traditional tribal beliefs at their respective tribal colleges.

Student affairs professionals and faculty members need to be aware of the influence of spirituality in the lives of students. In religious colleges especially, that awareness can be reflected in student life programming, curriculum development, counseling practices, and relationships with institutional personnel. For AI/AN students who are of the Christian faith, private Christian colleges such as American Indian College in Phoenix, Arizona have a staff and faculty comprised of credentialed ministers who seek to minister to student spiritual needs through counseling, chapel and church attendance, and ministry outreach to the inner city, reservations, and overseas trips. While not all institutions will incorporate religion to such an extent, it can have an impact at all institutions. To serve AI/AN student spiritual needs, some institutions such as First Nations University of Canada, (formerly known as Saskatchewan Indian Federated College, a college within the University of Regina) employ "elder services" in which tribal elders are available under the auspices of student services for counseling and traditional spiritual guidance. Therefore, some efforts can be made in student services to address this powerful aspect in the lives of AI/AN students.

Life Experiences

Student services professionals need to understand the ongoing dynamics of the reservation settings including the influences of substance abuse, growing gang violence, and the development of tribal enterprises such as tribal gaming. Since many of the communities are in constant flux, practitioners need to constantly monitor trends and stay abreast of these developments. Those working with AI/AN students need to attend, as well as present, workshops on current sociological trends in the life experiences of AI/ANs. Needless to say, more practical and scholarly research needs to be conducted in this area.

Teaching faculty and student affairs professionals need adequate training on how AI/AN students solve problems and deal with self-esteem issues and life experiences. Practitioners who work with large AI/AN populations will need regularly updated information as higher education researchers investigate emerging trends. Institutions employing faculty and student affairs professionals who work with AI/AN populations should consider offering workshops and training before employment begins so that these individuals can be proactive in their understanding and problem-solving skills. Workshops and seminars should focus not only on the problem, but also highlight students who have strong intrapersonal skills and are able to persist. Both Tierney (1995) and Saggio (2000b, 2001) discuss the importance of presenting good role models for AI/AN students. Using these students as models may bring clarity to a difficult issue.

Institutional Culture

Mainstream higher education institutions must adapt their services to meet the needs of the growing numbers of AI/AN students. This has been a challenge for colleges and universities across the country. Tierney (1992) recommends the following to mainstream institutions:

> Academe must do more than officially encourage students to attend college on mainstream society's terms, for when this is done [Native] students generally encounter institutional discouragement. Instead, participants in academic organizations need to develop rituals of empowerment that enable [Native] students to celebrate their culture and become critically engaged in the life of the institution, their tribes, their families, and themselves. To do so offers American society vast potential for the 21st century and fulfills an obligation to Native Americans that has yet to be met. (p. 165)

Yet, even in institutions that serve predominantly AI/AN students, the development of a sense of community is extremely important for first-year students. For example, Saggio and Dempsey (2003) indicate that American Indian College in Phoenix, Arizona, recently implemented a new three-day Welcome Week for first-year students planned around the themes of commitment, community, and communion. The purpose of the Welcome Week is to initiate first-year students into the college community through a series of games, bonding experiences, and rituals that culminate in students receiving special pins during a chapel communion service identifying them as full-fledged members of the campus community.

Mainstream institutions should develop strategies for recruiting, retaining, and graduating AI/AN students. Earlier research and theories on college student persistence in higher education have indicated the need for students to fit into the culture and norms of the institution (Astin, 1984, 1985a, 1985b; Tinto, 1975, 1987, 1993). As enrollment and retention data indicate, this has not been effective for AI/AN college students. Institutions can address this gap by reassessing the student services practices that typically have been based on mainstream premises and mainstream college student participation research.

Institutional adaptation to AI/AN students. The first interpersonal contact an institution has with an accepted student may indicate how that institution values its students. Since the admissions office is one of the first points of contact for new students, this interaction can be the deciding factor for enrollment. This is particularly poignant for AI/AN students who may find their acceptance to a college or university surprising. Given this, mainstream institutions should provide focused outreach programs to tribal communities. Special recruitment and/or orientation events should be planned within tribal reservation boundaries and in predominant AI/AN urban communities. In many cases, AI/AN families do not have the financial resources that would allow them to attend on-campus events; nevertheless, AI/AN parents and guardians want to be there for their students as any parent would. Outreach to tribal communities would provide family members access to university staff and an opportunity for parents to become informed about the processes of college admissions and registration. Through such outreach efforts, the university demonstrates its interest in recruiting students from underrepresented communities.

Provide relevant services to AI/AN students. When an AI/AN student is accepted and plans to attend a mainstream institution, the college/university should be committed to helping that student succeed. One innovative approach involves an intergovernmental agreement between an institution of higher education and a tribal government, such as the agreement between Arizona State University (ASU) and the Navajo Nation. In 1996, ASU's administration and the Advisor on American Indian Affairs to the university's president worked together to negotiate an intergovernmental agreement with the Navajo Nation. This agreement stipulates that all entering first-year students at ASU who are tribal members and who have been granted a tribal college scholarship are required to participate in the Native American Achievement Program, a university retention program established as a result of the intergovernmental agreement. Existing student service programs and departments were involved in the design of the program whose purpose is to closely monitor and track participants in order to help them navigate the campus and to intervene appropriately to retain them. Its intent is to ease the student's transition and provide a supportive and nurturing environment.

One of the keys to the program's success has been the agreement between ASU and the tribal communities to have participants' tribal scholarship sent to the institution in one lump sum for incremental disbursement to students who have demonstrated active participation in the program. By receiving incremental disbursements from the tribal monies sent to the university, the student is accountable to both the tribe and the university. More important, the institution confirms its commitment to these students and to their tribal communities through proactive programming geared toward American Indian student needs. This type of agreement validates the tribe's sovereignty and, therefore, is a significant point of reference for other mainstream institutions.

Staffing for the Native American Achievement Program was also carefully considered. The institution employs Native-American staff to maintain the cultural relevance of its services. For instance, it is common for the staff to escort program participants to unfamiliar offices or programs, adhering to the original intent of the program to provide a secure sense of community within a large bureaucracy.

The student requirements for the program include regular visits with the program staff, individual visits with instructors, and attendance at informational workshops dealing with topics deemed relevant to student needs. Orientation and social activities are incorporated into the program to provide a well-rounded experience for students.

The program was institutionalized after the first year of operation because of its impact on significantly decreasing Navajo students' attrition. Institutionalizing this program signifies to tribal communities ASU's commitment to retaining and graduating American Indian students. As a result, more tribes have signed an intergovernmental agreement with the University thereby increasing the number and diversity of program participants. ASU did not have to create or allocate a large budget to develop this program since it relies on the collaboration and cooperation of existing campus programs and services.

Another example of a program that has had solid success with Native student retention is the Navajo Freshman Year Experience (NFYE), a two-year program that features a partnership between Northern Arizona University (NAU) in Flagstaff, Arizona and the Navajo Nation. The program begins with a summer orientation for Native students and includes closely monitoring grades and meeting regularly with retention specialists who are trained to anticipate questions and concerns.

Admittedly, these programs may not work at all institutions. As with any program or strategy, the outcome will depend on a number of factors such as institutional culture, human resources, political climate, leadership from the administration, and proximity to AI/AN communities. Nevertheless, mainstream institutions need to reexamine their practices for direct student services and find ways to provide culturally relevant approaches that allow AI/AN students to realize their higher education goals.

Out-of-class learning experiences. Tierney (1995) recognizes the importance of out-of-class learning experiences for AI/AN students. In fact, institutions wishing to draw and retain AI/AN students should sponsor strong co-curricular activities that celebrate Native heritage. For example, the Native American Student Association at Northeastern Oklahoma A & M College in Miami, Oklahoma provides opportunities for AI/AN students to develop pride and tribal identification through its activities that include fall and spring pow-wows, regular meetings, films, tribal dinners, and special speakers. Northeastern State University in Muskogee, Oaklahoma provides opportunities for Native students to develop as learners and leaders through the Indian University Scholars Society (IUSS). The organizations' governing body consists of Native students who are both traditional and non-traditional religious believers and who possess leadership expertise in business, sciences, tribal councils, and literature publication.

Overall, participation in extracurricular activities should increase involvement (Astin, 1984, 1985a, 1985b) within the institution and help AI/AN students develop a strong cultural appreciation of themselves and other AI/ANs. By being involved, AI/AN students stand a much greater chance of becoming integrated into the fabric of the institution, enriching their total academic and social experience, and bonding with those with whom they have a strong ethnic and social affinity.

Validation. Institutions wishing to recruit a significant number of AI/AN students should strive to develop excellent faculty who understand the need to validate students' experiences (Rendón & Jalomo, 1993, 1995; Rendón, 1994) and know how to serve as cultural mediators, models, and translators (de Anda, 1984; Jalomo, 1995). Because faculty and staff members who are not culturally trained may actually negatively impact retention efforts, institutions need to hire carefully and train faculty, staff, and administrators to be sensitive to the needs of AI/AN students. Indeed, the type of personnel who will meet those needs will be those individuals who are willing to formulate strong, encouraging relationships with students (Pavel, 1999; Tierney, 1991, 1992, 1995; Wright & Tierney, 1991).

Since Rendón's (1994) research on validation is predicated on non-traditional students (e.g., older students, first generation, ethnic minorities), it is especially appropriate for use with AI/ANs. Rendón's model includes the following recommendations:

- Faculty and staff need to be oriented to the needs and strengths of culturally diverse populations.
- Faculty members need to be trained to validate students.
- A validating classroom needs to be fostered.
- A therapeutic learning environment must be fostered both inside and outside the classroom.

Her model should be reviewed to see how administrators, staff, and faculty could apply it appropriately.

Overall, AI/AN students, like many other students of color, benefit from validation and the personal attention that faculty, staff, and administrators can offer to help them feel that they are a vital part of the institution. Validation occurs when faculty members take an active role in getting to know students outside of class, call them by name, structure learning experiences that allow students to experience themselves as capable learners, show a personal interest in them, and encourage them to succeed (Rendón, 1994). Rendón's (1994) and Rendón and Jalomo's (1993, 1995) research closely parallels Pavel's (1999) recommendations in which he indicates:

> To improve outcomes for [AI/AN] students, institutions of higher education have to cultivate enduring academic advisor-advisee and intellectual mentor-mentee relationships. These faculty-student relationships should be characterized by caring attitudes conveyed through good communication skills, likable personalities, a willingness to learn cultural norms, respectful interactions, appreciation for different ways of knowing, and high expectations. (p. 249)

Retention Task Force. Finally, institutions serious about retaining AI/AN students should seriously consider forming a retention task force like American Indian College in Phoenix, Arizona. Their retention task force includes administrators, faculty, staff, and two students, at least one of whom is a first-year student. The task force seeks to monitor and enhance the retention of AI/AN students at that college, with a particular focus on first-year students. Meeting about three times per semester they exchange ideas, provide training, plan activities, and inform the administration of specific retention concerns at the campus. These efforts have resulted in a first-year retention rate in 2001 of 88% (American Indian College, Office of the Academic Dean, 2001).

Summary

American Indians and Alaska Natives hold a very unique place within today's society. They are U.S. citizens and members of individual tribes and tribal governments.

They are expected to practice and maintain their cultural customs and life-styles, defend their homelands and resources, and participate in the larger mainstream society. While it is true that pedagogical practices, curricula, teachers, and access to higher education and support programs have changed significantly in recent decades, falsehoods, movies, and school mascots that reflect stereotyping and misperceptions continue to impede the educational progress and cultural integrity of AI/ANs.

All public higher institutions must continue to collaborate with federal, state, and tribal governments to strive to meet the needs of AI/AN students. Research that will educate all parties involved, to the extent possible, must be undertaken from individual tribal perspectives. Given the extent of diversity among AI/ANs, "Pan-Indian" research must stop, if false perceptions and stereotypes are to be eliminated. Institutions must clearly articulate policies and programs that meet the intellectual and cultural needs of their AI/AN students (Pavel, 1999). Most importantly, the teaching-learning relationship must be a caring and mutually respectful one (Swisher & Tippeconnic, 1999). These relationships are essential for the educational success of these students.

Authors' Note

Throughout the chapter we have generally used AI/AN to designate American Indian/Alaska Native, which is the demographic term used by many when referring to the indigenous peoples of North America in the aggregate. We have done so because many of the social and educational issues affecting both groups are very similar. However, when referring specifically to Canadian Indians we have used the designation "First Nations," which is the preferred term used in Canada and also certain parts of the northern United States. Also, at times we have interspersed the term Native or Native American to refer specifically to the indigenous people in the "lower 48" states especially where that term seemed more appropriate.

References

Almeida, D. A. (1996). *Countering prejudice against American Indians and Alaska Natives through antibias curriculum and instruction.* (ERIC Digest Reproduction Service No. ED 400 146)

American Indian College. (2001). Raw statistical data. Office of the Academic Dean.

Astin, A. W. (1984). Student involvement: A developmental theory for higher ecducation. *Journal of College Student Personnel, 25*(4), 297-308.

Astin, A. W. (1985a). *Achieving academic excellence: A critical assessment of priorities and practices in higher education.* San Francisco: Jossey-Bass.

Astin, A. W. (1985b). Involvement: The cornerstone of excellence. *Change, 17*(4), 35-39.

Astin, A. W. (1991). Today's freshman: A puzzle and a challenge. In D. S. Fidler, (Ed.), *Perspectives on the freshman year* (Monograph No. 2) (pp. 23-32). Columbia, SC: University of South Carolina, National Resource Center for The Freshman Year Experience.

Benjamin, D. P., Chambers, S., & Reiterman, G. (1993). A focus on American Indian college persistence. *Journal of American Indian Education, 32*(1), 24-30.

Bowker, A. (1992). The American Indian female dropout. *Journal of American Indian Education, 31*(2) 3-20.

Boyer, E. L. (1989). *Tribal colleges: Shaping the future of Native America.* Princeton: The Carnegie Foundation.

Brown, S. V. (1996). Responding to the new demographics in higher education. In L. I. Rendón & R. O. Hope (Eds.), *Educating a new majority* (pp. 71-96). San Francisco: Jossey Bass.

Colbert, C. R. (1999). *The academic progress of American Indian/Alaska Native students at Arizona State University: A longitudinal six-year trend study of the 1989, 1990, and 1991 cohorts.* Unpublished doctoral dissertation, Arizona State University.

Creating role models for change: A survey of tribal college graduates. (2000, May). Prepared by the American Indian Higher Education Consortium, the Institute for Higher Education Policy, Sallie Mae Education Institute. Retrieved from: http://www.aihec.org/research.htm

Curley, G. (1984). *Self-esteem and Northern Cheyenne children of alcoholics.* (ERIC Document Reproduction Service No. ED 281 697)

Daughtry, L. M. (1992). *The development of a freshman orientation course for African-American students with a focus on Afrocentricity.* (ERIC Document Reproduction Service No. ED 347 259)

de Anda, D. (1984). Bicultural socialization: Factors affecting the minority experience. *Social Work, 29*(2), 101-107.

Deyhle, D., & Swisher, K. (1997). Research in American Indian and Alaska Native education: From assimilation to self-determination. *Review of Research in Education, 22,* 113-194.

Dehyle, D. (1992). Constructing failure and maintaining cultural identity: Navajo and Ute school leavers. *Journal of American Indian Education 31*(2), 24-47.

Demmert, W. G. (1994). *Blueprints for Indian education: Languages and cultures.* (ERIC Document Reproduction Service No. ED 372 899)

Demmert, W. G. (1996). Indian nations at risk. In L. I. Rendón & R. O. Hope (Eds.), *Educating a new majority* (pp. 231- 262). San Francisco: Jossey-Bass.

Duran, E., & Duran, B. (1995). *Native American postcolonial psychology.* Albany, NY: State University of New York Press.

Falk, D. R., & Aitken, L. P. (1984). Promoting retention among American Indian college students. *Journal of American Indian Education, 23*(2), 24-31.

Gardner, J. N. (1980). *University 101: A concept for improving university teaching and learning.* (ERIC Document Reproduction Service No. ED 192 706)

Gardner, J. N. (1990). *Guidelines for evaluating the freshman year experience.* Columbia, SC: University of South Carolina, National Resource Center for The Freshman Year Experience.

Garrod, A., & Larimore, C. (Eds.) (1997). *First person, first peoples.* Ithaca, NY: Cornell University Press.

Gilbert, W. S. (1996). *Bridging the gap between high school and college: A successful program that promotes academic success for Hopi and Navajo students.* (ERIC Document Reproduction Service No. ED 398 039)

Hill, N. (1991). AISES: A college intervention program that works. *Change, 23*(2), 24-26.

Hodgkinson, H. (1992). *The current condition of Native Americans.* (ERIC Digest Reproduction Service No. ED 348 208)

Hornett, D. (1989). The role of faculty in cultural awareness and retention of American Indian college students. *Journal of American Indian Education, 29*(1), 12-18.

Jalomo, R. E. (1995). *Latino students in transition: An analysis of the first-year experience in community college.* Unpublished doctoral dissertation, Arizona State University.

Kirkness, V. J., & Barnhardt, R. (1991). First Nations and higher education: The four R's-respect, relevance, reciprocity, responsibility. *Journal of American Indian Education, 30*(3), 1-15.

Kleinfeld, J., Cooper, J., & Kyle, N. (1987). Postsecondary counselors: a model for increasing Native Americans' college success. *Journal of American Indian Education, 26*(3), 9-16.

Ledlow, S. (1992). Is cultural discontinuity an adequate explanation for dropping out? *Journal of American Indian Education, 31*(3), 20-35.

Lee, W. Y. (1997). *Transitioning from high school to college: Surviving a clash of cultures.* ASHE annual meeting paper. (ERIC Document Reproduction Service No. ED 415 825)

Lin, R. (1990). Perceptions of family background and personal characteristics among Indian college students. *Journal of American Indian Education, 29*(3), 19-28.

Lin, R., LaCounte, D., & Eder, J. (1988). A study of Native American students in a predominantly White college. *Journal of American Indian Education, 27*(3), 8-15.

Martin, W. E. & Farris, K. K. (1994). A cultural and contextual path approach to career assessment with Native Americans: A psychological perspective. *Journal of Career Assessment, 2*(3), 258-275.

Melchior-Walsh, S. (1994). *Socio-cultural alienation: Experiences of North American Indian students in higher education.* Unpublished doctoral dissertation, Arizona State University.

National Center for Education Statistics. (2002). *Digest of Education Statistics.* Retrieved on February 16, 2004, from: http://nces.ed.gov/pubs2003/digest02/

Pavel, D. M. (1999). American Indians and Alaska Natives in higher education: Promoting access and achievement. In K. G. Swisher & J. W. Tippeconnic, (Eds.), *Next steps: Research and practice to advance Indian education* (pp 239-258). Charleston, WV: Clearinghouse on Rural Education and Small Schools.

Pavel, M. (1991). *Assessing Tinto's model of institutional departure using American Indian and Alaskan Native longitudinal data.* (ERIC Document Reproduction Service No. 339 324)

Pavel, M., & Colby, A. Y. (1992). *American Indians in higher education: The community college experience.* (ERIC Document Reproduction Service No. ED 351 047)

Pavel, M., & Padilla, R. V. (1993). American Indian and Alaska Native postsecondary departure: An example of assessing a mainstream model using national longitudinal data. *Journal of American Indian Education, 32*(2) 1-23.

Rehyner, J. (1991). *Plans for dropout prevention and special school support services for American Indian and Alaska Native students.* (ERIC Document Reproduction Service No. ED 343 762)

Rendón, L. I. (1994). Validating culturally diverse students: Toward a new model of learning and student development. *Innovative Higher Education, 19*(1), 33-51.

Rendón, L. I., & Garza, H. (1996). Closing the gap between two and four-year institutions. In L. I. Rendón & R. O. Hope (Eds.), *Educating a new majority* (289-308). San Francisco: Jossey-Bass.

Rendón, L. I., & Jalomo, R. E. (1993). *Validating students.* Paper presented at the annual conference of the American Association of Higher Education. Washington, D.C.

Rendón, L. I., & Jalomo, R. E. (1995). *Validating student experience and promoting progress, performance, and persistence through assessment.* (ERIC Document Reproduction Service No. ED 381 051)

Rendón, L. I., Jalomo, R. E., & Nora, A. (2000). Theoretical consideration in the study of minority student retention in higher education. In J. Braxton (Ed.), *Rethinking the departure puzzle: New theory and research on college student retention* (127-156). Nashville: Vanderbilt University Press.

Rendón, L. I., Nora, A., Gans, W. L., & Calleroz, M. D. (1997). *Student academic progress: Key data trends baseline 1995-96.* Urban partnership program: Funded by the Ford Foundation National Assessment Center.

Robert, E. R., & Thomson, G. (1994). Learning assistance and the success of underrepresented students at Berkeley. *Journal of Developmental Education, 17*(3), 4-14.

Russell, G. (1997). *American Indian facts of life: A profile of today's tribes and reservations.* Phoenix: Russell Publications.

Saggio, J. J. (2000a). Transcription of a focus group session occurring at American Indian College in Phoenix, Arizona, on February 12, 2000.

Saggio, J. J. (2000b). *Experiences affecting post-freshman retention of American Indian/Alaskan Native students at a Bible college.* Unpublished doctoral dissertation, Arizona State University.

Saggio, J. J. (2001). *The influence of institutional culture on institutional choice and post-freshman persistence of American Indian/Alaska Native students at a Bible college.* Paper presented to the First Annual Graduate Student Conference on American Indian Research held at Arizona State University on February 8, 2001. (ERIC Document Reproduction Service No. 451 978)

Saggio, J. J., & Dempsey, J. (2003). Creating positive institutional climates for American Indian/Alaska Native students. In S. E. Van Kollenberg, (Ed.), *A collection of papers on self-study and institutional improvement, Vol. 2* (pp. 117-122). Chicago: The Higher Learning Commission, A Commission of the North Central Association of Colleges and Schools.

Stein, W. J. (1999). *Tribal colleges: 1968-1998.* (ERIC Document Reproduction Service No. ED 427 913)

Swisher, K., & Hoisch, M. (1992). Dropping out among American Indians and Alaska Natives: A review of studies. *Journal of American Indian Education, 31*(2), 3-23.

Swisher K.G., & Tippenconnic, J. W., III (1999). Research to support improved practice in Indian education. In K. G. Swisher & J. W. Tippencconic, III (Eds.), *Next Steps: Research and practice to advance Indian education.* Charleston, WV: ERIC Clearinghouse on Rural Education and Small Schools.

Tierney, W. G. (1991). Native voices in academe: strategies for empowerment. *Change, 23*(2), 36-39.

Tierney, W. G. (1992). *Official encouragement, institutional discouragement.* Norwood: Ablex Publishing.

Tierney, W. G. (1995). Addressing failure: Factors affecting Native American college student retention. *Journal of Navajo Education, 13*(1), 3-7.

Tinto, V. (1975). Dropout from higher education: A theoretical synthesis of recent research. *Review of Educational Research, 45*(1), 89-125.

Tinto, V. (1987). *Leaving college: Rethinking the causes and cures of student attrition.* Chicago: The University of Chicago Press.

Tinto, V. (1993). *Leaving college: Rethinking the causes and cures of student attrition* (2nd ed.). Chicago: The University of Chicago Press.

Upcraft, M. L. (1991). *Evolving theoretical perspectives on freshman.* (ERIC Document Reproduction Service No. ED 334 881)

Upcraft, M. L., Gardner, J. N., & Associates. (1989). *The freshman year experience.* San Francisco: Jossey Bass.

U.S. Census Bureau. (2001). *Profiles of general demographic characteristics.* Retrieved on February 16, 2004, from http://www.census.gov/census2000/states/us.html

Wells, R. N. (1989). *The forgotten minority: Native Americans in higher education.* (ERIC Document Reproduction Service No. 317 346)

Wells, R. N. (1997). *The Native American experience in higher education: Turning around the cycle of failure II.* (ERIC Document Reproduction Service No. 414 108)

Winik, L.W. (1999, July 18). There's a new generation with a different attitude. *Parade Magazine, Arizona Republic,* pp. 6-8.

Wright, B. (1991). *American Indian and Alaska Native higher education: Toward a new century of academic achievement and cultural integrity.* (ERIC Document Reproduction Service No. 343 771)

Wright, B. (1985). Programming success: Special student services and the American Indian college student. *Journal of American Indian Education, 24*(1), 1-7.

Wright, B., & Tierney, W. G. (1991). American Indians in higher education. *Change, 23*(2), 11-18.

Wright, S. W. (2000). Survey confirms tribal college role in alleviating unemployment. *Black Issues in Higher Education, 17*(19), p.18.

Yates, E. L. (2001). American heritage. *Community College Week, 13*(11), p.6.

Programs That Serve AI/AN First-Year Students

A number of programs and resources are available to support AI/AN students as they navigate their collegiate experiences. However, finding programs that specifically target AI/AN first-year students is difficult. Many first-year programs exist in mainstream institutions and target mainstream college and university students. However, this section has attempted to capture a representative, and by no means exhaustive, sample of programs and institutions that address AI/AN first-year student retention. Tribal colleges, private sectarian colleges, and programs at regional public institutions are highlighted throughout the following pages.

Tribal Colleges

The American Indian Higher Education Consortium (AIHEC) consists of 33 colleges and universities in the United States and Canada. These institutions are bound together politically out of a sense of unified need and purpose (Stein, 1999). The vast majority of tribal colleges are two-year institutions, although some such as Haskell University of the Nations, Sinte Gleska University, Salish Kootenai, and Oglala Lakota offer baccalaureate degrees. Also, Sinte Gleska University and Oglala Lakota now both offer a masters degree program in education. In addition to the growing academic offerings of these colleges, one of their greatest attributes is their ability to enhance Native retention rates through an environment that is culturally sensitive to the unique needs of Native-American students (Boyer, 1989; Pavel, 1999; Stein, 1999).

American Indian Higher Education Consortium (AIHEC)
121 Oronoco Street
Alexandria, VA 22314
Telephone: 703-838-0400
FAX: 703-838-0388
Email: aihec@aihec.org
Web site: www.aihec.org/
(Links to the various tribal colleges and universities are provided at this site.)

Arizona State University

The Native American Achievement Program (NAAP) was created to serve Native American students from the Navajo, San Carlos Apache, and White Mountain Apache tribes. Each of these tribes is indigenous to the southwestern United States and has entered into an agreement with Arizona State University (ASU) to help students to persist and graduate. These tribes support the program by providing financial aid for students enrolled in the program. Students must remain in good academic standing with their respective tribe and the university, participate in an on-campus NAAP orientation each semester, and meet with their instructors and academic advisors at least twice per semester and with NAAP staff four times per semester. Students in the NAAP program also agree to become involved in peer mentoring and attend all required NAAP events.

Native American Achievement Program
Student Life/Multicultural Student Center
P.O. Box 871112
Tempe, AZ 85287-1112
Telephone: (480) 965-6060
Fax: (480) 727-7592
Web site: http://www.asu.edu/studentlife/msc/naap.html

Northern Arizona State University

Native American Student Services (NASS) is a program at Northern Arizona University (NAU) that provides culturally sensitive support services for Native students. This program especially targets first-year and transfer students with an eye towards helping them make the transition to a university setting. In 2000, NAU saw a 60% increase in Native-American student enrollment at their statewide campus and a 2% increase at their mountain campus. NAU ranks second among all institutions in the United States for conferring bachelors degrees on Native-American students.

Working in conjunction with NASS is the Navajo Freshmen Year Experience Program (NFYE), specializing in working with Navajo students, who are indigenous to the region served by NAU. The NFYE is a two-year program that features a partnership between NAU and the Navajo nation. The program begins with a summer orientation for Native-American students and includes close monitoring of their GPA and regular meetings with their retention specialists. Trained staff members provide a wide range of information about how to navigate the collegiate experience successfully. Students in this program are reportedly more likely to persist. Financial aid is available.

Native American Student Services (NASS)
Northern Arizona University
PO Box 5653
Flagstaff, AZ 86011
Telephone: (928) 523-8086
FAX: (928) 523-5653
Web site: http://www2.nau.edu/nass/

Humboldt State University

Humboldt State University in Arcata, California houses two outstanding student services support programs: the Indian Natural Resource, Science & Engineering program (INRSEP) and the Indian Teacher & Education Personnel Program (ITEPP). Although these programs do not specifically focus on first-year students, they promote retention and socialization into higher education and first-year students are among those greatly benefiting from them.

The INRSEP provides an environment that seeks to provide Native students with a balance of traditional western science and a respect for traditional Native views of science.

The program works hard to promote academic retention and career placement through strong academics and the acculturation of Native students into the greater collegiate community. It reports a 90% placement of its graduates.

The ITEPP program currently has a very high retention rate (84-92%) and has served as a national model since 1969. Like the INRSEP, it promotes retention and career advising. Over the past few years, the ITEPP has reported a retention rate that fluctuates between 84% and 92%.

Indian Teacher and Educational Personnel Program (ITEPP)
Humboldt State University
Spidell House #85
Arcata, CA 95521
Telephone: (707) 826-3672
Web site: http://www.humboldt.edu/~hsuitepp/2.aboutitepp.html

Indian Natural Resource Science & Engineering Program (INRSEP)
Humboldt State University
Campus Office: Walter Warren House, #38
Arcata, CA 95521
Telephone: (707) 826-4994
Web site: http://www.humboldt.edu/~inrsep/

Northeastern State University

Northeastern State University with campuses in Tahlequah and Muskogee, Oklahoma has the highest enrollment of Native American students in the United States. Northeastern also confers more bachelor's degrees on Native Americans than any other institution in the United States. The Indian University Scholars Society (IUSS) is a campus-recognized organization that focuses on developing leadership, scholarship, and the study of sovereignty vis-à-vis Native peoples.

The Native American Student Association (NASA) promotes leadership, education, and social development within the context of political, cultural, and community projects. The program includes mentorship for Native high school students, as well as assistance to first-year, transfer, and continuing students regarding enrollment, scholarships, and educational program information.

Northeastern State University (Muskogee Campus)
P.O. Box 549
Muskogee, Oklahoma 74402
Telephone: (918) 683-0040
FAX: (918) 458-2106
Web site: http://www.nsuok.edu/muskogee/index.htm

Montana State University

Montana State University located in Bozeman, Montana offers assistance to first-year AI/AN students through their Center for Native American Studies. The Center places a high premium on teaching, research, public service, and student services. The Center's focus on Native student retention and success is reflected in its student services programming. Student services for first-year students include Native American peer advisors who are upperclass students, mentoring programs, grade monitoring, and the opportunity to participate in the American Indian Council, which provides various social services including pow-wows, Christmas gifts, and talking circles.

In addition to its student services for AI/AN students, the Center for Native American Studies offers a minor in Native American Studies, as well as a Master of Arts degree program.

Montana State University
Center for Native American Studies
Student Advising, Advocacy, and Counseling
Room 1 Wilson Hall
Telephone: (406) 994-4880
Web site: http://www.montan.edu/wwwcat/opportunities/spec6.html

University of Alaska

The University of Alaska at Anchorage has an office of Native Student Services that seeks to improve both the retention and success of AI/AN students through academic advising, educational and vocational planning, and providing financial aid information and opportunities for interactions with other AI/AN students and faculty.

The Della Keats Enrichment Program provides interested college students who meet threshold requirements a chance to have a six-week pre-collegiate experience during the summer at the University of Alaska. This program is specifically designed for AI/AN students wishing to pursue careers in medicine, dentistry, psychology, social work, dental hygiene, or other health care professions.

The First Step Program is similar in scope to the Della Keats Enrichment Program, but specializes in reaching high school students interested in careers in engineering, business, electronics, aviation maintenance, food services, or the Alaska petroleum industry.

The University of Alaska, Anchorage
Native Student Services
3211 Providence Drive
BEB 108
Anchorage, AK 99508
Telephone: (907) 786-4000
FAX: (907) 786-4009
Web site: http://www.uaa.alaska.edu/nss/

First Nations University (formerly Saskatchewan Indian Federated College)

Unique among institutions, First Nations University is an integral part of the University of Regina in Canada and provides First Nations students the chance to be a part of an aboriginal college within a regional university. The First Nations University student services is host to a First-Year Services Entrance Program (FYS) that seeks to help students navigate the pivotal first year. Academic counselors assist with academic, personal, and social development. Also, Elder Services assists students who wish to develop their spiritual formation through the promotion of traditional aboriginal beliefs under the mentorship of recognized elders. First Nations University has seven campus locations throughout Regina including five locations on the main campus and the old campus, as well as two off-campus locations.

First Nations University
Regina Campus
1 First Nations Way
University of Regina
Regina, Saskatchewan, Canada
S4S OA2
Telephone: (306) 546-8489
Web site: http://www.firstnationsuniversity.ca/about/campuses.htm

Private Sectarian Institutions

American Indian College of the Assemblies of God, located in Phoenix, Arizona, is a regional college of the Assemblies of God, a conservative Protestant denomination. A small college of less than 100 students, AIC prides itself on being able to give its students substantial individualized attention. In 2001, the College reported an 88% first-year student retention rate.

American Indian College's retention efforts include: Freshman Experience, Retention Task Force, academic intervention strategies, validation, and cultural sensitivity (Saggio & Dempsey, 2003). These components impact both first-year students and others by making the college-going experience richer and more relevant to their unique needs and expectations.

Freshman Experience. First-year students take the Freshman Experience Seminar I and II to become acclimated to higher education and to better understand their unique vantage point as AI/AN college students. First-year student orientation is supplemented by an orientation session for both students and family members meeting with faculty and administrators to help with the transition into higher education. First-year students participate in a three-day "Welcome Week" planned around the themes of commitment, community, and communion. The "Welcome Week" festivities culminate in a special chapel service in which new students are presented with a special pin and formally welcomed into the campus community.

Retention Task Force. The Retention Task Force is an interdisciplinary group that includes administrators, instructors, student affairs personnel, and students who monitor retention trends. They meet several times per year and report their findings to other key stakeholders within the college community. Data comes from assessment instruments such as locally developed surveys and the College Student Inventory® (Noel-Levitz).

Academic Intervention Strategies. The College uses various academic intervention strategies to assist first-year and other students who encounter difficulties in their class work. These include academic alerts, midterm grades, and special classes for students on academic probation. American Indian College also has a Learning Resource Department (LRD) that provides remedial coursework in reading, writing, and basic math skills for underprepared incoming first-year students. The LRD also includes a tutoring center.

Validation. At American Indian College students are validated through positive interactions with faculty, staff, and administrators. Students are affirmed through in- and out-of-classroom experiences that stress warm interpersonal relationships, which according to Saggio (2000b, 2001) was a major reason for first-year students' persistence.

Cultural Sensitivity. American Indian College strives to be culturally sensitive to the unique needs of AI/AN students. Family members are involved in admissions decisions and invited to orientation sessions for new students. Also, face-to-face encounters are stressed when recruiting students. Instructional practices favor hands-on learning rather than highly theoretical abstract approaches. Graduation and chapel services frequently feature Native American leaders who serve as role models to the students. Finally, the Colleges' outreach and service projects favor both urban and rural Native communities as their highest priorities.

American Indian College
10020 N. Fifteenth Avenue
Phoenix, Arizona 85021-2199
Telephone: (602) 944-3335, (800) 933-3828 [Toll Free Admissions]
FAX: (602) 943-8299
Web site: http://www.aicag.edu

Private Non-Sectarian Institutions

Dartmouth College has instituted a Native American Program (NAP) that seeks to graduate a substantial number of AI/AN students. According to Garrod and Larimore (1997), they have managed to graduate 75% of Native American students enrolled in the program. In 2001, Dartmouth had 117 AI/AN students enrolled. The NAP has been established to provide support services to AI/AN students who attend Dartmouth so that they can succeed. The program provides spiritual, emotional, and personal support, and includes counseling and advising. The program also seeks to foster greater understanding of Native cultures to other constituencies both on and off the campus.

Native American Program
Dartmouth College
201 Collis Center
Dartmouth, NH 03755
Telephone: (603) 646-2110
Web site: http://www.dartmouth.edu/~nap/

Resources

This section briefly highlights some of the books, journals, and videos that may be helpful for those who work closely with AI/AN students. Needless to say, this is only a representative list, with only some key resources listed.

Books

Carney, C. M. (1999). *Native American higher education in the United States.* Rutgers, NJ: Transaction Publishers.

A comprehensive history of higher education for American Indians in the United States beginning with the colonial period, including attempts by Harvard, Dartmouth, and The College of William and Mary to make educating the American Indian a part of their institutional missions. Includes extensive discussion on the development of American Indian higher education from early neglect extending from the time of the Revolutionary War to the 1960s, as well as events leading up to the present time, including the development and success of tribal colleges. Discussion also includes the current role of the federal government in its responsibility towards ensuring ongoing educational opportunities for American Indians in higher education.

Garrod, A., & Larimore, C. (Eds.) (1997). *First person, first peoples.* Ithaca, NY: Cornell University Press.

An anthology of first-person accounts of Native Americans who have successfully persisted to a bachelor's degree at one of America's most elite institutions, Dartmouth College. The contributors include a tribal court judge, a professional baseball player, and a surgeon. Also, these individual authors come from a wide variety of tribal backgrounds including Tlingit Eskimo, Lakota Sioux, Navajo, Rosebud Sioux, and Houma.

Huffman, T. G. (1999). *Cultural masks: Ethnic identity and American Indian higher education.* Buckhannon, WV: Stone Creek Press.

Included in this book are data drawn from 69 in-depth interviews of Native American students who are primarily Lakota Sioux. The interviews took place over a five-year period and reveal that the students' ethnic identity was a central, unifying theme in their respective experiences. The interviews also uncovered four cultural masks that typified the students' experiences: (a) assimilated, (b) marginal, (c) estranged, and (d) transculturated.

Swisher, K. G. & Tippeconnic, J. W., III (Eds.) (1999). *New steps: research and practice to advance Indian education.* Charleston, WV: ERIC/CRESS.

This work contains 13 chapters written entirely by Native educators and covers issues in Native education at the elementary, secondary, and higher educational levels. Topics covered include the history of American Indian education and appropriate assessment practices for Native students. Edited by two leading scholars in American Indian education, this work covers a wide range of issues in Indian education.

Tierney, W. G. (1992). *Official encouragement, institutional discouragement.* Norwood, NJ: Ablex Publishing Corporation.

Tierney has interviewed more than 200 AI/AN students, and key informants such as faculty, staff, and administrators from several different institutions who have had close contact with these students. Using a critical theorist approach, Tierney demonstrates that the educational system has in many cases failed AI/AN students by providing an institutional climate that suppresses Native cultural values. Positing that a change in institutional approaches will enhance AI/AN retention, Tierney points out that institutions of higher learning must take the initiative in creating an environment conducive to AI/ANs or continue to risk losing them.

Journals

These journals are published by AI/AN researchers and are produced for an audience that includes both researchers and practitioners who deal with AI/AN students.

Journal of American Indian Education. This journal has been published under the auspices of Arizona State University since 1961 and features articles on basic and applied research directly relevant to AI/ANs at various educational levels including higher education. It is published three times per year (fall, winter, and spring).

Journal of American Indian Education
Center for Indian Education
College of Education
Arizona State University
P.O. Box 871311
Tempe, AZ 85287-1311
Telephone: (480) 965-6292
FAX: (480) 965-8115
Web site: http://jaie.asu.edu

Tribal College Journal of American Indian Higher Education. This publication focuses on educational issues relevant to American Indian higher education, and in particular, issues specific to tribal colleges. *Tribal College Journal* has been published since 1989 under the auspices of the American Indian Higher Education Consortium, a voluntary association of 33 tribal colleges and universities located throughout North America (including one in Canada).

Tribal College Journal of American Indian Higher Education
PO Box 720
Mancos, Colorado 81328
Telephone: (970) 533-9170
FAX: (970) 533-9145
Web site: http://www.tribalcollegejournal.org/contact.htm

Winds of Change: A Magazine for American Indians. Specifically written for AI/AN college students, this quarterly publication focuses on AI/AN role models and stories of personal achievement and leadership. This magazine also features career development and job position listings, as well as an *Annual College Guide for American Indians* in September that includes financial aid, college programs, and statistics on AI/AN retention and graduation rates from colleges and universities throughout the United States.

Winds of Change: A Magazine for American Indians
AISES
P.O. Box 9828
Albuquerque, NM 87119-9828
Telephone: (505) 765-1052
FAX: (505) 765-5608
Web site: http://www.winds.uthscsa.edu

Wicazo Sa Review: A Journal of Native American Studies. A bi-annual journal of Native American Studies published since 1985, the *Wicazo Sa Review* seeks to advance Native American studies as a scholarly field. The journal specializes in publishing articles dealing with book reviews, curriculum designs, syllabi, and discussions of appropriate pedagogical techniques to use with AI/AN students. The journal also includes poems, essays, and short stories published by AI/ANs.

Wicazo Sa Review: A Journal of Native American Studies
University of Minnesota Press
111 Third Ave. South, Suite 290
Minneapolis, MN 55401-2520
Telephone: (612) 627-1970
FAX: (612) 627-1980
Web site: http://www.upress.umn.edu/journals/wsr/default.html

Videos

The videos in this section include selections that are both entertaining and informative. Those that are entertaining still provide a "slice of life" that will help educators and practitioners have a better understanding of AI/AN cultures.

Keep Your Heart Strong: Native American Pow-Wows and Celebrations. This hour-long documentary provides an inside look at the traditional Native American pow-wow through the eyes and words of its participants. This video also portrays the importance and relevance of traditional Native American art forms to today's Native-American people. Winner of the 1987 National Indian Education Association, Outstanding Media Award.

Keep Your Heart Strong: Native American Pow-Wows and Celebrations
Available through Prairie Public TV
P.O. Box 3240
Fargo, ND 58103
Telephone: (701) 241-6900 and (800) 359-6900
FAX: (701) 241-7650
Web site: http://www.redeyevideo.com/
VHS-Running Time 58 minutes

Lakota Woman: Siege at Wounded Knee. This 1994 made-for-TV movie tells the story of Mary Crow Dog, a Lakota Sioux woman who grows up on reservation, attends a boarding school, and later joins the American Indian Movement (AIM) and becomes involved in the Siege at Wounded Knee. The video stars Irene Bedard as Mary Crow Dog. Available in VHS format through Amazon.com.

Smoke Signals. This film tells the "coming of age" story of two young Native men, Victor Joseph and Thomas Builds-the-Fire, on a bus trip from their reservation in the Pacific Northwest down to Phoenix, where they are going to collect the ashes of Victor's late father. Made by Native film-makers and featuring a Native cast, *Smoke Signals* is written by Sherman Alexie and based on his book *The Long Ranger and Tonto Fistfight in Heaven.* Available in VHS and DVD format through Amazon.com. Running time is 89 minutes. Rated PG-13.

Warriors: Native American Vietnam Vets. This video captures the first-hand accounts of Indians who served in the Vietnam War during the 1960's and 1970's. Of the 86,000 Native Americans who enlisted in the military, close to 90% of them volunteered, the highest percentage of any ethnic group. This video captures their wartime experiences, the reasons behind why many of these men volunteered so willingly for this war, and what life was like for them upon their return from the war.

Warriors: Native American Vietnam Vets.
Available through Prairie Public TV
P.O. Box 3240
Fargo, ND 58103
Telephone: (701) 241-6900 and (800) 359-6900
FAX: (701) 241-7650
Web site: http://www.redeyevideo.com/
VHS-Running Time 56 minutes

Chapter 11

Transfrming the First-Year Experience for Multiracial/Bicultural Students

Raechele L. Pope,
Timothy R. Ecklund,
Teresa A. Miklitsch,
and Radhika Suresh

Rita has successfully navigated the challenges of her first year in college and is looking forward to her sophomore year as an education major at a state college in the northeastern United States. She is biracial—half-Irish American and half-Native American. Rita grew up on a Reservation and strongly identifies with the culture and beliefs of Native Americans. Her parents were divorced when she was 10 and she moved to the suburbs to live with her White maternal grandmother until she completed high school. Rita then enrolled in a nearby state college.

Samantha is now a first-semester student at a state college in the northeastern United States after a failed attempt at a nearby community college. She was enrolled last semester but had to withdraw because of academic difficulties. She is biracial and does not strongly identify with the racial heritage of either parent. Her mother was born in Korea and met her father, a White American, while he was stationed in Korea as a soldier. Her parents separated when she was a teenager because her father is an alcoholic. Samantha has a two-year-old daughter whose father is Latino. Samantha does not appear to think much about her racial identity or what it means to be a multiracial person.

Derrick is in his second semester at a city college in the Midwest. He is succeeding academically but having difficulty socially. He is multiracial, with an African-American and Native-American father and a White mother. He grew up in predominantly White suburbs of a major, mid-western city where most of his friends are White. Now that he is attending an urban campus, he finds that most of his friends are Black and grew up in the city. He tries to fit in and has difficulty finding any peer group with whom he can relate. He is an accomplished student majoring in engineering and is currently in a relationship with an African-American woman for the first time.

Madonna just completed her first semester of college and is already focused on graduate school. She is biracial; her dad was African American and her mom is White. Her father died when she was young. She has always been very close to her mother. Madonna has never had difficulty identifying as a biracial person. She is very light-skinned, and it is not uncommon for individuals to assume that she is White. She is clear about who she is and does not let the assumptions and biases of others affect her self-identity as an African-American woman.

The biological basis of our identity is only one aspect of who we are. Race and racial identity are social constructs informed by our personal, interpersonal, familial, and educational experiences as well as the expectations, legacies, and cultures that surround and influence us. How others identify us racially and how we *choose* to self-identify are essential pieces of the complex issue of racial identity. Recent theories of racial identification (e.g., Myers, 1988; Root, 1992) provide equally critical frameworks to assist us in understanding and addressing the concerns of students with multiracial background and identities.

The students profiled in this chapter self-identified as multiracial. The life experiences of these students and more specifically, their experiences in college, shed light on the unique realities of multiracial students during their first year in college. During this crucial developmental period for all first-year students, multiracial students have additional and unique concerns. They need to balance typical psychosocial and academic development tasks with their own exploration of racial identity and integration of who they are as individuals into a new environment.

Challenges of the First Year in College

During the first year, students face important challenges. For many traditional-aged first-year students, this is a time to learn how to be independent; make decisions for themselves; and explore relationships, work demands, career paths, and academic interests. Tinto (1993) suggests that college presents multiple transitions that influence students' success during the first year and beyond. The higher education literature is rich with research that illustrates the importance of academic and social integration during the first year (Astin, 1996; Tinto, 1993). Tinto, in particular, explored the level of integration that needs to take place, both academically and socially, for students to persist and succeed. Integration refers to the extent to which students share the attitudes and values of peers and faculty and how much they subscribe to the expectations of the larger community or the smaller sub-groups within the college (e.g., fraternities, sororities, and other student organizations). As students try to achieve academic and social integration, they go through various stages that are characterized by separation from familiar surroundings and home life; adjustment to campus life; the formation of new relationships with students, staff, and faculty; and the exploration of the new dimensions of their lives (Tinto).

Rendón, Jalomo, and Nora's (2000) research on retaining students of color argues that first-year programs and services should incorporate frameworks and practices that allow students from diverse backgrounds and experiences to transition to college without separation from their current culture. First-year transitions and opportunities for social involvement and integration assume that students are comfortable with who they are and will be able to find peer groups that affirm their identity. It must be remembered that for the most part, research on first-year transitions and the practices of most first-year programs are typically based on the experiences and realities of White students. The experiences of students of color and their adjustment processes are likely not the same as White students. The many differences that exist among students of color only add to the complexity of understanding and meeting their needs. For example, multiracial students, who are raised within families and communities where there is more than one community with which to form a connection and identity, have challenges that go beyond even those of monoracial students of color. As the number of multiracial college students continues to increase, more understanding about who they are and their unique experiences, expectations, and needs warrants further study.

In the literature exploring the experiences of students of color, Smedley, Myers, and Harrell (as cited in Sax, Gilmartin, Keup, DiCrisi, & Bryant, 2000) have suggested that students of color on predominantly White campuses often experience stress that affects their ability to integrate and adjust to their new surroundings. Schwitzer, Griffin, Ancis, and Thomas (1999) also investigated the connection between students' of color adjustment to college and their interaction within the campus social environment. They offered several recommendations for increased positive social adjustment including increasing student-faculty interaction and community-level intervention. Similarly, Nora (2001) reported increased retention of students of color when relationships were established with significant individuals (e.g., faculty, administrators, counselors) within the campus environment.

In the first ever, comprehensive, national study of the experiences of first-year students, Sax et al. (2000) reported that while students "feel a sense of comfort" during the first year in college, most students admitted to the presence of personal challenges. These challenges included being "uncomfortable with their physical appearance, lonely or homesick, depressed, and 'forced' to interact with students they dislike" (p. 23). More than half of the students surveyed admitted to feeling worried about their health, meeting new people, and breaking away from their home and family in order to succeed on their own. These problems reflect the challenges of integrating into a new environment often without the safety net of parental presence and intervention. The study also found gender differences in how women and men dealt with these issues. Women generally were affected by these personal challenges to a greater degree, especially during the first year. While this report makes no mention of the impact of race when it comes to challenges during the first year, it is likely that many students of color have unique issues that add another layer of complexity to their first-year experience.

Although the data exploring the experiences of first-year students of color is limited, there is modest growth in research that explores the experiences and attitudes of students of color and their effect on the students' psychosocial growth (See for example, Cokley, 2001; Itzkowitz & Petrie, 1986; Jordan-Cox, 1987; Pope, 1998, 2000; Taub & McEwen, 1991). Research suggests that student development theories may not adequately explain the growth and development of students of color, because these studies often ignore or minimize the effect that cultural context may have on these students. Also, research often has not incorporated variables that account for significant within-group differences such as racial identity and acculturation (Pope, 1998).

The significance of racial attitudes and identity in higher education has been increasingly established (Pope, 1998, 2000; Taub & McEwen, 1991). On college campuses across the country there are ongoing multicultural interventions that strive to improve relationships among racially diverse students. Racial identity theory offers some understanding of how students of all races view themselves and others who are racially similar or different from themselves. This awareness helps higher education professionals better appreciate the attitudes, identity, and experiences of students of color, which ideally translates into improving the interventions and services offered.

As higher education professionals gather information about the various groups with whom they are working, they develop a better appreciation of how student experiences, values, and cultural background may affect collegiate experience. However, gathering knowledge about diverse cultures is not enough. It must also influence the teaching and helping process. It is imperative that higher education professionals gather more accurate and extensive information about various cultural groups and be conscientious about how they use such knowledge. Learning about important cultural constructs like racial identity and its impact on how first-year students make meaning of their experiences, their cultural background, and their relationships with others is vital to building effective helping relationships. If the unique relationship and experiences that students have with their cultural group are not explored, content knowledge, by itself, may perpetuate a cookbook or stereotypic approach where the faculty or staff member does not individualize or apply this knowledge to the distinctive world view or experiences of individual students.

Educators must ask: Did the student grow up in a racially homogenous or heterogeneous environment? Was race a salient issue in their family or upbringing? Is college the student's first experience in a racially mixed environment? Is this the first time the student has experienced being a numerical minority? Racial identity theory offers no absolutes and should never be used to explain the behavior of all students. Instead, it provides the framework to challenge our assumptions and to view students as individuals whose unique identity and experiences profoundly shape who they are and what they can contribute to their college environment.

Cross and Fhagen-Smith (2001) offer a life span model of Black identity that can be used as a framework to better understand the experiences and perspectives of students of color and specifically multiracial students. The life span approach is vital because it reminds us that prior to coming to college students of color have been shaped and influenced by their families and communities and have had significant experiences that profoundly influence how they view themselves and others. According to Cross and Fhagen-Smith, individuals are raised in families where race is experienced on a continuum as having high or low salience, or importance, in their lives. In low-race salience families, little significance is placed on race (beyond being one of many identities), and a group racial identity may be completely rejected. This does not mean that individuals reject their race or even feel badly about who they are; it just may not be immediately relevant or significant in their view of themselves or the world. In high-race salience families, parents often emphasize race and culture in the home and larger social environment and actively strive to build a strong racial identity and self-concept. Some diversity in attitudes and values exists within this high-race salience category, where individuals may view themselves in a variety of ways (e.g., Black nationalist, Afrocentric, bicultural, or multicultural).

The most significant contribution of this conceptualization of racial identity is the importance of not making assumptions about the meaning of race in students' lives without gathering some information and understanding about that student. Therefore, getting to know and appreciate individuals from their own point of reference is vital to providing relevant and meaningful programs and services. No matter how well-developed a sense of self these first-year students of color may have when they first come to college, those initial college experiences and the students' racial identity development process can have a profound impact on their ability to make a smooth transition to college life during the first year.

Multiracial Identity Development Theories

Examining the experiences of multiracial students in light of some of the current theories on multiracial identity development will help us understand them more fully. This section briefly explores some of these theories and applies them to the life experiences, values, and attitudes of several multiracial students. Many of the models developed have specifically focused on biracial identity development; however, their frameworks are easily adapted to address the realities of students whose racial heritage incorporates more than two racial groups.

Poston (1990) developed a progressive, multiracial identity development model that identifies five stages. The first stage, *Personal Identity,* usually encompasses very young individuals to whom the idea of race is just becoming salient. Their identity is based on what they learn from their family. According to Poston, some multiracial individuals are exposed to both cultures as part of their upbringing. Others may be exposed to only one cultural group, and some are not raised in any particular cultural tradition. Most college students have moved beyond this stage prior to coming to college. During the second stage, *Choice of Group Categorization*, multiracial individuals are often forced to choose an identity, usually a monoethnic one. Society often pressures them to make choices in order to facilitate their participation in social groups, peer relationships, and family groups. Factors such as parents, peer groups, demographics of the home neighborhood, physical appearance, knowledge of the culture, and individual personality differences influence these choices. Rita is an example of a student at this stage. She is part Irish American and part Native American and grew up on the Iroquois reservation until she was 10. Her sense of self as a Native American is strong; however, when her parents divorced and she moved in with her mother's grandmother who is White, her transition proved difficult at times. She rarely acknowledged her multiracial background and did not like to answer questions about being multiracial. Her friends saw her as only Native American.

During the third stage, *Enmeshment and Denial*, multiracial individuals typically experience a lack of comfort with their chosen identity. This may be characterized by feelings of guilt, self-hatred, and perhaps even a lack of acceptance from one or more groups. Again we turn to Rita, whose relationship with her relatives and friends on the reservation was complicated. Since her Iroquois culture emphasized a maternal lineage and Rita's mom was White, Rita was not allowed to participate in certain ceremonies, including her grandmother's funeral, which was very upsetting to her. In addition, because of some negative relationships with some of the Native-American men she dated, she has over-generalized these experiences and has developed biases against dating Native-American men. She has now decided that if and when she marries it will be to a White man. Another student, Derrick, also struggles with this third stage. Although Derrick strongly identifies as an African-American male, he sometimes struggles with the lack of acceptance he feels from his Black peers. Often they tease him as being "too White," because of his lack of awareness of urban Black culture (e.g., music, clothing, language). Even his new girlfriend, who is African American, sees how he acts and dresses as being more similar to their White peers.

It is during the fourth stage, *Appreciation* that many multiracial individuals begin to value their rich and diverse backgrounds. They often learn more about the different aspects of their identity but may still only identify with one group. For instance, Derrick has absorbed as much African-American culture as possible since he was a child and has always valued that part of his heritage. During high school, he realized that he knew very little about his father's Native American background and had spent very little time exploring his mother's White racial and ethnic heritage. As part of a senior project in high school, he studied his mother's family history, which made him feel closer to his mom and helped him feel more whole. Still, when asked about his racial background, Derrick generally states that he is African American, although privately he does acknowledge that he is multiracial. Like Derrick, Rita also claims both a public and private identity. Rita definitely recognizes her multiracial background and claims it privately. Yet in public, she identifies herself only as a Native American. This hesitation to more fully integrate their multiracial identity and publicly acknowledge it is why they have only achieved a level of *Appreciation*.

The final stage, *Integration*, exemplifies a fully integrated sense of identity. These individuals tend to recognize and value all aspects of their identity, and the result is one of acceptance, security, and integration of all their different cultural backgrounds. For example, Madonna came to college fully understanding and appreciating all aspects of her cultural background. While she has no memory of her father, her mother's involvement in the Black community made it easy for Madonna to develop a strong sense of identity as an African-American woman. She also has always been close to her mother's family and explored her White ethnic heritage on that side of the family. Madonna openly talks about being multiracial and understands that others want to put her in identity boxes that do not suit her. She is comfortable living in both worlds and suggests that it is not her problem when others have concerns or negative reactions to her racial background or identity.

Root (1990) offered another model of multiracial identity development that is flexible, non-linear, and not based in a developmental stage framework. In her model, it is possible for individuals to move between different options at different points in their lives. According to Root, multiracial identity development is viewed as a complicated process, and her dynamic model recognizes the multiple and ongoing challenges in choosing an identity.

The first option of the Root (1990) model is the acceptance of the identity that society assigns. This is a passive decision in which the individual usually accepts an identity as a person of color. There is a tendency to identify a non-White person exclusively as a person of color. For example, although Samantha is multiracial, she has made limited attempts to explore her racial background or identity. She is strongly aware of her mother's culture and is sometimes frustrated by her mother's Korean values and behaviors. While she does not deny her racial background, she makes no effort to connect with other Asian students or understand Asian culture. She was surprised when she received a letter during her first semester on campus from the Asian Student Organization and wondered how they received her name. She chose not to get involved.

Root's (1990) second identity option is for individuals to identify with both racial groups. There is a realization of the similarities and differences between both groups and the individual chooses to identify actively with both. In fact, there may be an effort to work with both groups in an attempt to reconcile one with the other. This is the case for Derrick and Rita. Rita is comfortable in both the Native American and White communities because of her varied life experiences; however, she works hard to keep those communities separate and does not really blend her different groups of friends. Similarly, Derrick has spent significant time in White culture and is comfortable there. While he has spent less time in African-American culture and with Black peers, he is very aware of the culture and enjoys it. At college, he has both White and Black friends but typically socializes with them separately.

The third option within Root's model is for the individual to identify actively with a single racial group. Although a person may primarily identify with one racial group, it does not mean she is denying other aspects of her identity. Nevertheless, there is a conscious decision to identify with only one part of the self. Rita never publicly identified as being multiracial, because she did not want to deal with other people's questions or issues. At some level, she worries that it would dilute the view of her as a Native American as well as further distance her from aspects of her Native American culture and community.

The fourth and final option available to a multiracial individual in Root's model is to create a new racial group—multiracial. The individual openly declares multiracial identity and positively relates to other multiracial people. Unfortunately, this goal can sometimes be challenging and elusive. Madonna has embraced this notion. She actively looks for other multiracial individuals because she feels a connection to them regardless of their racial background. At times, her friends challenge her choice to equally identify as multiracial and as African American; however, Madonna feels no hesitation in her decision.

Building on Root (1990), Reynolds and Pope (1991) created the Multidimensional Identity Model (MIM) that encourages individuals to examine their identity in dynamic and multidimensional ways. In addition to being used to explore multiracial identity, this framework can help individuals conceptualize the various aspects of their identity beyond race such as gender, class, or sexual orientation. The authors define four different identity preferences that multiracial individuals can explore as they develop as individuals. The key characteristic of the MIM model is that the options are not mutually exclusive, nor are they hierarchical. The borders among the four identity options are porous, allowing an individual to move freely among alternatives, depending on the needs of the moment (see Figure 1).

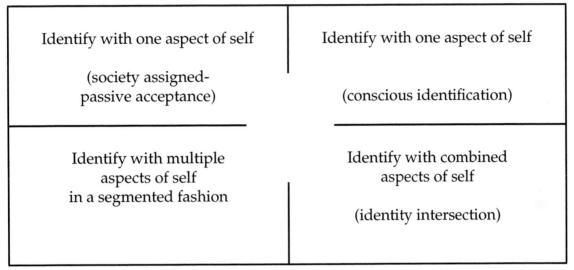

Figure 1. *Multidimensional Identity Model.*

Note. From "The Complexities of Diversity: Exploring Multiple Oppressions," by A. L. Reynolds and R. L. Pope 1991, *Journal of Counseling and Development, 70,* 174-180. Copyright 1991 by American Association of Counseling and Development. Reprinted with Permission.

A final model that provides a useful framework to examine the students' experiences and better understand the complex nature of the development of a multiracial identity is provided by Renn (1998). Her study focused on the influence of campus culture and peer interactions on students' attempts to make sense of their racial identity in college. Based on a qualitative analysis of three college campuses, Renn delineated five patterns that described how students grouped themselves in terms of their multiracial identity. These patterns are quite similar to the previously described frameworks.

One way that students identify themselves racially is to choose one racial category with which to affiliate. The second way involves students moving between or among their different heritage groups and choosing not to identify with one racial identity or group all the time. In a third approach, students create a new category called multiracial, depending on whether or not they are able to find support on campus. The fourth category includes students who avoid being labeled as belonging to any racial group. The fifth and final category involves students who use one or more of the first four options when different situations suggest different ways of affiliation.

Using these multiracial identity theories to examine the experiences of Samantha, Derrick, Madonna, and Rita, it is clear that these students move freely between the various options although few are comfortable identifying as multiracial. Samantha is very passive in her identity process and may continue to be so unless some event occurs that causes her to rethink her identity. Derrick actively identifies as being African American and strives to fully integrate into that community even though he does not always fit in. He also tends to keep his different identities and friends separate. Madonna strongly identifies as African American and multiracial and sees no incongruity in doing so even when others do.

To highlight one student's story a little more closely, Rita has been both active and passive in her racial identity development. She is active in not wanting to be seen as multiracial yet has often switched allegiances between her Native-American and White roots as the situation warrants. Rita identified herself as a Native American, yet has no problems in wanting to marry a White individual. As a Native American, she chooses to go to a predominantly White school rather than a tribal college. While she takes pride in her Native-American heritage and clearly enjoys that culture and its customs, Rita also has no trouble identifying and relating to mainstream America's values of seeking career success, a secure life, and stable income with a husband who will be a good provider. Ultimately, alternating between the White and Native-American communities may cause her to feel fragmented and not truly secure in who she is.

Lessons from Multiracial Students

The experiences of multiracial first-year students and the theories that describe multiracial identity development make apparent that there are important issues to consider as administrators and faculty strive to make the first year more meaningful and relevant. First of all, there is no end point or final resolution to identity development. During the first year, even students from monoracial backgrounds are attempting to forge separate identities for themselves. In the case of multiracial students, the situation is more complex. They are in the middle of discovering and/or establishing their multiracial identity in a new setting.

As the various models illustrate, students have their own way of coming to terms with their multiracial heritage. There are many options and identities that multiracial students can explore, and having an accepting campus environment makes it easier for them to embrace all aspects of their identity. Multiracial students may not overtly choose to be known as multiracial, even though they may acknowledge it privately. Being forced to choose a single identity may make it difficult for them to be true to themselves and where they are in their own racial identity development. What we do know is that the situation is both dynamic and fluid. Experiences of multiracial students are very diverse. No two multiracial students are ever going to make meaning of their experiences and identities in the same way. There is no one size that fits all when it comes to designing programs and services. Sensitivity to multiracial students' unique situations and understanding the complex nature of their identity development is essential to fostering a supportive environment during their first year.

Summary of Key Issues in Working with Multiracial Students

For student affairs professionals who are vested with the responsibility of creating and fostering a supportive learning environment for multiracial students, especially during the first year in college, the following are some of the key issues to remember:

- During the first year in college, multiracial students are exploring the nuances and complexities of their multiracial background while they deal with academic challenges and learn to live independently.
- Student affairs and other higher education professionals need to have some

degree of multicultural awareness, knowledge, and skills that will provide them with tools to work effectively with diverse groups of students and help them address students' needs (Pope, Reynolds, & Mueller, in press).

- Professionals directly responsible for first-year programs and services need to be familiar with important cultural constructs like racial identity and acculturation and how these influence the teaching and helping process. This knowledge is vital to building effective helping relationships.
- Racial identity theory offers no absolutes and should never be used to explain the behavior of all students. Rather, it provides the framework to challenge our assumptions and to view students as individuals whose unique identity and experiences profoundly shape who they are and what they can contribute to their college environment.
- It is important to remember that all students, especially multiracial students, have been shaped and influenced by their families and have had experiences that affect how they view themselves and the world around them.
- In order to provide meaningful programs and services, it is important to get to know and understand multiracial students from their own point of reference.
- Student affairs practitioners must refrain from trying to view multiracial students in unidimensional ways, even as they attempt to provide a nurturing environment during the first year at college. Multiracial students may not overtly choose to be known as multiracial, even though they acknowledge it to themselves.

In summary, it cannot be emphasized enough that experiences of multiracial students are very diverse. As mentioned previously, sensitivity to their situation and understanding the complex nature of their identity development is essential to providing a supportive environment during their first year.

Strategies for Colleges

So, how *do* colleges and universities create campuses that are more supportive and responsive to first-year multiracial students? Each institution needs to explore the unique nature of its campus and the diversity found there. What is important is that colleges be open to change, make a commitment to fostering a supportive atmosphere, and above all, be willing to experiment. Strategies that may work for a small college, where size is already conducive to creating comfortable student communities, may have no impact on a large research university. Whatever the size and nature of the institution, it takes both the administration and the faculty working together to create an environment that will support, nurture, and celebrate multiracial students' quests to develop their identity and experience academic success.

The following suggestions may help administrators and faculty enhance the first-year experiences of multiracial students:

1. *Update materials.* When asking for racial data, a wide variety of institutional forms may not offer "multiracial" as a category. Multiracial students must often choose among identities to complete these forms. Something as simple as updating institutional forms can send a powerful message of inclusion.

2. *Update training.* Training programs should include information on the experiences and concerns of multiracial students to provide faculty, staff, and administrators with critical knowledge and strategies to serve diverse populations of students.

3. *Include multiracial issues in all diversity awareness programming.* Programs that assume students are monoracial or make them identify with only one aspect of their ethnic heritage may create frustration and conflict for students. Activities should be modified to include such issues as multiple identities and cultural/racial backgrounds.

4. *Consider creating a student organization for multiracial students.* College and university students often associate with other students from their cultural or racial background. As a result, multiracial students often have to negotiate affiliation with other students through one of their racial or cultural heritages. Sometimes they are not fully accepted by any group. The creation of a separate group for multiracial students may have many benefits. Primarily, having such a group allows students to maintain all of their racial/cultural identities and affiliate with students who have similar experiences.

5. *Create an environment that values diversity.* Activities, programs, policies, and procedures that are designed to foster diversity have natural benefits for multiracial students. Multiracial students are well suited to be leaders in this type of environment. Recognition and validation of the challenges and difficulties they face everyday will be more easily addressed on a truly diverse campus.

6. *Be prepared to support the growth and development of multiracial students.* The research on student development and on racial identity development of college students includes limited information on multiracial students. Providing a supportive environment that is designed to foster their exploration of the issues surrounding identity development is essential. Staff should continue to familiarize themselves with the emerging literature in this important area of student development.

7. *Understand that peer group affiliation is a complicated process.* We know that establishing a peer group is extremely important to first-year students. Multiracial students may choose to affiliate with a group that is representative of one of their racial/cultural heritages and reject the others. However, other multiracial students may deal with this process much differently. In some cases, multiracial students may reject any group affiliation to avoid having to make a choice. Campus programs and organizations should make room for the many approaches that these students may choose as they become involved in the campus community.

Resources for Colleges

The development of multicultural campus communities is central to the healthy psychosocial development of students. "Helping students develop openness to diversity and challenge requires assessment, planning, self-reflection, risk-taking, and effort on the part of faculty, staff and students" (Whitt, Edison, Pascarella, Terenzini, & Nora, 2001, p. 200). Renn's (1998) research on the notion of space and impact of culture has added to the critical dialogue regarding multiracial students. Assisting first-year multiracial students as they adjust to the academic and community life requires a multifaceted approach and a diverse support system. Securing and providing racial identity resources that address the distinct needs and issues of multiracial students can be an important way to support their adjustment process.

Developing student and faculty communities that are welcoming of multiracial students requires campus-wide commitment and initiatives that increase interracial contact and provide requisite resources to achieve multicultural competence. Resources may include writings, films, and shared conversations regarding multiracial identity; counseling services; student personnel programs/workshops, discrete courses, and curriculum infusion that discuss multiracial identities; and social networking that builds connections between students of color and White students.

Multicultural resources and relevant materials are often accessed through various student development or diversity offices (e.g., multicultural or minority student services offices, counseling centers, campus ministry centers, and residence life offices). While resources specific to multiracial students remain limited, it is a growing area.

Authors' Note

The authors interviewed each of the students profiled in this chapter. The names and other identifying information have been changed to protect anonymity.

References

Astin, A. W. (1996). *What matters in college? Four critical years revisited*. San Francisco: Jossey-Bass.

Cokley, K. O. (2001). Gender differences among African American students in the impact of racial identity on academic psychosocial development. *Journal of College Student Development, 42,* 480-487.

Cross, W., & Fhagen-Smith, P. (2001). Patterns of African American identity development: A life span perspective. In C. L. Wijeyesinghe & B. W. Jackson (Eds.), *New perspectives on racial identity development: A theoretical and practical anthology* (pp. 243-270). New York: New York University Press.

Itzkowitz, S. A., & Petrie, R. D. (1986). The Student Development Task Inventory: Scores of Northern versus Southern students. *Journal of College Student Personnel, 27,* 406-412.

Jordan-Cox, C. A. (1987). Psychosocial development of students in traditionally Black institutions. *Journal of College Student Personnel, 28,* 504-512.

Myers, L. J. (1988). *Understanding an Afrocentric world view: Introduction to an optimal psychology* (2nd ed.). Dubuque, IA: Kendall/Hunt.

Nora, A. (2001). The depiction of significant others in Tinto's "Rites of Passage": A reconceptualization of the influence of family and community in the persistence process. *Journal of College Student Retention, 3*(1), 41-56.

Pope, R. L. (1998). The relationship between psychosocial development and racial identity among Black college students. *Journal of College Student Development, 39,* 273-282.

Pope, R. L. (2000). The relationship between psychosocial development and racial identity of college students of color. *Journal of College Student Development, 41,* 302-312.

Pope, R. L., Reynolds, A. L., & Mueller, J. A. (in press). *Multicultural competence in student affairs*. San Francisco: Jossey-Bass.

Poston, W. S. C. (1990). The biracial identity development model: A needed addition. *Journal of Counseling and Development, 69,* 152-155.

Rendón, L. I., Jaloma, R. E., & Nora, A. (2000). Theoretical considerations in the study of minority student retention in higher education. In J. M. Braxton (Ed.), *Reworking the student departure puzzle* (pp. 127-156). Nashville, TN : Vanderbilt University Press.

Renn, K. A. (1998). *Check all that apply: The experience of biracial and multiracial college students.* ASHE Annual Meeting Paper, Miami, FL. (ERIC Document Reproduction Service No. ED 427 602)

Reynolds, A. L., & Pope, R. L. (1991). The complexities of diversity: Exploring multiple oppressions. *Journal of Counseling and Development, 70,* 174-180.

Root, M. P. P. (1990). Resolving "other" status: Identity development of biracial individuals. In L. S. Brown & M. P. P. Root (Eds.), *Complexity and diversity in feminist theory and therapy* (pp. 185-205). New York: Haworth Press.

Root, M. P. P. (Ed.). (1992). *Racially mixed people in America.* Newbury Park, CA: Sage.

Sax, L. J., Gilmartin, S. K., Keup, J. R., DiCrisi, F. A., III, & Bryant, A. N. (2000). *Designing an assessment of the first college year: Results from the 1999-2000 YFCY pilot study.* University of California, Los Angeles, Higher Education Research Institute.

Schwitzer, A., Griffin, O. T., Ancis, J. R., & Thomas, C. R. (1999). Social adjustment experiences of African American college students. *Journal of Counseling and Development, 77,* 189-197.

Taub, D. J., & McEwen, M. K. (1991). The relationship of racial identity attitudes to autonomy and mature interpersonal relationships in Black and White undergraduate women. *Journal of College Student Development, 33,* 439-446.

Tinto, V. (1993). *Leaving college: Rethinking the causes and cures of student attrition* (2nd ed.). Chicago: The University of Chicago Press.

Whitt, E. J., Edison, M. I., Pascarella, E. T., Terenzini, P. T., & Nora, A. (2001). Influences on student's openness to diversity and challenge in the second and third years of college. *Journal of Higher Education, 72*(2), 172-204.

Additional Resources on Biracialism

Antonio, A. L. (2000). *Developing leadership skills for diversity: The role of interracial interaction.* Paper presented at the Annual Meeting of the American Educational Research Association, New Orleans, LA. (ERIC Document Reproduction Service No. ED 443 321)

Brandell, J. R. (1988). The treatment of the biracial child: Theoretical and clinical issues. *Journal of Multicultural Counseling and Development, 16,* 176-187.

Foeman, A. K., & Nance, T. (1999). From miscegenation to multiculturalism: Perceptions and stages of interracial relationship development. *Journal of Black Studies, 29*(4), 540-557.

Fukuyama, M. A. (1999). Personal narrative: Growing up biracial. *Journal of Counseling and Development, 77*(1), 12-14.

Funderburg, L. (1994). *Black, white, other: Biracial Americans talk about race and identity.* New York: William Morrow.

Gibbs, J. T. (1989). Biracial adolescents. In J. T. Gibbs, L. N. Huang, & Associates (Eds.), *Children of color: Psychological intervention with minority youth* (pp. 322-350). San Francisco: Jossey-Bass.

Gillem, A. R. (1998). The multiracial experience: Racial borders as the new frontier [Review]. *Journal of Black Psychology, 24*(4), 476-479.

Grove, K. (1991). Identity development in interracial, Asian/white late adolescents: Must it be so problematic? *Journal of Youth and Adolescents, 20,* 617-628.

Ingram, D. (2000). Valuing a growing population: Biracial youth. *Journal of Family and Consumer Sciences, 92*(3), 10.

Johnson, T. P., Jobe, J. B., O'Rourke, D., Sudman, S., et al. (1997). Dimensions of self-identification among multiracial and multiethnic respondents in survey interviews. *Evaluation Review, 21*(6), 671-687.

Kenny, M. E., & Stryker, S. (1996). Social network characteristics and college adjustment among racially and ethnically diverse first-year students. *Journal of College Student Development, 37*(6), 649-658.

Kerwin, C., Ponterotto, J., Jackson, B., & Harris, A. (1993). Racial identity in biracial children: A qualitative investigation. *Journal of Counseling Psychology, 40*, 221-231.

Motoyoshi, M. M. (1990). The experience of mixed-race people: Some thought and theories. *Journal of Ethnic Studies, 18*(2), 77-94.

Nakashima, C. L. (1996). Voices form the movement: Approaches to multiraciality. In M. P. P. Root (Ed.), *The multiracial experience: Racial borders as the new frontier* (pp. 79-97). Thousand Oaks, CA: Sage.

Nishimura, N. J. (1998). Assessing the issues of multiracial students on college campuses. *Journal of College Counseling, 1*(1), 45-53.

Phelps, R., Altschul, D. B., Wisenbaker, J. M., Day, J., Cooper, D., & Potter, C. (1998). Roommate satisfaction and ethnic identity in mixed-race and white university roommate dyads. *Journal of College Student Development, 39*(2), 194-203.

Phinney, J. S., & Alipuria, L. L. (1996). At the interface of cultures: Multiethnic/ multiracial high school and college students. *The Journal of Social Psychology, 136*(2), 139.

Ramirez, D. A. (1996). Multiracial identity in a color-conscious world. In M. P. P. Root (Ed.), *The multiracial experience: Racial borders as the new frontier* (pp. 49-62). Thousand Oaks, CA: Sage.

Root, M. P. P. (1996). A bill of rights for racially mixed people. In M. P. P. Root (Ed.), *The multiracial experience: Racial borders as the new frontier* (pp. 3-14). Thousand Oaks, CA: Sage.

Root, M. P. P. (1996). The multiracial experience: Racial borders as a significant frontier in race relations. In M. P. P. Root (Ed.), *The multiracial experience: Racial borders as the new frontier* (pp. xiii-xxviii). Thousand Oaks, CA: Sage.

Seward, R. J., Giordano, N. G., Goldsworthy, S. B., Stallworth, T. C., & Stevens, K. L. (1998). *A content analysis of the four major journals in counseling psychology: Multiracial and multiracial literature over the last decade.* East Lansing: Michigan State University, Department of Counseling and Educational Psychology. (ERIC Document Reproduction Service No. ED 418 340)

Swartz, W. (1998). *The identity development of multiracial youth.* (ERIC Document Reproduction Service No. ED 425 248)

Thornton, M. C. (1996). Hidden agendas, identity theories, and multiracial people. In M. P. P. Root (Ed.), *The multiracial experience: Racial borders as the new frontier* (pp.101-120). Thousand Oaks, CA: Sage.

Torres, V. (1999). Validation of a bicultural orientation model for Hispanic college students. *Journal of College Student Development, 40*(3), 285-298.

Williams, C. B. (1999). Claiming a biracial identity: Resisting social constructions of race and culture. *Journal of Counseling and Development, 77*(1), 32-35.

Web Sites of Interest

Project RACE:
Project RACE advocates for multiracial children and adults through education, community awareness, and legislation. The main goal of Project RACE is for a multiracial

classification on all school, employment, state, federal, local, census, and medical forms requiring racial data.
http://www.projectrace.com

Association of MultiEthnic Americans (AMEA):
This comprehensive site maintains current resources, web links, newsletters, as well as information regarding legal and health issues pertinent to multiethnic individuals.
http://www.ameasite.org

Multiracial Activist:
This site provides journal coverage of issues related to biracial, multiracial, interracial, and transracial individuals and families.
http://www.mulitracial.com

MAVIN:
This site provides information on MAVIN, a nonprofit organization that is redefining diversity by celebrating multiracial and transracially adopted youth. MAVIN publishes a magazine, hosts a national conference, sponsors Matchmaker Bone Marrow Program, provides diversity consulting, and has published a 40-chapter book to educate parents and educators about the needs and concerns of multiracial youth.
http://www.mavin.net

Y? The National Forum on People's Differences:
This site provides a place to ask questions, seek information, and to engage others, in the areas of ethnic and cultural backgrounds. This site actively encourages students to post questions on diversity.
http://www.yforum.com

Tolerance – a web project of the Southern Poverty Law Center:
This site promotes tolerance and diversity, and provides educational materials, legal information, and diversity-oriented resources for all populations.
http://www.tolerance.com

Section 4

Moving Toward the Future

Chapter 12

Transforming the First-Year Experience for Students of Color: Where Do We Begin?

Laura I. Rendón

This monograph invites student and academic affairs professionals involved in shaping first-year programs to become transformative educators who view their roles more broadly than merely offering services or imparting knowledge to students. Transformational practice involves a paradigm that places major change at its core. Creating this kind of change requires a critical approach that probes deeply into belief systems, conventions, practices, power structures, and politics to see and understand the complexities involved in framing an education that is truly transformative, supportive, and enriching for students of color. The authors of this monograph believe that a critical cultural perspective provides a useful framework for creating transformational change.

A critical cultural perspective is rooted in the tradition of critical theory. Darder (1989) poses that "critical educators perceive their primary function as emancipator and their primary purpose as one committed to creating conditions under which students can learn skills, knowledge, and modes of inquiry that will allow them to examine critically the role that society has played in their transformation" (p. viii). As such, transforming the first-year experience becomes more than simply offering services that foster retention and social and academic growth. A transformative first-year experience for students of color would also include a social justice agenda that challenges existing structures and those they privilege, favoring democratic structural changes where power and privilege are shared among different constituencies. Of course, this agenda carries tensions, because so much is at stake. It is only by acknowledging issues that have been detrimental to students of color that we can come to terms with them. This chapter provides educators with a theoretical framework for entering into a critical dialogue about transforming the first-year experience. I also outline the essential elements for designing a transformative first-year experience for students of color. The basis for a transformational first-year experience is that faculty and student affairs administrators can create educational experiences that are academically rigorous, compassionate, nurturing, empowering, liberating, and democratic.

A Framework for Transforming the First-Year Experience

A transformative framework for first-year initiatives builds on democratic ideals, respect for diverse cultures, justice, and equity. These values are reinforced in the classroom, in the overall program environment, and by academic and student affairs personnel who are involved with the program. They constitute what Rhoads and Black (1995) call a "critical cultural perspective." The work of educational theorists such as Paulo Freire, bell hooks, Peter McLaren, Donaldo Macedo, Antonia Darder, Henry Giroux, and Bill Tierney exemplify critical cultural views that ask educators to create institutional conditions that allow for individual development as well as collective communication and cooperation. It is useful to consider critical approaches that can help educators transform the first-year experience in the classroom, in the context of the program, and in the behaviors and beliefs of the academic and student support staff involved with the program.

Critical Pedagogy

Critical pedagogy is rooted in critical theory and addresses the power imbalances among different social groups that result in limited social justice, freedom, and empowerment for subordinated groups. This critical perspective requires faculty to think about, negotiate, and transform the relationship among classroom teaching; the production of knowledge; the structures of the educational institution; and the social and material relations of the wider community, society, and the nation (McLaren, 1998). Educators who subscribe to critical pedagogy argue against the oppressive "banking model" (Freire, 1970) of education where faculty, who consider themselves the sole experts in the classroom, become depositors of knowledge. Instead, Freire argues that education should be liberatory and that students should be helped to develop a critical consciousness that allows them to envision themselves as social change agents empowered to create a more democratic society. Applying a critical perspective to teaching and learning in the first college year means that all who teach would be engaged in a critical analysis of curricular content, pedagogical approaches, and the relationships between teachers and students. The goal is to create an inclusive, multicultural curriculum that reflects the lives and experiences of students of color; connects what is being learned to student lives; allows students to become actively engaged in learning; and establishes meaningful relationships among teachers, students, and peers. Connected teaching and holistic learning approaches can help educators reach this goal (Belenky, Clinchy, Goldberger, & Tarule, 1987; Palmer, 1998; Rendón, 2002). Additionally, students would have multiple opportunities to engage in critical thinking about the meaning of education for them, their families, and their cultures.

Cultural Democracy

The context of the first-year experience also merits careful attention. Ramirez and Castañeda (1974) argue that educational systems should reflect "cultural democracy," a philosophy that affirms the right of individuals to be educated in their own language and their own learning style. Employing cultural democracy in the context of all aspects of a first-year program means that all first-year college staff should strive to help students establish and maintain a multicultural identity. In other words, students should have experiences that reflect their cultures of origin while learning and integrating the values, conventions, and traditions of a new academic environment.

In an era where some educators would prefer to follow a "color-blind" education reform agenda, some may ask: Why adopt different strategies for educating students of color? Why should these students merit special attention? The dangers of adhering to a color-blind mentality are numerous, because a color-blind consciousness masks more than just color. A color-blind approach to education reform usually ignores or diminishes the historical context of marginalized groups, which includes numerous instances of oppression. The majority of African-American, American-Indian/Alaska Native, Asian/Pacific American, and Chicano/Latino students have experienced a long history of exclusion, invalidation, invisibility, stereotyping, trivialization, and marginalization in schools, higher education institutions, and the larger American society. This history includes long and difficult struggles for civil, voting, and language rights; access to college; equal educational and work opportunities; and financial aid. A color-blind consciousness can also overlook the fact that dominant groups usually have rights and privileges that they often take for granted. It may conceal the fact that many of the rights won in the past have been opposed at the level of implementation. It can confirm the erroneous notion that making a difference for students in the first year of college is about simply setting up programs, rather than viewing students as whole, multilayered human beings who defy the essentialism that reduces them to bottom-line commonalities. Moreover, a color-blind agenda masks the fact that institutions of higher education are sites in which power relationships usually result in dominant groups reaping benefits at the expense of oppressed groups. Consequently, setting up a culturally democratic context that honors, respects, and embraces diversity is integral to any first-year program that seeks to work more effectively with students of color.

Darder (1994) outlines the characteristics of a culturally democratic institution. They are included here because they are relevant to building the features of a culturally democratic first-year experience program. Darder begins by advocating that institutions view culture as an integral and fundamental component of the collective and for individuals in the collective. Cultural differences are understood and accepted, as well as engaged as common and ongoing occurrences. Darder argues that the context of historical struggles for voice, participation, and self-determination is the basis for the institution's ideology. Emphasis is on creating conditions for social justice and cultural equality through dialogues that are continuously redefined. The distribution of power allows for shared political influence and control, representativeness, fairness, and cross-cultural dialogue. People of color become active owners of the institution and are actively involved in shaping the institutional culture as equal participants. Diversity is recognized and understood, language differences are accepted, and multilingualism is supported.

Transformative Student and Academic Affairs Practice

Rhoads and Black (1995) were among the first theorists to bring critical theory perspectives to student affairs practice. The researchers outline seven principles that may assist student affairs administrators in acting as transformative educators. These principles also apply to academic support staff and are summarized below:

1. Student affairs practitioners must be actively engaged in shaping the larger campus community, including working with faculty and other staff in creating campus change. In other words, student affairs professionals should view themselves as capable of shaping both student and academic affairs practice.
2. Staff should build empowering social and cultural contexts in which student development is presumed to occur, as opposed to focusing solely on individual development. Empowering social settings allow students to develop their "fullest potential as community members and as democratic citizens" (p. 419).

3. Student affairs administrators should structure an ethic of care and a commitment to democracy in order to foster an empowering student experience.

4. Staff should create structures and opportunities that allow multiple constituencies to participate in inclusive decision-making structures. This allows students to see their connections to others and to society while encouraging a sense of social responsibility.

5. Student affairs personnel should accept and respect cultural differences, as well as support and protect the rights and liberties of marginalized groups even if it requires adopting unpopular positions.

6. Transformative educators should move beyond the mentality that the profession is simply about "offering services" and enter into engagement with students that treats them as equals.

7. Student affairs administrators must embrace conflict as an opportunity to transform the college community rather than avoiding conflict because it threatens organizational harmony. Chaos can be healthy if dealt with in a productive manner. As Williams (1997) points out: "Creating community...involves this most difficult work of negotiating real divisions, of considering boundaries before we go crashing through, and of pondering our differences before we can ever agree on the terms of our sameness" (p. 6).

Critical cultural perspectives, whether in the classroom or in student and academic affairs practice, acknowledge and work for organic connections within and outside the institution. For example, they strive for inclusion of and openness to nontraditional methodologies and epistemologies, willingness to work through tensions and differences, and the presence of democratic structures that allow the participation of multiple constituencies.

Essential Elements for Designing a Transformative First Year

Working with students of color requires a great deal of care and attention to multiple issues. The tools that transformative educators bring to designing the next wave of first-year experience programs include a critical consciousness that asks challenging questions and looks widely and deeply at the following elements.

Creating a Culturally Democratic Context for Working with Students of Color

To engage in transformational practice, student and academic affairs professionals must first examine the complexities of social belief systems that rationalize a status quo and place students of color at a disadvantage. To what extent does the program honor, respect, and embrace diversity as opposed to following a color-blind agenda? Working with students of color requires attention to difference and the politics of diversity. Questions such as the following will need to be addressed:

- How have political forces shaped the current structures in the first-year experience?
- Is there anything about the current first-year framework that is oppressive in nature?
- Who or what has benefited from the current structure or lack of structure?
- To what extent have students in the program come to believe they have or lack power? How have these beliefs affected their participation?

- Are dominant groups aware of their privileges in the program? How is this privilege manifested?
- Where is this program physically located (center/margin), and how is it funded (hard/soft)?
- What are the implications of location and funding?

A transformative first-year experience program for students of color must exist in relationship to the entire campus. Transformative educators should examine the history of the institution in terms of whom it serves and does not serve. How has this history changed? What policies, power structures, and programs privilege majority and minority students? To what extent are White faculty, staff, and students sensitized to issues related to students of color? To what extent do students of color understand issues related to White students? Programmatic issues that need to be addressed include creating a validating campus climate that fosters intergroup relations, reduces culture shock, and promotes student involvement in the campus social and academic life. In addition, programs should contain curricular materials, educational approaches, staff, and activities that are sensitive to the student's history, sociopolitical reality, and cultural orientation (Darder, 1989).

Understanding and Addressing the Characteristic Complexities of Students of Color

Making truly significant changes that result in greater numbers of students of color succeeding in the first year of college requires engaging in a critical dialogue about the characteristic complexities of these students and their experiences. Too often, educators succumb to the temptation to treat these students as a homogenous cohort. As noted throughout this monograph, students of color are not monolithic in nature. Reducing them to bottom-line commonalities neglects the complexities inherent in their lives and school experiences, which are interfaced with issues of class, gender, and sexuality, as well as disability, age, religion, and world view. Among the nuances educators must understand are regional differences and diversity within and across groups. Students of color also vary along the lines of learning styles, identity development, values, aspirations, prior school experiences, spirituality, and family relationships. Young (1990) elaborates on these points:

> Especially in a large, complex, and highly differentiated society, social groups are not themselves homogeneous, but mirror in their own differentiations many of the other groups in the wider society. In American society today, for example, Blacks are not a simple unified group with a common life. Like other racial and ethnic groups, they are differentiated by age, gender, class, sexuality, region and nationality, any of which in any given context may become a salient group identity. This view of group differentiation as multiple, cross-cutting, fluid, and shifting implies another critique of the model of the autonomous, unified self. (p. 48)

Educators may also address questions such as:

- What has been the history of students of color in this community? At this institution?
- How do students of color differ from White students?
- What are the views of dominant students toward oppressed groups? What are the views of oppressed groups toward dominant students?
- If there is no reference to difference or oppression, why not?

Facilitating the Transition to College

The transition to college for students of color is fraught with positive and negative tensions as students move away from an old, familiar culture and enter a totally new context. Dislocation and relocation can create anxiety even when students experience the excitement of meeting new people and learning new things. A first-year experience must address structural issues such as:

- To what extent is the program set up to benefit primarily majority students?
- To what extent do faculty and staff understand what college transition means from the student's perspective?
- What are the positive and negative factors associated with attending college for students of color?
- To what extent are students allowed to establish and retain multicultural identities?

In terms of programmatic issues, attention will need to be given to validation, involvement in campus academic and social life, financial aid, separation anxiety, academic preparation, and identity development.

Recruiting, Hiring, and Training Culturally Responsive Faculty and Staff

Culturally responsive faculty and staff from diverse races and ethnicities are absolutely essential to working effectively with students of color. These educators are more likely to embrace transformation and understand the intersections among race, class, gender, and sexuality. They know how to access resources to assist students of color. They understand that a mentoring relationship entails connecting with individuals not just as students, but also as human beings. As such, structural issues that may work against having culturally responsive educators will need to be examined. These structural barriers may include existing hiring practices, as well as the characteristics and belief systems of current faculty and staff. Faculty and staff development programs should be designed to engage in critical pedagogy, as well as to create and sustain social and cultural contexts which foster community, care, social justice, and democracy.

Transforming Teaching and Learning Practices

A critical pedagogical practice is integral to a transformative first-year experience program. In terms of structural issues, faculty will need to examine the existing canon.

- To what extent does the canon privilege majority and minority students?
- Who is excluded and included in the canon?
- What are the politics of knowledge in the classroom?
- To what extent are diverse student voices and experiences welcome in the classroom?
- How do faculty view themselves in relationship to students?

Programmatically, faculty will need to create a curriculum of inclusion that embeds multiple forms of knowledge. They must also be able to create holistic teaching and learning approaches that focus on intellectual development as well as social, emotional, and spiritual growth (Rendón, 2002; Burgis, 2000; Palmer, 1998).

Fostering Student Retention

Student retention is critical to the first year and beyond. Structural issues that should be examined include the extent to which academic and student support strategies are designed for specific student populations. Who do they really benefit? Why have strategies remained the same if retention rates are flat or have gotten worse over time? Transformative educators will need to design programs that foster high student retention rates. These include learning communities; mentoring programs; thematically linked courses; validating in- and out-of-class environments; and connections among faculty, students, and peers.

Engaging in Environmental Assessment and Planning

Transformative educators will need to examine structural issues that are related to the first-year program environment. For example, they should consider the following questions:

- What do power structures of the first college year look like? Who do they privilege?
- What organizational barriers stand in the way of inclusion?
- What is needed to create a more just and equitable first-year learning environment?
- What are the emerging frameworks that seek to change college and university cultures?

Educators will also need to examine programmatic issues such as conducting an environmental assessment that employs both qualitative and quantitative methods. This assessment should be used to foster and monitor the progress of a first-year teaching and learning environment that is conducive to students of color. Questions to ask when planning such assessment efforts include: What needs to be assessed? What are the appropriate methods to conduct the assessment? Who should benefit from this assessment?

Enacting a transformative first-year experience for students of color represents the next wave of program development in this educational movement that has by now served thousands of students in diverse educational settings. This monograph outlines specific programs and strategies that transformative educators can use to work with students of color. However, more will be needed in terms of training first-year student and academic services personnel to become transformative educators who are able to work from a critical cultural perspective. This chapter offers a preliminary framework that may be embraced to achieve this end. Developing an in-depth understanding of the forces that have worked against students of color and acting in pursuit of social justice and democratic structures will add new meaning to first-year experiences and to the lives of students of color. The authors in this monograph invite all first-year academic and student services faculty and staff to join us in shaping this exciting next wave of transformative education.

References

Belenky, M., Clinchy, B., Goldberger, N., & Tarule, J. (1986). *Women's ways of knowing: The development of self, voice, and mind.* New York: Basic Books.

Burgis, L. (2000). *How learning communities foster intellectual, social and spiritual growth in students.* Unpublished doctoral dissertation, Arizona State University, Tempe.

Darder, A. (1989). *Critical pedagogy, cultural democracy, and biculturalism: The foundation for a critical theory of bicultural education.* Unpublished doctoral dissertation, Claremont Graduate University, California.

Darder, A. (1994). Institutional research as a tool for cultural democracy. In D. G. Smith, L. E. Wolf, & T. Levitan (Eds.), *Studying diversity in higher education.* (New Directions for Institutional Research No. 81) (pp. 21-34). San Francisco: Jossey-Bass.

Freire, P. (1970). *Pedagogy of the oppressed.* New York: Continuum.

McLaren, P. (1998). *Life in schools: An introduction to critical pedagogy in the foundations of education* (3rd ed.). New York: Longman.

Palmer, P. (1998). *The courage to teach.* San Francisco: Jossey-Bass.

Ramirez, M., & Castañeda, A. (1974). *Cultural democracy: Bicognitive development and education.* New York: Academic Press.

Rendón, L. (2002). *Invoking the wisdom of the heart and the intellect in the classroom.* Veffie Milstead Jones Endowed Lecture. The College of Education, California State University, Long Beach.

Rhoads, R. A., & Black, M. A. (1995). Student affairs practitioners as transformative educators. *Journal of College Student Development, 36*(5), 413-421.

Williams, P. J. (1997). *Seeing a color-blind future: The paradox of race.* New York: Noonday Press.

Young, I. M. (1990). *Justice and the politics of difference.* Princeton, NJ: Princeton Unversity Press.

About the Contributors

James A. Anderson James A. Anderson is vice president and associate provost for institutional assessment and diversity at Texas A & M University, where he also holds a tenured faculty appointment in psychology. From 1992 to November 2003, Anderson served as vice provost for undergraduate affairs at North Carolina State University where he supported faculty development; undergraduate research; assessment of student learning; general education, university courses, and curricula; the Honors Program, and all academic support programs. His faculty appointment was in the department of counselor education. His research has focused on differences in student cognitive and learning styles across culture, race, class, and gender and how these styles interact with teaching styles in different classroom settings. Anderson earned a B.A. degree from Villanova University where he also sits on the Board of Trustees. He received a Ph.D. in psychology from Cornell University. He has been selected as an American Council on Education (ACE) Fellow and a Danforth Fellow.

Mistalene Calleroz Mistalene Calleroz is associate director of residential life at Arizona State University. Before coming to residential life, she was assistant to the vice president for student affairs, where she worked with enrollment management and student services units. Prior to this position, she served as a policy analyst for the Arizona Board of Regents, focusing on university policy issues, specifically transfer articulation. She also worked for two years with the Ford Foundation Urban Partnership Program (UPP) Assessment Center in ASU's College of Education, analyzing quantitative and quantitative data (e.g., graduation rates, persistence rates, community collaborations) from K-16 initiatives in 16 cities across the nation. She has co-authored three articles, and has taught undergraduate and graduate courses on leadership and student affairs administration. She received her Ph.D. in educational leadership and policy studies from ASU and holds a B.S. in Spanish and English education from the University of Nebraska-Lincoln and an M.Ed. in higher education from ASU. Her research interests include the experience of mixed race students in universities and colleges, recruitment and retention of students of color, and access to higher education.

Charles R. Colbert Charles R. "Bo" Colbert is a tribally enrolled member of the Muskogee (Creek) Nation of Oklahoma. He received his Ed.D. in higher and adult education from Arizona State University and has considerable past experience as a teacher and administrator in the education of Native Americans. He was instrumental in the formation of the recently created American Indian Studies Program at Arizona State University and currently serves as lecturer for the program.

Timothy R. Ecklund Timothy Ecklund is associate vice president for residence life and auxiliary services at Buffalo State College. Prior to this, he served as director and associate director of residential life at the University of Buffalo and as assistant director of residence life at the University of Illinois Champaign-Urbana. He is an adjunct faculty member in educational foundations at Buffalo State and the Graduate School of Education at the University at Buffalo. Ecklund is also a doctoral student in higher education administration in the Educational Leadership and Policy program at the University at Buffalo. His area of research concerns the experiences of American Indian college students, and he is currently studying the relationship of psychosocial development and acculturation among American-Indian college students.

Kris Ewing Kris Ewing is interim director of the Intergroup Relations Center (IRC) and faculty associate in the College of Education's Education Leadership and Policy Studies program at Arizona State University. Her teaching and research interests focus on intergroup relations, women's lives and experiences, and the study of diversity in higher education. She is leading an IRC faculty team study that focuses on students' experiences in the classroom and how these experiences influence thinking about different social issues. She consults regularly with faculty, staff, students, and community groups on intergroup dialogues and training.

Xiaomei Feng Xiaomei Feng is assistant director of institutional research at Tufts University. Feng has extensive experience in outcomes assessment, program evaluation, and survey studies. She has presented her research studies at local, regional, and national conferences. Two of her studies regarding children's cognitive development were published in China (*New Psychological Exploration*, 1987; *Acta Psychologic Sinica*, 1988). She received her Ph.D. in special education from Utah State University, an Ed.S. in special education, from University of Nevada, Las Vegas, and an M.A. in educational psychology from Washington State University.

Mildred García An educator and scholar with extensive administrative and teaching experience at all levels of higher education, Mildred

García serves as president of Berkeley College. Her research has concentrated on equity in higher education and its impact on policy and practice and led to her selection as an evaluator for the Ford Foundation's Campus Diversity Initiative. Her work in this initiative, along with that of three other scholars, resulted in the 1995 coauthored monograph, *Diversity in Higher Education: A Work in Progress.* Their most recent book, *Assessing Campus Diversity Initiatives* (2002), underscores the importance of assessment and evaluation. Her other publications include *Affirmative Action's Testament of Hope: Strategies for a New Era* (1997) and *Succeeding in an Academic Career*, which both focus on diversity issues in higher education. García holds a doctorate and master's degree from Teachers College, Columbia University; a master's degree from New York University; a B.S. from Bernard Baruch College of CUNY; and an A.A.S. from New York City Community College of CUNY.

Kenneth P. Gonzalez

Kenneth P. Gonzalez is associate professor of education at the University of San Diego. Gonzalez's scholarship examines the role of campus culture in the persistence of Chicano undergraduate students, Latina/o doctoral student socialization, and the expansion and constriction of college opportunities for Latinas. His work appears in such journals as the *Journal of College Student Development*, the *International Journal of Qualitative Studies in Education, Urban Education*, the *Journal of College Student Retention*, and the *Journal of Hispanic Higher Education*.

Romero E. Jalomo, Jr.

Romero E. Jalomo, Jr. is director of Extended Opportunity Programs and Services at Hartnell College in Salinas, California. He is a former assistant professor of higher education administration at New York University. His research examines the transition to college and first-year experiences of first-generation college students. He is a co-editor of the *ASHE Reader on Community Colleges* (3rd ed.) (2003, Simon & Schuster). Jalomo has authored a number of articles relating to culturally diverse students, student transitions to college, orientation programs, student assessment, and community colleges.

Kevin Kinser

Kevin Kinser has been an assistant professor in the department of educational administration and policy studies at the University at Albany, SUNY since 2001. He received two master's degrees and a doctorate from Columbia University's Teachers College and has taught in the higher education programs at Teachers College and Louisiana State University. As a researcher, Kinser studies non-traditional and alternative higher education, particularly the organization and administration of for-profit and virtual universities. He also is interested in the various ways in which institutions of higher education choose to serve and support students. He is the co-editor of *Higher Education in the United States: An Encyclopedia* (2002, ABC-CLIO) a comprehensive two-volume overview of American postsecondary education since World War II.

Wynetta Y. Lee   Wynetta Y. Lee is professor of education and assistant provost for institutional effectiveness and research curriculum/ director of undergraduate research at Dillard University. Prior to coming to Dillard University, Lee was associate professor of higher education at North Carolina State University where she worked with doctoral students who were planning careers in assessment, student affairs, and higher education leadership. She has extensive experience in evaluation and impact assessment of education and social programs. Her primary research interest focuses on factors that contribute to educational equity, cultural diversity, and parity in academic success at all points along the education pipeline. Her contributions to the field include serving as an assessment consultant for state, national, and international organizations; serving as a board member to national professional organizations; publishing in peer-reviewed journals and edited books; and presenting at peer-reviewed research conferences.

Teresa A. Miklitsch   Teresa A. Miklitsch is currently completing doctoral work in educational leadership and policy at the University at Buffalo. She has previously worked as a higher education administrator and secondary school guidance counselor. Her current research interests include multicultural competence, diversity, and first-year experiences.

Louis Olivas   Louis Olivas is assistant vice president for academic affairs and associate professor of management at Arizona State University. He has an extensive background in executive development; public education; and teaching at secondary, community college, and university levels. Olivas joined Arizona State University (ASU) in 1979 as the assistant director for the Center for Executive Development and served as the director from 1982 to 1986. He is a tenured professor in the management department, College of Business. His teaching and research emphasis is in entrepreneurship and small business management. He has been awarded the "Outstanding Teaching Award" by ASU undergraduate students and the "Teaching Excellence Award" from ASU's Center for Executive Development. He has published in the fields of personnel, management, training, and small business operations.

Nana Osei-Kofi   Nana Osei-Kofi currently serves as evaluation and assessment consultant to the National Council for Community and Education Partnerships in Washington, D.C. In this capacity, she is presently working on a grant funded by the James Irvine Foundation aimed at increasing access to higher education for underserved student populations through strengthening K-16 community-education partnerships. Osei-Kofi also teaches as an adjunct faculty member in the Graduate School of Education and Information Studies at the University of California Los Angeles (UCLA). Her research interests include critical and feminist social theories; the political economy of higher education; critical higher education theory and practice; and the politics of race, class, gender, and sexuality in education. Osei-Kofi received her Ph.D. in education from Claremont Graduate University.

Dawn Person

Dawn Person is professor of counseling and student development in higher education at California State University, Long Beach in California. She serves as co-director of the CSU/UC, Irvine Joint Doctoral Program in Educational Administration and Leadership, Higher Education-Community College Emphasis. She also coordinates a masters degree program emphasizing student development in higher education. Prior to her decade of college teaching, she served as a counselor, advisor, and administrator in student affairs, coordinating programs and services in support of students of color, international students, first-year students, and student athletes. Person serves as a consultant to colleges and universities on program evaluation, student retention, organizational change, and multicultural issues. She was the principal investigator of a longitudinal study on Black and Hispanic student retention in math, science, and engineering funded by the William Penn Foundation. She was co-author of the book *How Minorities Experience College* (2002) and has published articles and book chapters on student retention for African-American men, women, and student athletes of color. She has written about student cultures in higher education and success factors influencing the retention of students of color. Among her many honors and awards, she received the American College Personnel Association Diamond Honoree, a lifetime achievement award.

Raechele L. Pope

Raechele L. Pope is an associate professor of higher education and student affairs administration in the Department of Education, Leadership, and Policy at the University of Buffalo. Prior to her work at the University at Buffalo, she was an assistant professor in higher and adult education at Teachers College, Columbia University. She earned her doctorate in organization development from the University of Massachusetts at Amherst, and her M.A. in student personnel administration from Indiana University of Pennsylvania. With more than 20 years of experience in college student affairs, she has worked at several institutions in a variety of functional areas, including residential life, academic advising, and diversity education and training. Her primary teaching and research interests and publications are focused on the creation of multicultural campus environments. She is the co-author (along with Amy L. Reynolds and John A. Mueller) of *Multicultural Competence in Student Affairs* (Jossey-Bass, 2004). In addition, she has published several book chapters and refereed journal articles on multicultural organization development, multicultural competence, and psychosocial development of students of color. She has served as a reviewer or as a member of the editorial boards of the *Journal of College Student Development, ACPA Media*, and the *Journal of College Student Retention: Research, Theory, and Practice.*

Laura I. Rendón   Laura I. Rendón holds the Veffie Milstead Jones Endowed Chair at California State University, Long Beach. In 2003, the *Chronicle of Higher Education* named Dr. Rendón as one of the nation's leading experts in the field of Hispanic students and faculty. Her current research focuses on access, retention, and graduation of low-income, first-generation students and teaching and learning addressing intellectual, social, emotional, and spiritual student development. Rendón earned a Ph.D. in higher education administration from the University of Michigan, Ann Arbor; an M.A. in counseling and guidance and psychology from Texas A&M University, Kingsville; a B.A. in English and journalism from the University of Houston; and an A.A. from San Antonio College. She serves on several national organizational boards and on the editorial boards for the *Review of Higher Education, Educational Researcher, Journal of Latino Education, About Campus, Journal of Chicana/Latina, Studies* and *Journal of Women and Minorities in Science and Engineering.* She has been a fellow of the Fetzer Institute and has directed research projects funded by the Ford Foundation and the Office of Educational Research and Improvement, U.S. Department of Education. She is co-editor of two books, *Educating a New Majority* and the *Racial and Ethnic Diversity in Higher Education* ASHE Reader. She is currently working on another book, *Sentipensante (Feeling/Thinking) Pedagogy.*

Sandra L. Richards   Sandra L. Richards is a doctoral student in the School of Educational Studies and Certificate Program in Africana Studies at Claremont Graduate University. She is also program director for the Ontario Community-University Partnership, a collaborative grassroots "think tank" funded by the U.S. Housing and Urban Development (HUD) Office of University Partnerships, and sponsored jointly by Claremont Graduate University and Pitzer College. Richards received her B.A. degree in English and Sociology from Rutgers College, Rutgers University and an M.A. degree in Student Personnel Administration from Teachers College, Columbia University. Her research interests are in the areas of Black education, Diaspora studies, community studies, and educational development in underserved regions. Currently, she is examining the schooling experiences of students in the youth homes of Jamaica, West Indies. Through liberatory education, Ms. Richards strives to secure a future for some of the most vulnerable children of Jamaica and to contribute to improved conditions of economic well-being for Black people throughout the Diaspora.

Joseph J. Saggio

Joseph J. Saggio has served as the academic dean at the American Indian College of the Assemblies of God in Phoenix, Arizona since 1994 and also presently serves as an adjunct professor for the Assemblies of God Theological Seminary in Springfield, Missouri. An ordained minister since 1984, he is actively involved as a missionary educator and speaker in promoting awareness of American Indian/Alaska Native educational and spiritual needs. Saggio has been published in both religious and educational publications. He received his Ed.D. in higher and adult education from Arizona State University and completed the Management Development Program in higher education leadership at the Harvard Graduate School of Education.

Daryl G. Smith

Daryl G. Smith is professor of education and psychology at the Claremont Graduate University. Prior to assuming her current position in 1987, Smith served as a college administrator for 21 years. Her current research is in the areas of organizational implications of diversity, planning, governance, student affairs, and the impact of women's colleges and other special purpose institutions. In addition to numerous articles and papers, she is an author or co-author of *Achieving Faculty Diversity: Debunking the Myths* and *Diversity Works: The Emerging Picture of How Students Benefit*. Smith has consulted with numerous foundations and campuses across the country. She has served as a member of a National Science Foundation visiting panel for the Chemlinks Chemistry National Reform Project, consulted on the evaluation of Project Kaleidoscope, a national science reform effort, and served on numerous accreditation teams. She has chaired the editorial board for *The Journal of Higher Education*, served on the Board of the Association for the Study of Higher Education, and currently serves on the Editorial Board for the *Review of Higher Education* and the *NASPA Journal*. Smith earned her Ph.D. in social psychology and higher education at the Claremont Graduate University.

Radhika Suresh

Radhika Suresh is director of graduate admissions and student services in the Graduate School of Education at the University at Buffalo. She is responsible for enrollment management, marketing, recruitment, admissions, and student services. She has an MPA in public administration from the University of Cincinnati, an M.S. in public policy and a Ph.D. in Higher Education Administration, both from the University at Buffalo.

Dawn Tato   Dawn Tato is a member of the Seneca Nation of Indians. She is completing her Ph.D. in educational leadership and policy studies at Arizona State University in Tempe, Arizona. She is the coordinator of a U.S. Department of Education Title III Strengthening Institutions Program grant at Haskell Indian Nations University in Lawrence, Kansas.

Corlisse D. Thomas   Corlisse D. Thomas is currently associate dean of student affairs at Columbia University. For more than 14 years, she has held a variety of positions within areas of student affairs including student activities, Greek life, multicultural affairs, and admissions. She co-wrote, "Cultural Dynamics and Issues in Higher Education," a chapter in *Addressing Cultural Issues in Organizations* (1999, Sage). Her research interests include the experiences of students of color within higher education and the impact of popular culture on student values. She completed her masters and doctoral degrees in higher education at Teachers College, Columbia University.

Jesús Treviño   Jesús Treviño is the associate provost for multicultural affairs and director of the Center for Multicultural Excellence at the University of Denver. Prior to DU, he was at Arizona State University where he held the positions of director of the Intergroup Relations Center in the Office of the Senior Vice-President and Provost and assistant dean for cultural diversity in the Office of Student Life. He has also held the position of coordinator of Hispanic Student Services at Southern Methodist University. His areas of expertise include campus climate issues, campus intergroup relations, diversity training, and the collegiate experiences of students of color. He earned a B.A. and an M.A. from Eastern Michigan University. Treviño also earned an M.A. and Ph.D. in education with an emphasis on higher education from the University of California, Los Angeles.

Xiaoyun Yang   Xiaoyun Yang is the director of information reporting services at Office of the President, University of North Carolina. She has experience in data collection, reporting, and analysis at both the community college and university levels and has presented her research studies at various conferences. One of her studies about Asian students was published by *Community College Review* in 1994. Yang is also the 1998 recipient of the North Carolina Association for Institutional Research's (NCAIR) "Best Paper Award." She received both her doctoral and master's degrees from North Carolina State University.

Titles on Improving the Teaching and Learning
Experience for First-Year Students

Monograph 34. Service-Learning and The First-Year Experience: Preparing Students for Personal Success and Civic Responsibility. *Edward Zlotkowski, Editor.* Produced in association with Campus Compact. This monograph combines a research-based argument for the value of service-learning in the first year of college with a practical discussion of the issues related to implementation. Readers will find program and course models from a variety of disciplines, curricular structures, and institutional types. Connecting service-learning to the broader issues of the first college year, this monograph allows readers to examine where and how learning best takes place. 167 pages. ISBN 1-889271-38-1. $35.00

Monograph 26. Learning Communities: New Structures, New Partnerships for Learning. *Jodi H. Levine, Editor.* Learning communities have become one of the most widely used structures for achieving both academic and social integration of new students. This monograph describes various successful models, links theory with examples of good practice, and describes how learning communities can facilitate faculty development. In addition, chapter authors outline strategies for dealing with logistical concerns and provide comprehensive resource listings and recommendations for building learning community programs. 180 pages. ISBN 1-889271-27-6. $30.00

Learning Interdependence: A Case Study of the International/ Intercultural Education of First-Year College Students. *David J. Bachner, Laurence J. Malone, and Mary C. Snider.* Challenging the notion that study abroad programs are best suited for "mature" students, faculty and administrators at Hartwick College designed an intercultural, interdisciplinary course for first-year students, spanning an entire academic year. The book includes information on program development and student outcomes, with an appendix featuring syllabi from six courses based on the model. 203 pages. ISBN 1-889271-35-7. $30.00

Moral Action in Young Adulthood. *Ralph L. Mosher, David Connor, Katherine M. Kalliel, James M. Day, Norma Yokota, Mark R. Porter, and John M. Whiteley.* This book is an extension of the Sierra Project, which began at the University of California, Irvine, in the mid-1970s. The original Sierra Project was both a curricular initiative for first-year college students and a longitudinal study of character growth and development over four years of undergraduate study. In this groundbreaking follow-up, the researchers have returned to the original Sierra students to measure their continuing growth in moral reasoning and to understand the nature and meaning of moral action in response to the dilemmas inherent in everyday life. 280 pages. ISBN 1-889271-26-8. $30.00

Use the order form on the next page to order any of these titles from the National Resource Center.

Use this form to order additional copies of this monograph or to order other titles from the National Resource Center for The First-Year Experience & Students in Transition.

Prices advertised in this publication are subject to change.

Item	Quantity	Price	Total
Monograph 38. *Transforming the First Year of College for Students of Color*		$35.00	
Monograph 34. *Service-Learning & The First-Year Experience*		$35.00	
Monograph 26. *Learning Communities*		$30.00	
Learning Interdependence		$30.00	
Moral Action in Young Adulthood		$30.00	

Shipping Charges:	**Order Amount**	**Shipping Cost**	Shipping & Handling	
U.S.	$0 - $50	$ 6.50 US		
	$51 - $150	$10.00 US	Total	
	over $150	$15.00 US		
Foreign	For orders shipped outside of the United States, customers will be billed exact shipping charges plus a $5.00 processing fee. Fax or e-mail us to obtain a shipping estimate. Be sure to include a list of items you plan to purchase and to specify your preference for Air Mail or UPS Delivery.			

Name _____   Department _____

Institution _____   Telephone _____

Address _____

City _____ State/Province _____ Postal Code _____

E-mail Address _____

Select your option payable to the University of South Carolina:

❏ Check Enclosed   ❏ Institutional Purchase Order   Purchase Order No. _____

Credit Card: ❏ VISA   ❏ Mastercard   ❏ Discover

Card No. _____   Expiration Date _____

Name of Cardholder _____

Billing Address _____

City _____ State/Province _____ Postal Code _____

Signature _____

Mail this form to: National Resource Center for The First-Year Experience & Students in Transition, University of South Carolina, 1728 College Street, Columbia, SC 29208. Phone (803) 777-6029. FAX (803) 777-4699. E-mail burtonp@sc.edu Federal ID 57-6001153.